Praise for ***The Body of Christ in a Market Economy***

"Gawain de Leeuw offers us a tutorial in modern economics in dialogue with theological themes rooted as deep as the foundation of the world. This is no small feat, and he brings it all home with a suite of practical applications suitable to church structures as intimate as the parish and as encompassing as the Communion."

Tobias Stanislas Haller, BSG, Church of the Advent, Baltimore

"In one of the more obscure sayings attributed to Jesus in the gospels, 'the parable of the dishonest manager,' Jesus warns his disciples that 'the sons of this world are more shrewd in dealing with their own generation than are the sons of light' (Luke 16:8). One possible reading of this parable is that it criticizes the followers of Christ for their lack of sophistication in matters of money, stewardship, and economics, or perhaps, for failing to love God even as much as the wicked love riches.

"If it is read carefully, perhaps this new book by the Rev. Gawain de Leeuw could help remedy this weakness.

"Ambitious and expansive, de Leeuw takes aim at faith that remains uninformed by economic theory. But he offers much more than a dry discussion of 'economics.' This is a call for the Body of Christ to rethink money, markets, community and work from the ground up. And it is a practical guide to changing the way we engage with the world."

Matthew Baldwin, Professor of Religion and Philosophy at Mars Hill College

"There's always call for a fresh book explaining how it's possible people can remain faithful followers of Jesus within the capitalist economic system. Gawain de Leeuw's work steps up to the challenge with wisdom, brio and cutting-edge anthropology. Filled with insights, his study wrestles over and over with the aporias separating the reckless giving of the gospel from a market system based in debt, exchange and commodification, or between the relationship of love modeled by Jesus and the fetterless desire and rivalry modeled by money. The fact that capitalism has proven the best way of increasing productivity while satisfying endless wants does nothing to lessen the othering and exploitation at its heart. Gawain offers us the church's dream of the sabbath as antidote, a time and place where competition and inexhaustible demand are replaced by rest, community, and blessing. But how can the church enable this practically? He suggests the successful management of rivalry as the core church practice, through sacraments, prayer, good governance, and cooperative networks. But perhaps the most radical impact of de Leeuw's work is to continue to knead the leaven of the gospel into our economic worldview until the times really do catch up with Jesus. As he vividly puts it, 'By ingesting Jesus, (we are given) the power to reconsider the game, the rat race, the system of materialism that creates a status war with others.'"

Anthony Bartlett

The Body of Christ in a Market Economy

Studies in Episcopal and Anglican Theology

C. K. Robertson
General Editor

Vol. 10

The Studies in Episcopal and Anglican Theology series
is part of the Peter Lang Humanities list.
Every volume is peer reviewed and meets
the highest quality standards for content and production.

PETER LANG
New York • Bern • Berlin
Brussels • Vienna • Oxford • Warsaw

Gawain de Leeuw

The Body of Christ in a Market Economy

An Anglican Inquiry into Economic Thinking

PETER LANG
New York • Bern • Berlin
Brussels • Vienna • Oxford • Warsaw

Library of Congress Cataloging-in-Publication Data

Names: De Leeuw, Gawain, author.
Title: The body of Christ in a market economy: an Anglican inquiry
into economic thinking / Gawain de Leeuw.
Description: New York: Peter Lang, 2019.
Series: Studies in Episcopal and Anglican theology, vol. 10
ISSN 2168-3891 (print) | ISSN 2168-3905 (online)
Includes bibliographical references and index.
Identifiers: LCCN 2018044980 | ISBN 978-1-4331-2848-6 (hardback: alk. paper)
ISBN 978-1-4539-1747-3 (ebook pdf) | ISBN 978-1-4331-6173-5 (epub)
ISBN 978-1-4331-6174-2 (mobi)
Subjects: LCSH: Economics—Religious aspects—Christianity.
Economics—Religious aspects—Anglican Communion.
Classification: LCC BR115.E3 D355 2019 | DDC 261.8/5—dc23
LC record available at https://lccn.loc.gov/2018044980
DOI 10.3726/978-1-4539-1747-3

Bibliographic information published by **Die Deutsche Nationalbibliothek.**
Die Deutsche Nationalbibliothek lists this publication in the "Deutsche
Nationalbibliografie"; detailed bibliographic data are available
on the Internet at http://dnb.d-nb.de/.

29 Broadway, 18th floor, New York, NY 10006
www.peterlang.com

Table of Contents

	Acknowledgments	vii
	Introduction	1
1	Reading Scripture	7
2	Engaging Economics	55
3	Theological Responses	99
4	Learning to Desire	119
5	How Jesus Saves	139
6	The Church and Salvation in a Commercial World	153
	Bibliography	197
	Index	203

Acknowledgments

This book is the product of twenty years of steady reading on economics, mimetic theory, and sociology. I'd like to thank a few of those who have provided invaluable support along the way.

My brother Kabir de Leeuw for listening to me talk for years.

Anthony Bartlett, Matthew Baldwin, Tobias Haller, Katy Herron, Sam Jackson, Tom Nichols, Gary Perscesepe, Joyce Schroeder, Joseph Shepley, Mark Usher, Jesica Vega, and Ashley Warner, either read or cheered.

My brothers and sisters of the Order of the Ascension inspired me to connect Benedict, Martin Thornton, and economics.

Thank you to Bianca Cappellini, Tiffany Card, Noelle Damico, Joel Daniels, John Denson, Andy Dietsche, Greg Dvorak, Neil Dvorak, Brad Dyche, Cornelius Eady, Jennifer Flowers, Michael Gecan, Meredith Garmon, Jeffrey Geary, Mary Glasspool, Colin Goundry, Margret Grebowicz, Helena Gronberg, Leigh Hall, Jonathan Huyck, Dawne Moon, Matthew Moretz, Andrea Meyges, Sarah Micklem, Clara Mun, Christopher Oldi, Daniel Radosh, Allen Shin, Devin Singh, Jim Steen, Jeffrey Taylor, Elizabeth Werner, Frederick Wherry, and who all supplied me with data, support and encouragement.

Thank you to Ellen Wondra and Bill Burrill, each mentors in faith. Charles Mathewes offered suggestions and kept me reading.

The Lilly Foundation gave me time to rest. The Luce Foundation had great expectations.

Rabbi Geoff Mitelman and Sinai and Synapses gave me the opportunity to learn about the intersection of science and religion.

Charles Henderson and Auburn Seminary was where this project began to find words, and especially Ivan Petrella, Elizabeth Hinson-Hasty, Hannah Holfheinz, and Jennifer Leath, who each offered useful suggestions.

Thank you to the members of the Union Vision Team: Jason Ferris, John Flack, Melissa Hinnen, Julie Hoplamazion, Amy Kienzle, Cheri Kroon, Sara McCaslin, Eric Mull, Drew Paton, Sara Searight, Arden Strasser, Adrien Thorne, Seth Wax, Chris Shelton, Linda Taryy-Chard, Jane Huber, and Serene Jones.

The members of St. Bartholomew's Church supported this long project with their endurance and patience. The White Plains Religious Leaders received regular updates.

Thank you to The Anglican Theological Review and Cross Currents, who have published some of these ideas in nascent form. I have enormous gratitude for those who shaped me intellectually: Mike Michalson, Harlan Wilson, Norman Care, George Rainbolt, Paul Griffiths, Brian Gerrish, Katherine Brekus, and Bert Harrill.

Brian Kenney from the White Plains Library helped me find books and articles.

The members of the White Plains Rotary who kept discussions of economics practical.

Gratitude for my editor Chuck Robertson, for his persistence and patience, who heard my pitch and believed it mattered, and to Megan Simpson and Janell Harris of Peter Lang.

To my family, especially Amy de Leeuw, who provided me a room in Isla Mujeres to write. David Buhler, Sanjiv Das, and Peter Ray each confirmed how rivalry works in capitalist firms. And for all the family across five continents who have waited.

Shreela Ray and Hendrik de Leeuw each gave me a love of reading widely, of the written word, and a commitment to justice. I dedicate this book to their memory.

Introduction

Rivalry costs. Find Jesus, or prepare to spend.

Churches teach Jesus Saves. Salvation through Christ has consequences for the way persons live in the world, including at the intersection of money, debt, sin, and desire. This book disentangles various threads that weave through economics and behavior, by highlighting the connections between envy, market systems, debt, sin, and salvation.

This book seeks to unpack the stories of scripture and contemporary life to explain how people engage markets. The economist Paul Heyne once wrote, "storytelling is a legitimate form of science" for "it is through the telling and hearing and critical consideration of stories that people come to understand how market systems work."[1] Churches tell stories of their impact in communities—through charity, building projects, partnerships, investments, and stewardship. So economics matters, and should matter, to Christians.

I began formulating my thoughts about this book after the financial crash of 2008 led to the loss of the entire endowment of my parish, in spite of being managed by a highly regarded firm. It is a story that has shaped the life of this community and forced some reflection about how churches make market decisions. However, my interest in economics as a moral discipline first began when I was the president of the Oberlin Student Cooperative Association (O.S.C.A), a six-hundred member student organization. It was responsible for feeding its members and housing nearly one hundred and fifty. It ran by consensus and mutual reciprocity, allocating resources through the intensive mechanics of managing and directing people in a way that was different from a traditional command structure.

I discovered the skills of living cooperatively, such as consensus and mutual accountability, required training. Students away from home for the first time often were not inculcated with these disciplines. Learning self-management required time and patience. There was also a tension, for example, between holding people accountable and the desire to be open, inclusive, and free. However, the everyday realities of training, education, and skill development, weren't found in the economic models I was familiar with. Those models assumed that people are perfectly rational actors, and didn't account for variables such as time, training, or other aspects of human behavior.

A central problem was that effective management, time, training, and collaboration are each costs within institutions and markets. Social connections and other non-financial rewards could also be incentives that directed individual choices. So economic descriptions of self-interest contrasted with insights about what individuals truly need and desire. The costs and benefits comparing money with social connections highlighted different views of rationality, freedom, exchange, cooperation and money. While incentives mattered, describing, identifying, and governing them remained perplexing.

Christians have something to say about economics. It understands that there are different values than only individual self-maximizing returns. Like members of cooperatives, congregants have a direct stake in churches. Both churches and cooperatives have some business-like characteristics and must coordinate of individuals to complete the tasks they seek to accomplish. Churches are entrepreneurial and sell things. They build affordable housing, offer summer camps, create credit unions, and run thrift stores.

However, theologians don't always understand why economists think the way they do. In 1996 I met with the Episcopalian and economist Paul Heyne, who helped me identify some challenges economists pose to theologians. Heyne was famous for his commitment to teaching undergraduates and his groundbreaking introductory textbook, *The Economic Way of Thinking*. Heyne identified a few specific ideas from economics that he thought were overlooked by progressive Christians. For example, he defined markets as systems of coordination driven by incentives rather than as merely systems of competition. Markets were places of social interaction and not merely of human calculators.

Because of these misunderstandings, I wanted to demystify the relationship between church and firm, offering a clearer way for Christians to engage economics and be less timid around harnessing money. Our lack of clarity about our nature as an economic institution has coddled our sentimentality and misdirected the able use of our wealth. My intuition is that the fear of money challenges our emotional capacity to make good decisions that will benefit the church, and that this fear begins with a justified suspicion of desire and wealth.

Money, wealth, and markets are all of a central concern to Christianity. The faith has used economic metaphors to describe its work from the beginning. Jesus calls us to be generous; he declares that one cannot serve both God and Wealth (Matt 6:21), and many parables have economic undertones. The bible connects the relationship of sin and debt, almsgiving and redemption. Theologians argue that Christianity has a preferential option for the poor. Therefore, as Christianity is concerned with the arranging of resources, it will be concerned with economies. However, there is a diversity of opinion between biblical scholars, ethicists, economists, and theologians about what this entails for persons in churches.

I believe that a fundamental key understanding Christian concerns about economics requires recognizing how societies and their institutions manage rivalry. The literature of the economics of firms and behavior provides a way to explore rivalry that is congruent with Christian concerns about desire and envy. Rivalry, which is expressed through acquisitive desire, provides a common thread within scripture, economics, theology, ecclesiology and liturgy. A clearer understanding of the mechanics of desire and rivalry can help us explain how desire impacts our social life. I will suggest the problems that arise out of rivalry are what connect concerns of desire, debt, and sin.

A couple presuppositions throughout the book deserve clarifying. First, economics does not always distinguish between its work as a descriptive or analytical enterprise or as a normative one. This confusion needs to be disentangled. Second, a religious, Christian, or even Anglican view is not necessarily distinct from other religious views. I take the view that economics *does* make moral claims and that Anglican Christians make justifiable critiques. There are shared analogies and homologies between theology and which can be translated and aid in their mutual understanding. I do not know, however, if Anglican Christians will say much that is distinctive.

Furthermore, I believe individuals experience spirituality also as materialistic, through the things, objects, and persons around them. The salvific power of Jesus not only concerns heaven, but changes how we desire, behave, and act in the world. I also assume that the atonement matters to Christians, and that our primary conversation partner in understanding our work remains the scripture handed down through the church. I define "neoclassical" as an economic tendency that presumes that the individual and its aggregates are useful ways to analyzing markets. I define *The Body of Christ* as, most broadly, the church—and this includes all sorts of Christian congregations.

The first chapter argues that the religious constraints around debt and money arise from the need to regulate rivalry and desire in order to diminish the social tensions that arise from the accumulation of wealth due to debt bondage. Market networks are placed in the context of social networks. I explore the relationship between sin, debt, money, and envy and show how scripture tries to regulate it.

My second chapter explains the mechanics of markets by exploring institutional and behavioral economists. I will introduce and clarify the language economists use to describe how markets work and individuals make decisions. This will include how institutions reduce the costs of making those decisions. I show how economists give theologians a value-neutral way to describe sin.

The third chapter reviews a selection of theological responses to economics. This will include a critique of the economic way of thinking, of markets, and of its presumptions toward being value free. Theologians have explored the challenges of consumption, why a belief in the market is misplaced, and where the economic description of the individual is flawed.

In chapter four, I patch a missing element through describing the mechanics of desire through Rene Girard's theory of mimesis. Mimetic theory shows how individuals model others, and this imitation leads to social tension. It offers an explanation for how individuals make decisions in markets and other sorts of social networks. It explains both why and how individuals desire. While scripture and economics each show desire drives our behavior, the mimetic anthropology of Rene Girard's explanation of desire links both of them. It also provides a link to how Jesus fits into the consequences of that desire.

In the fifth chapter, I show how the atonement suggests *how* Jesus saves has *economic* content. The atonement rearranges what a Christian desires by rearranging who Christians are to model. If Jesus saves, Christians engage our choices differently. Individuals are now invited to be formed not by the market or by models that are perpetually dissatisfied, but through following Jesus. Through Jesus, individuals have the grace to eschew rivalry and choose alternative paths to behaving and existing in the world. Therefore, being saved means engaging in the market differently.

My last chapter will look more at how this fits in with the Anglican tradition. I will explore how our liturgy and the rule of the church may help us handle the spiritual complexities of rivalry. Baptism, Eucharist, and the rule of prayer in the church offer some intriguing analogues for developing a spiritual practice that helps us put rivalry in perspective. The atonement shows how the church might be governed without rivalry—as Christlike. I will explore a bit what governance means, and its relationship to previous traditions, such as the Benedictine rule. Church governance invites us to develop techniques that make it easy to arrange resources for the common good. This includes reaffirming the Sabbath, taking a central role in building social networks between institutions, and increasing the quality of our public institutions.

This book offers neither a blanket defense nor a general critique of markets. I present markets as one kind of network, and the neo-classical perspective allows us to measure using the unit of the individual. In some sense, the default unit and position of the individual in the neoclassical tradition still remains central to the project. I do not challenge the literature prioritizing the commitment of Christians to the poor. I hope the reader will recognize that discipleship is an economic discipline, and that the church has a role in forming people. Followers of Christ are free, but with a new understanding of wealth, it is now possible to truly flourish.

"Is it possible to think intelligently about Economy without being a professional economist? It is an urgent necessity."[2] This book is an attempt by a priest to read economics so you don't have to. That said, you should. May this be a suitable introduction.

Notes

1. Heyne, Paul T. 2008 "Teaching Economics by Telling Stories." In *"Are Economists Basically Immoral?": And Other Essays on Economics, Ethics, and Religion*, edited by Geoffrey Brennan and Anthony Michael C. Waterman, 327. Indianapolis: Liberty Fund.
2. Dupuy, Jean-Pierre. *Economy and the Future: A Crisis of Faith*. Translated by Malcolm B. DeBevoise, 15. East Lansing: Michigan State University Press, 2014.

1 Reading Scripture

Scripture shapes how the church addresses economics. It offers stories, prohibitions, mandates, and exhortations for arranging resources in households and communities. So I begin with the foundational texts that inform the Christian religious, spiritual, and ecclesial intuitions. Christians allocate, distribute, and receive wealth, which impacts relationships between persons and with God. The social consequences of ownership and money matter.

While the task of interpreting scripture can be remade in each generation, I assume Christians engage sacred texts as conversation partners and sources of guidance and wisdom. Through scripture, Christians identify how to be responsible in Christ and his Church in a complex economy. While it may not give specific details about what sorts of cereals to purchase, what fashion to wear, whether to rent or buy, or how to tax, it helps discern how to understand the world and guide a social life. Reading scripture matters to Christians.

Certainly some scholars have been chary about using scripture to commend specific sorts of policies to states or governments. It can be argued that scripture both praises the justly prosperous and chastises the overly acquisitive; it neither trusts the trader nor endorses sophisticated bureaucracies. Scripture is alternately suspicious of political power and hierarchy, and accommodating toward the ways societies organize. It holds a tension between an attitude of realism about human behavior and institutions, and a vision of a more perfect future instituted by God. Scripture reflects the multivocal experiences of persons and the times they inhabit.

I believe that this tension is relieved, in part, through a better anthropological understanding between individuals and the institutions that shape them. Instead of assuming the individual is a self-defined, atomistic, distinct unit, I begin with a model of human action that recognizes that institutions shape the minds of persons and assumes persons are embedded in human culture and relationship. Scripture offers such a description of humanity. It understands persons as having relationships with other persons, and it seeks an economy where God is present.

The use of money and the impact of debt creates tensions between different networks of social power. The experience of desire and envy intensifies these tensions. Money, debt, desire, and envy are intertwined. This nuance will be familiar to casual readers of scripture, as the writings comment strongly about the relationship of God to wealth and the prohibitions against covetousness. These views impact any Christian understanding of economics.

Scripture both describes and prescribes human activity. Description and prescription are intertwined. Scripture illustrates, through story and law, what people value, what they see, and so how they decide, respond, and act. Sometimes it offers examples of human behavior without judgment or moralizing. Other times, scripture illustrates how the people of God engage God, and then may prescribe a solution or a warning. Often, the description is seen through the prescription; the normative, ethical command points to a real action that has happened or practiced. The positive prescription that commands refraining from murder only makes sense when people murder. Scripture commands "thou shalt not covet" because people covet. Therefore, prescriptions can themselves be descriptions; one only prohibits acts that people are likely to commit. God tells us not to make idols, because this is precisely what human beings are inclined to make when God seems distant and uncooperative.

Scripture also provides some insights into the complexities of communities. It warns of idolatry and covetousness, even though God provides plenty; it warns that money, or wealth, has godlike characteristics that misdirect us away from God; third, of the righteous care for the vulnerable and the stranger; fourth, that the people of Israel are dependent upon each other and God; and that while abundance is a gift, material poverty is not a punishment. Scripture seeks to steer markets away from exploitation and violence. To show how it does so, I will connect sin and debt; money, idolatry, and envy; and redemption, charity, and the Sabbath.

> Proverbs 22:
> [4]The reward for humility and fear of the Lord
> is riches and honor and life.
> [7]The rich rule over the poor,
> and the borrower is the slave of the lender.

Networks in Ancient Israel

Economics helps understand the arrangement of resources in the household, the *oikonomia* (Greek: οἰκονομία), which defined the ordering of goods and relationships between people in the home and the broader network. I understand economies are kinds of networks, and networks are *paths of connection*, where information, goods, and relationships can be given, distributed, or exchanged. It is a deliberately broad concept to describe the multiplicity of the ways persons, things, and ideas move. It can include physical networks like roads or a relationship with the environment, kinship, or culture.

Market networks are arranged through an exchange system made possible by the technology of money and the accounting of debt. Regulation Theory, as proposed by the biblical scholar Roland Boer, illustrates how scripture seeks to diminish the social tensions caused by markets. This theory allows us to begin a stronger framework for understanding what is at stake.

Regulation Theory: How the Scripture Approaches Economics

The priorities and social mechanisms that undergirded ancient Israel had little in common with our own market economy. Our sophisticated commercial economy calculates transactions much differently than ancient agricultural networks. Surplus capital moves at the speed of light, with the help of technology, a division of labor, and diminished transaction costs. A subsistence economy moves at the speed of the seasons, dependent upon the natural cycles of the world.

Yet we can also trace some commonalities. Roland Boer, in his illuminating book *The Sacred Economy of Ancient Israel*,[1] contrasts the networks of the ancient Israelites and those of commerce. Boer explains the priorities of Israelite social life by applying a broad model, regulation theory, to show the way networks worked. Regulation theory holds that *the structures of society were oriented around minimizing the social tensions that threaten to tear apart society when social crises arise.* Thus, culture is managed through systems of restraints and compromises, our actions circumscribed by patterns of culture that permit a subsistence economy to be maintained with as little conflict as possible. The ancient world prioritized stability and security over modern economic values such as reinvesting surplus value. Innovating for the purpose of creating surplus would have been secondary to the desire to ensure stability, regularity, and consistency in a world where surplus was rare. The prohibitions and rules valued the prevention of rivalry and the establishment of peace.

Boer therefore puts the market economy in the context of the many other sorts of networks upon which the ancient worldview was constructed. The foremost of these networks was kinship—people connected through genealogy and a shared history or story: "Production and consumption appear as one beneath the umbrella of kinship; it was not a question of individuals sharing, but the simple assumption that any labor and usufruct belonged to the collective."[2] Such networks were not static, but flexible, and changed according to the context, whether through war or marriage.

Boer shows the social network in scripture prioritized the importance of kinship, which also included ancestors and livestock. It "went well beyond blood relations, yet even living bodies were not the only bodies that counted. The dead were counted as well, as were domesticated animals of various descriptions. Animals and human beings were part of the same continuum."[3] Boer shows that communities were fundamentally preoccupied with networks other than markets.

Regulation theory distinguishes between what early and modern societies calculated. The subsistence economies did not seek to create surplus, but prioritized sustaining connections based on more immediate survival needs. Boer writes, "A household comprises the rhythms of life and flexible constructions of space within and without a distinct structure or collection of structures that may be more or less permanent, which is made possible by the social and economic context in which it is found." It includes the everyday life of ordinary people, but "they involve constant rhythms, of movement within… households are eminently flexible, constantly reusing items for different purposes, and reconfiguring internal and external space in multiple ways, depending upon the needs of the moment."[4]

Boer makes several points about how society was organized in scripture. First, everyday life did not always include exact calculation of cost and benefits to identify surplus value. The need to get things done, to move, to reap, to sow, meant that tasks were performed simply because they needed to be done, by whomever was available. Work was not specialized. Customs and laws regulated relationships in the midst of crisis. Networks presumed[5] broader and wider relationships than the clearly defined boundaries of blood relatives. Boer writes, "The sheer resilience of kinship-household and subsistence survival, along with its creative adaptation to ever-changing conditions, was itself the constitutive force."[6] The immediate relationships within an extended network provided the nexus of sustainability, a way to manage the crises and precarity that would have been constant.

Boer posits that exchange with money was a type of *patronage*. Unlike a simple exchange of cash for services, monetary exchanges expressed the power of the person who had it. With money, one person would provide food, shelter, or expertise, establishing dependence of one person upon another. And while those with resources can distribute, they also represent the power to extort. The power to move others that money provides is a coercive power, one that also underlies the power to take and plunder.

Scripture reveals the priority of relational, physical, and geographical networks before markets. The culture sought to maintain the network of chains of emotional support and intensive investment to get the work done, which would become fraught and tense especially in the midst of crises. Each network, whether it mediated money, kinship, or political structures, was intertwined and interdependent with other networks. The financial network was seen as being one that increased tension within other networks.

Boer thus shows us why prescriptions about envy were so important. By identifying and restraining envy, societies could curtail the tensions that would lead to greater violence and strife. Financial markets and debt were exacerbated by envy. Therefore rules, rituals, and habits that coordinate human life around money were demonstrations of restraining it. The mechanics of the market were by no means universally powerful. An empire's administration could not be everywhere or record every transaction. But it would ask for more than people need, demanding surpluses, seeking immediate windfalls through plunder and violence.[7] Markets, therefore, were directly associated with this exploitation. Merchants were like "busybodys"[8] who traded expensive, precious goods that signaled prestige for the wealthy rather than produced objects that were practically valuable.[9] They were merely middlemen guilty of hoarding and taking the best for themselves (Isa 23:2–3, 7–8; Ezek 17:3–4; 38:13; Hos 12:7–9; Nah 3:16).

In an agricultural economy, vast surpluses did not exist. Transportation was expensive and laborious. The network of the market was distinguished from other networks of kinship and it didn't provide what most people valued—stability. Instead, the role of empires and merchants in plundering, in remembering debts, in trading objects of rivalry and desire, would have been seen as socially destabilizing. In a pre-industrial subsistence economy, money has the power to burden a life by becoming a debt to another person.

Societies sought to regulate kinship and stability through offering a critique of larger economic and imperial networks that impacted the community. Because markets encouraged plunder, stimulated rivalry, and led to debt slavery, scripture sought to diminish the harm that such practices caused to the networks of kinship through a variety of restraints.

The practice of the Sabbath was one primary way markets were kept in check. Keeping the Sabbath brings stability and peace because it places the market into its proper role in social life. During Sabbath, the values of surplus, of utility, and the mechanics of plunder have to stop. It limits the power of debt. The Sabbath allows for slaves to stop working. It prevents a variety of activities that arise from the seduction of money by being a time and space that is meant to be redirected toward God. The Sabbath allows the individual to redirect desire.

Sin and the Economics of Debt

Sin and debt can help explore how religion shows how to reduce social tension. Sin reflects or causes tension in a community; sacrifice of some kind redeems it. Sin is related to debt, and debt is linked with money. Sin is therefore also an economic concept and not only a spiritual stance. It does not just concern the condition of the heart but also describes our relationships in markets, in economies where bodies buy and sell. Therefore, the redemption of debt implies something about what God intends for the economy.

The Hebrew scholar Gary Anderson[10], in *Sin: A History*, explores how sin shifted from burden to debt. Sin could explain the punishment of Israel and the desolation of Jerusalem. Because Israel did not keep the Sabbath, it had to pay off a debt to account for its transgression. By violating the Sabbath, its punishment was compounded until the debt ran its course.

Anderson affirms the metaphorical connection between sin and debt. However, if Israel's disobedience was reflected by an economy where there was a concentration of wealth in the hands of a few who could hold others in bondage, then sin is an economic relationship. Jubilee was therefore a radical way of reorienting the economy. It redeemed by cancelling economic debts, reorienting the power between the lender and the debtor.

Sin is thus connected with money because money provides the technology of counting debts. It is further related to the state as the state mints coin. Money intrinsically represents the value of a person's life energy, the work required to be free of debt to another person. Eventually, sin itself becomes calculated by prices.[11] The links between debt-slavery, economic inequality, and the condemnation of Israel by the prophets shows that financial debt, not just the spiritual metaphor, was a concern for the people of God.

Debts changed relationships. The anthropologist David Graeber describes this viscerally. He writes, "A debt is just the perversion of a promise. It is a promise corrupted by both math and violence."[12] A debt reduces a specific living person to a number, a fungible object that can be substituted, replicated, and counted. A person who had been embedded in a web of relationships is extracted and removed from one context, such as their family, to another. Money becomes the tool that permits the coerciveness within a social network. The concrete relationship becomes replaced and signified by something substitutable, replaced by a number, a coin. One person can now be substituted for another.

A debt, as Graeber notes, requires counting—and thus, is dependent upon money because it makes counting possible; doing so renders a human being as an abstract commodity. Debt "requires a relationship between two people who do not consider each other fundamentally different sorts of being, who are at least potential equals, who are equals in those ways that are really important, and are not currently in a state of equality, but for whom there is some way to set matter straight… It is just an exchange that has not been brought to completion… Debt is strictly a creature of reciprocity and has little to do with other sorts of morality."[13]

The market is not the totality of human experience, or the only kind of network humans create. Graeber reminds us, "All human interactions are not forms of exchange. Only some are. Debt is what happens in between: when the two parties cannot yet walk away from each other because they are not yet equal."[14] And so we begin to have a sense of what sin looks like: sin is when we diminish the human being before us by rendering them as a replaceable object in the market; when money makes a person into a tool. Economic markets are only one network among many which people would have valued.

Usury and Interest

Money has the power to intensify debt because it can charge for its own use. Debt begins with a loan. Not all loans are pernicious: "In most cases, the debtor needed a loan to survive a bad harvest to pay taxes, for a wedding… The flow of wealth allowed some space for the debtor to survive."[15] Debt becomes a problem when we consider interest, which is a price imposed upon the use of money. Interest extracts extra labor from the debtor to the lender. For this reason, scripture calls interest a vulgarity (Ezek 22:9–12) and a "punishment" (Isa 24:2, 50:1, Ps 112:5–6). The nature of acquisitiveness is not only demonstrated by plunder, legal manipulation, or tipping the scales, but by extorting people through interest.

Money creates more money through interest. It magnifies its ability to substitute for another good. It becomes not merely a substitute for another good, a dowry, or for labor, but a substitute for itself *over time*. This interest is a bet on the future of another person, with the hope of payback. Time is an important element of how money has power. *It can command commitments in the future.*

Boer writes about the impact of such a debt: "The landlord would have little incentive to see the debt repaid promptly, for it was in his interest for the laborer to work longer on his estates."[16] These debts locked workers into specific kinds of labor, making it more difficult for them to move into other kinds of work.[17] Uncertainty makes them difficult to repay, because fortunes change, disasters happen, and people become disabled and unable to work. Because the ability to pay for the use of the money depends on other factors beyond the control of the borrower, it can also lead to such indebtedness that the recipient may not be able to pay back the cost of the original money itself.

When a person is unable to repay the debt, usury puts one person in bondage to another (Prov. 22:7). The laws regarding the Jubilee years constrain the amount and length of debt, mitigating usury's coercive power over another person's life or death. Scripture's corrections to this relationship, the Sabbath and Jubilee, suggest that liberation from debt is at the heart of God's work, and that redemption is defined as the unshackling of bondage. Usury is sin because it is inherently exploitive; it is a means by which one person becomes enslaved to another through the exploitation of a power and resource asymmetry. Sin is *economic* because it reflects the power of debt. It is relational and intensified through the use of money and interest.

The traditional prohibitions of usury in scripture and the history of the church are the link between debt and sin, redemption and liberation. Usury is not a sin because loaning is wrong, but because it holds people in bondage, by restricting the debtor's life energy by putting it into the hands of a lender. Because it is now measurable, more can be demanded, and it becomes conceivable for one to enslave oneself. Money makes it easy to extract more labor. This debt is seen as a disorder of God's desire for our relations with one another, therefore justifying regular corrections through mandating the Sabbath and the Jubilee year.

Scripture critiques the use of charging interest upon interest, and limits the extent to which we can charge interest upon the poorest (Ex 22:25; Deut 23:19–20). The impact of charging interest potentially impoverishes the individuals who cannot pay the loan in a timely fashion. And so the covenant includes ways by which debt can be forgiven so that no person would lose their freedom completely. Over seven years, and even over fifty, their debts would be forgiven. As an example, Roland Boer writes, "Jubilees were barometers of economic instability… They functioned as short-circuits to ensure that the crisis-ridden system continued to survive. And they provided extraordinary occasions for political spin."[18]

Money functions as a way for the state to compensate for the work of its soldiers to protect its interest. The state offers stamped coins as a substitute for other goods. It signifies, as well, an implicit debt to the state. As one accumulates coin, it suggests that the accumulation of money is an accumulation of the sins of others. Perhaps redemption is to keep money moving out of one's own hands. It suggests that the urge to accumulate money—a signifier of another's debt and sin—is an emotional disorder that distracts us from the real purpose of money. Money must keep moving out of any individual person's hands. To redeem ourselves from this sin, we give it away, as charity, as sharing, or in the market. Perhaps redemption may be about getting rid of money, not as a tool, but by circulating it as widely as possible.

Liberation from sin is economic because it is linked in scripture to our relationship with debt. Redemption thus implies a freedom from debt (Ro. 6:23). Therefore, a redemptive practice may be spending (or giving) generously to get rid of money, or even the "debt" that one carries; it could mean reducing one's work so that one is not held hostage by the urge to make more. It could be forgiving someone else's debt, or one's own debt being forgiven (Ps. 37:21). It implies that it is not the accumulation of money that is virtuous, but the generous dispersal of it, in any fashion.

The Market and Other Networks

1 Samuel 8:1–22

When Samuel became old, he made his sons judges over Israel. The name of his firstborn son was Joel, and the name of his second, Abijah; they were judges in Beer-sheba. Yet his sons did not follow in his ways, but turned aside after gain; they took bribes and perverted justice. Then all the elders of Israel gathered together and came to Samuel at Ramah, and said to him, "You are old and your sons do not follow in your ways; appoint for us, then, a king to govern us, like other nations." But the thing displeased Samuel when they said, "Give us a king to govern us." Samuel prayed to the Lord, and the Lord said to Samuel, "Listen to the voice of the people in all that they say to you; for they have not rejected you, but they have rejected me from being king over them. Just as they have done to me, from the day I brought them up out of Egypt to this day, forsaking me and serving other gods, so also they are doing to you. Now then, listen to their voice; only—you shall solemnly warn them, and show them the ways of the king who shall reign over them." So Samuel reported all the words of the Lord to the people who were asking him for a king. He said, "These will be the ways of the king who will reign over you: he will take your sons and appoint them to his chariots and to be his horsemen, and to run before his chariots; and he will appoint for himself commanders of thousands and commanders of fifties, and some to plow his ground and to reap his harvest, and to make his implements of war and the equipment of his chariots. He will take your daughters to be perfumers and cooks and bakers. He will take the best of your fields and vineyards and olive orchards and give them to his courtiers. He will take one-tenth of your grain and of your vineyards and give it to his officers and his courtiers. He will take your male and female slaves, and the best of your cattle and donkeys, and put them to his work. He will take one-tenth of your flocks, and you shall be his slaves. And in that day you will cry out because of your king, whom you have chosen for yourselves; but the Lord will not answer you in that day." But the people refused to listen to the voice of Samuel; they said, "No! but we are determined to have a king over us, so that we also may be like other nations, and that our king may govern us and go out before us and fight our battles." When Samuel had heard all the words of the people, he repeated them in the ears of the Lord. The Lord said to Samuel, "Listen to their voice and set a king over them." Samuel then said to the people of Israel, "Each of you return home."

Nehemiah 5:3–7

There were also those who said, "We are having to pledge our fields, our vineyards, and our houses in order to get grain during the famine." And there were those who said, "We are having to borrow money on our fields and vineyards to pay the king's tax. Now our flesh is the same as that of our kindred; our children are the same as their children; and yet we are forcing our sons and daughters to be slaves, and some of our daughters have been ravished; we are powerless, and our fields and vineyards now belong to others." I was very angry when I heard their outcry and these complaints. After thinking it over, I brought charges against the nobles and the officials; I said to them, "You are all taking interest from your own people." And I called a great assembly to deal with them,

The institutions of debt and money depend upon the existence of the state. The state defends property claims and it stamps coins. Money has worth because of institutions that can create and guarantee the stability of the claim. In the above story about Samuel, scripture offers an origin story between the state and resources. The institution of kingship, a primordial bureaucracy, offers protection at a cost. Samuel makes his warning, outlining a brief description of the etiology of the state. Having protection, a civilization, or a king requires taxes. With taxes begins coinage. The passage illustrates how the market and the state have been firmly intertwined.

This leads to a moral principle: the lives of the people of Israel are intertwined. The abundance we have is dependent in part upon our relationship with the one true God and also on our interdependence with one another as a nation in relationship to God. Individuals are dependent upon each other, their inheritance, environment, *weltanschauung*, and, ultimately, God. Markets reflect our interdependence as systems of exchange that happen over time, between persons. They can be mediated by money and organized by governing institutions such as the state. They are networks. Beliefs that set individuals outside of this dependence are revealed as seductive fictions.

The passage from 1 Samuel describes how the state forms networks for protection, in the form of armies. The people of Israel wanted an army to defend themselves, and instead of offering sacrifices, they were to coin money to fund the state. Nehemiah expands this model by illustrating the connection between the land, taxation, and the institution of the monarchy through the act of borrowing, interest, and slavery. Money renders the inhabitants of the land powerless under the state, which coins currency and demands a tax. Instead of a network where grain is shared, where surplus is offered to feed the starving, the market system becomes a way of introducing bondage through debt.

The importance of markets hinges upon the establishment and the backing of money. The coordination the market depends first upon a political structure that has already organized aspects of our social life together. Money is a tool and a symbol, a sign value that increases the range, speed, and impact of exchanges between any two persons. For this reason, a fuller understanding of money will be essential to exploring the contours of scripture's understanding of markets.

Understanding Money

Money arises as a tool in organizing the sacrifices that defined the relationship between gods and persons. As believers and their gods exchanged sacrifices for protection, money evolved as a substitute for the animal flesh and crops that were once offered (Lev. 27:30–32; Deut. 14:24–25).[19] From this practical necessity, money provides both a tool and the beginning of a language to understand humanity's relationship with the transcendent through sacrifice and debt.

The Classicist Richard Seaborn describes money as having the following characteristics. First, it is an interchangeable sign that allows us to meet our obligations to other people, by enabling us to exchange things of value and pay our debts. Second, *this sign can be counted* and measured. Third, as a measurement, *it allows us to establish and compare value*, which facilitates exchange.[20] Fourth, *other people accept it* as a form of exchange. It is accepted in part because it has a sign—a symbol upon it—a stamp that enters the consciousness that creates the trust necessary for it to become the accepted unit of exchange. Money combines value with convenience; it is an object, but it is also a relationship. Money has its objective value *because* of its ability to depend on the confidence created by its symbolic power.[21] Lastly, as Devin Singh the historian agrees, money is related to state power. Money "as a sign and representation of sovereign power to aid in the governance of subjects… Money circulates as an extension of sovereignty, creating tendrils of control that generate the exchange relations of subjects and eventually shape evaluations of reality and consequent communal formation." Because of money's ability to pay for debt, including taxes, it is entangled in political relationships of power.[22]

Money increases markets' viability and effectiveness because it abstracts and substitutes for other goods. It makes transactions simpler because it allows people an easier way to assess value. However, money is not merely a convenient mechanism that allows for easy exchange; it also depends on the existence of other institutions and systems, such as accounting and the state, to be useful. Money is not merely a tool of transaction; it also relies on other institutions of the empire that enforce obligations, build trust, and express power. As Boer notes, "Coinage provides an ingenious solution to the logistics of supply, and with coinage a new type of abstraction becomes possible and tangibly real."[23] This abstraction simplifies transaction costs, provides an easy way to substitute one good for another, and designates value. It is a *sign-value* that allows people to measure worth.

Boer explains, "A coin has an objective value, instituted by the monarch who punches, stamps, or presses it. It has the same objective value for the peasant who sells his produce as it does for the hungry mercenary who purchases that produce and will never be seen again."[24] Boer further explains, "Markets spread to provision armies. The soldiers were paid in coin; and taxes were then paid in coin, so farmers would seek to acquire coin from the soldiers."[25] It moves armies, builds roads, and assesses value; it buys food, beer, music, and women.

The anthropologist David Graeber describes money as a symbol of a life-debt.[26] Money is a price on the life of a person. Money renders a distinctive, embedded life substitutable for others. It is both a symbol of debt to the state, which by nature owns and guarantees the money, but also an "an acknowledgment of the existence of a debt that cannot be paid," a life. It substitutes for what is un-substitutable. He says, "Money emerges from the recognition of an absolute debt to that which has given your life… Society is our debts."[27]

Money is therefore connected and given its value to and from the state, backed by its armies, and related to its power to tax. Money also has the power to reproduce itself through the power of interest on debt, which expresses the obligation of one person to another. One person with surplus resources to lend can impose their will upon another person. Scripture circumscribes this power, especially charging interest upon interest, the charging of money to use money. These prohibitions (e.g. Lev 25:36–7) limit the extent to which one can own another and impose debts.

Money is a tool. It facilitates commerce by offering a replicable sign that measures what the value of a good is. Its flexibility allows for quicker circulation, longer supply chains, and for more sophisticated needs to be satisfied. The principle of substitution eases the exchange by offering a clear point from which to negotiate. We enter a market and buy with money that we have earned by people compensating us for the work we do. Money facilitates an exchange of different kinds of labor with relative ease, especially between strangers. Furthermore, through the practice of pricing, money expresses value allowing individuals to prioritize goods that are important. However, the view that money is strictly neutral and has no necessary impact on consciousness or social relations is flawed. While money facilitates exchanges that other sorts of desirable objects cannot, it also represents obligation and relationships, requires institutional power, and represents a complex weaving of social relations.

In scripture, money is also a social animal, one that looks a lot like a divinity. It disembeds people from their contexts, making specific relationships replaceable and substitutable, counting what was previously incalculable. Our inheritance, our reputation, and our lives now have a price. However, while money illustrates the power of bondage, it also offers a way of understanding redemption.

The Changing Nature of Sacrifice

Sacrifice helps explain both the origins and uses of money. Ritual sacrifice placates the gods through erasing sins. Offering a victim, a person, or an animal as a substitute restores and corrects the relationship. Sacrifice does this by substituting one sort of violence for another. Its constrained violence seeks to prevent divine violence so the participants receive the benefits of security and prosperity.[28] Eventually, one symbol substitutes for another, less costly symbol; an animal substitutes for a person; an animal substitutes for the image of God, whose power can then be ingested. Money substitutes for the flesh, the shared divine offering,[29] and facilitates an exchange between the debtor and God.

Exchanges can be seen as a substitute for direct sacrifice. Initially, ritual sacrifice was an act of generosity, where a costly, extreme, and radical sacrifice, such as a person, was offered in exchange for peace. Over time, money, however, substitutes for a costly sacrifice, where both the buyer and the seller know what they are getting, and seems as effective as the costlier version. In another sense, markets represent how sacrifice changes over time: on one hand sacrifice implies the offering of one specific thing, a symbol on behalf of another. Whether it is a virgin, an animal, money, or a symbol of the broken body, sacrifice implies a substitute and is at the heart of an exchange between God and the community. This exchange is mediated by what is sacrificed or ordered by the priest. God offers forgiveness, peace, and order in exchange for a life, or money, or our good intentions. Money facilitates exchange in markets where things and persons may be substituted, calculated, and replaced. It represents and yet conceals the institutional relationships that make the money effective, or even allow the possibility of money.

Money looks a lot like God because it has become a substitute for Him in sacrifice. But it now helps organize armies and incentivizes the labor of other people. It creates more of itself through the power of interest. It also has the power to quantify the value of a life. These are some reasons money is fascinating. As such, it looks a lot like an idol.

Idolatry and Community

Scripture understands money as powerful. As such, it seeks to constrain its impact on the community. One way to understand scripture's regulation of money is through its condemnation of idolatry, and money as having the qualities of idols. Out of the book of the covenant (Ex 20:22–23:33), which compiles the laws that delineate the "guiding principles" (Ex 21:1) behind the expectations of the people of God, it's possible to examine the shape of such constraints.

The first commandment expresses the supremacy of the one God, and that there are no other gods but Him (Ex 20:2–5, Dt 5:6–10). The law thus distinguishes the practices of worshiping the one God of Israel and other gods; it is holy to worship *the* one God, profane to worship any others. The following commandments prescribe relationships within the Israelite community and indicate what acts become transgressive or disordered. They circumscribe the non-voluntary allocation or transfer of private property, through theft, and end with a prohibition of envy or covetousness.

The prohibitions against idolatry arise out of connecting it to a separation from the one true God and the consequences for the people of Israel. Covetousness is a consequence of idolatry that corrodes relationships. Scripture insists that abundance is because of God's beneficence and that our relationships with others matter. An individual does not create themselves, but is dependent upon God. Conversely, idols corrode our relationship with God and destabilize our relationships with one another.

The fundamental orientation toward God is followed by prohibitions against theft or envy, connecting idolatry with the economy of the community. Idols are a false substitute for our relationship with God, undermining the primary covenant with Him, which requires us, primarily, to respect others and their property, and to love our neighbor as ourselves. Idolatry breaks the covenant with God and corrodes the community by breaking the foundation of trust that beings achieve through believing in Him. Acts of idolatry amplify and intensify our desires, shedding the sense of mutual obligation, directing away from our commitments with others. They replace God with the titles, honor, and pretty baubles that are seductive to individuals. But the commandments in scripture affirm that the love of God must be prioritized above all competing desires. Instead of investing spiritual life in what is lifeless, scripture seeks to direct economic behavior toward life. The intention of the law is to redirect desire away from ourselves toward the value of God and persons.

Furthermore, idols also reveal the mechanics and power of desire. Desire can intensify our emotional life enough to break the covenant and our obligations to one another. It conceals and diminishes our dependence upon God and our interdependence with other people. The tension between individual desire and this fundamental interdependence with one another is one way to describe the tension between idolatry and true worship.

The image of the golden calf (Ex 32:15–24) can be compared to the worship of wealth itself. Money expresses a power that is akin to an alternative god. The story offers an understanding of our origins, illustrates behavior patterns, and mandates prohibitions. By freeing us from God, by breaking up the covenant, we can easily substitute our own desires for God's, which is the essence of idolatry. Insatiable human desires will replace, when broken, the prohibitions of the covenant which restrain the desires that can overwhelm a community. Idols are disposable, but it is impossible to perceive them as such because one's desire is overwhelming.

Idols, such as money, capture human imagination and attention. This is not necessarily due to the idols' inherent significance, but because others also have been captivated. They are a social contrivance, powerful spectacles that pull our collective attention into a self-constructed frenzy. They reflect the intensity of human desire over other people and God: "What man begins possess and the desire to possess more, whether in material goods, influence, sex, or other matters, has the potential to become the primary center of meaning and value in life, the ultimate value and thus the claim that has the force of another God."[30] This potential threatens to divide the community.

The relationship of wealth to the community is clear. Economist and theologian Daniel Finn writes, "The Israelites fundamentally understood themselves as members of a community in relationship to God," not as individuals first. Their tradition and customs were not perceived as chafing, but as a reflection of the nature of the "precious inheritance that each generation receives from its ancestors" back to Abraham.[31] To this end, the people who were dependent remained central to the covenant's description of wealth.[32]

Covetousness and anxiety leads to idolatry. It reflects a worry that God will not provide for the needs of the people. And so "we covet because we're worried that what God provides won't be enough." Idols mislead into other promising possibilities even though nothing else, except the one true God, will save us. Wealth, as an idol, invites taking our salvation into one's own hands.[33] Idolatry places a mirror of the people's desires at the center of worship, replacing God with persons, misplacing the true source of power.

The Prophets and Idols

The prophets routinely associate the problem of idol worship with the impact of wealth. The prophet Hosea, at a time when the state of Israel was more centralized and wealthy, connects the lifestyles of the wealthy with forgetting the worship of

God (Ho. 13:2). The repeated use of comparing Israel to one who fornicates with whores can be explained in part by Israel's fertility worship. But Hosea also suggests that this is connected with the economic conditions and strife that arose at this time. That Hosea bought a woman out of penury (Ho. 3:2) indicates that a crucial aspect of Israel's abandonment of the covenant was reflected in the oppression implicit in a society that was blind to the inequality within it. Whoring is a sin not only because of its sexual immorality, but also because it involves the buying and selling of women. The impact on society was infuriating to the prophet: "They shall eat, but not be satisfied," suggesting that the powerful couldn't determine if they had enough (Ho. 4:10). Furthermore, when he says, "a trader in whose hands are false balances, he loves to oppress," Hosea suggests that this wealth creation was, at least in part, generated by fraud (Ho. 12:7). Israel gets rich through the buying and selling of women, and by doing so, abandons the covenant. Hosea, who himself marries someone who has been part of this system, struggles to make sense of it (Ho. 1).

Jeremiah, in his temple sermon (Jer. 7:1–15), declares that the responsibility of Israel is to care for the vulnerable, repeating five of the commandments as part of remembering the covenant with God. He states that obedience to the covenant, not ritual sacrifice, is the basis of Israel's relationship with God. Plainly, practices that seem idolatrous cannot replace the requirement for moral behavior and the protection of the most marginalized (Jer. 7:21–28). Again, the protection of the poor is contrasted with the rituals and practices of worship.

Amos also excoriates the people by complaining about how the rich are having a good time, denouncing people who lie on beds of ivory while they have no concern for the nation at large (Amos 6:4–7). He declares he hates all the festivals that are being thrown, while there is so much injustice and unrighteousness (Amos 5:21–24). Again, the prophets make a connection between the habits of the rich, their indifference, and their worship of false Gods.

The prophet Isaiah also rages against the people for their decadence in the face of injustice:

> 11 What to me is the multitude of your sacrifices?
>   says the Lord;
> I have had enough of burnt offerings of rams
>   and the fat of fed beasts;
> I do not delight in the blood of bulls,
>   or of lambs, or of goats.
>
> 12 When you come to appear before me,
>   who asked this from your hand?
> Trample my courts no more;

13 bringing offerings is futile;
  incense is an abomination to me.
New moon and Sabbath and calling of convocation—
  I cannot endure solemn assemblies with iniquity.
14 Your new moons and your appointed festivals
  my soul hates;
they have become a burden to me,
  I am weary of bearing them.
15 When you stretch out your hands,
  I will hide my eyes from you;
even though you make many prayers,
  I will not listen;
  your hands are full of blood. (Is 1:11–15)

Isaiah connects the sacrifices with the injustice of fraud and exploitation. People engage in liturgical activity, see the presence of God and yet are not protecting the vulnerable. This harsh critique makes clear that ritual activities could not replace the moral accounting between God and the people of Israel. Their economic expectation was that their shared abundance as a nation was a measure of this accounting, while the abandonment of the vulnerable was reflected in ineffective sacrifices to both God and to His rivals. By forgoing the neediest, the sacrifices were idolatrous.

Money and Jesus

I assume that Jesus remains central to the Christian narrative and that his ministry is foundational to how the Body of Christ is to understand markets and money. The Sermon on the Mount, central both to the Catholic Catechism and to Christian theology, provides the most foundational description of Christian ethics. I presume that they are common texts for our understanding and are central in forming the Christian worldview.

Jesus says, "You cannot serve both God and Wealth" (Mt 6:24). Wealth represents power, reflected in networks of relationships that include the empire. The stark choice between the power of God and wealth can be understood as both prescriptive and descriptive. God and wealth are distinct; sometimes one has to choose. However, for a Christian, money is not necessarily God, even if the emperor is printed upon it. Therefore "to serve" and "to use" are distinguished. One can use money, even if it is a peril, and not serve it. Money symbolizes and facilitates multiple sorts of shared activities among different sorts of social networks. However, Jesus knows that money requires a network of institutions to have power.

When the Pharisees challenge Jesus about paying taxes, he responds with a reflection about the relationship between the state, money, and God (Mt 22:15–22). The coins have an image of the Emperor, who is himself, a god. In this passage, Jesus connects money and tax, recognizing the power of the stamp of the emperor and its command over the empire. His answer, to the Pharisees who challenge him about whose coin it is, is suggestive, if not ambiguous: "*Give therefore to the emperor the things that are the emperor's, and to God the things that are God's*" underscores that money is like a god, and even contains his image. And yet, it is not God. Of course, all things finally belong to God, and even the emperor cannot undermine that reality. Jesus' contempt for wealth extends to the way even his disciples measure how money can be used to solve social problems; when the poor widow pours expensive oil upon him, he chastises the disciples for their miserliness (Luke 21:1–4). Even they have been seduced by the need to measure another's generosity.

Scripture confirms that money, which represents a sign and value, is itself not value-neutral as an object, but conveys a network of relationships of power which include institutions that have the authority to coin, record, and measure. As such, it cannot be merely considered a tool or as a method of establishing equivalent value between goods. It also represents, in part, a symbol of debt to the state and thus expresses political power. Money may redeem sin if it commends the possibility of purchasing freedom, of generosity, and of gift. Money expresses sociability and interdependence, and can provide a liberation from debt. As a tool, it provides a way to share the sacrifice made to appease a God. It provides a symbol of trust as a replicable sign. It is, of course, presented as a sacrificial substitute. It solves the problems it creates.

If money has a relationship to debt and if debt and sin are homologous, then money has a relationship to sin also. Sin reflects a debt to God (Nh 5:3–7; Am 2.6, 8.2). The correspondence of religious language and economic language is not accidental or incidental, but complementary and congruent. Insofar as economics was concerned with obligations, so is the teaching of the church, as both are about organizing social life.

Nonetheless, conflict between individuals often arises out of envy and desire. The impulse toward sin arises from such feelings. It is to this sentiment we now attend.

> Proverbs 28:25: The greedy person stirs up strife, but whoever trusts in the Lord will be enriched.

> Mark 12: 38–40: As he taught, he said, "Beware of the scribes, who like to walk around in long robes, and to be greeted with respect in the market-places, and to have the best seats in the synagogues and places of honour at banquets! They devour widows' houses and for the sake of appearance say long prayers. They will receive the greater condemnation."

Covetousness, Property, and God's Law

Regulating tension is a crucial concern of scripture, and that this was reflected by an accounting of sin, debt, and money. These are highlighted through the problem of desire and covetousness. The list of specific transgressions in the Decalogue ends with the more general prohibition that signifies the urge to covet, to have what another has. The commandment is deliberately comprehensive; the writer implies a single commandment could encapsulate most of human conflict through this single prohibition. As one biblical commentator writes, "The Tenth Commandment thus functions as a kind of summary commandment, the violation of which is a first step that can lead to the violation of any one or all the rest of the commandments. As such, it is necessarily all-embracing and descriptive of an attitude rather than a deed. It was perhaps set last in the Decalogue precisely because of this uniquely comprehensive application."[34] As such, coveting takes a central place in biblical life. The composer of the ten commandments realizes that the list of objects possibly desired was endless. And so, the previous commandments are emphasized, but it remains comprehensive enough to include what was not considered. Envy corrodes human cooperation. It can be easily intensified and disruptive.

Desire is the root of envy. Rivalry is one of its components. A central concern in the relationships described in the bible are how close relatives want what others want. The relationship of Cain and Abel (Gen 4:1–16), Sarah's relationship to Hagar (Gen 16), David and Uriah (2 Sam 11–12), Jacob and Esau (Gen 25:19–34), Ahab and Naboth (1 Kings 21:1–15) all describe the impact of envy upon the people of Israel. Yet each story also reveals a transcendent response to the reality of these actions. The prohibition insinuates that the problem of coveting and envy, especially between people who are close, is particularly fraught and real. It affects both families and firms, neighborhoods and nations. And scripture recognizes that these prohibitions are required to ensure a peaceable kingdom.

Envy occurs in our closest relationships, extended networks, and with God. Elements of envy include elevating our own needs above others and forgetting, diminishing, or ignoring our interdependence. Envy, a social comparison with others, expresses a fear of loss. Envy increases our dissatisfaction and anxiety about the future. Scripture's attempts to regulate envy highlight how powerful it is, including its condemnation of acquisitiveness.

Envy, Status, and Money

Scriptures allude, however, that wealth, power, and status corrupt those who have it. The widows become oblivious to the scribes (Mark 12:38–40). Individuals become more concerned with status and having what another has (1 Kings 21:1–15) that focus the attention of the eyes of others. While the ones who envy may not appear envious, they are the individuals who are seen, who gather attention, and recipients are of other people's envy. The envied may not be aware to the degree they also envy.

The desire to have more, to accumulate, encourages practices that exploit aliens, orphans, and widows. Someone who has economic power, with physical backing, can manipulate measurements; steal lands through physical force; and influence the legal system. Bruce Longenecker calls this during the Roman Empire "Elite Acquisitive Manipulation."[35] The wealth that the prophets condemn has been acquired through violence, stealing, or other sorts of injustice. The inclination to acquire begins with envy and desire to have what another has. Even correctly performed rites cannot redeem the exploitation of the poor and erase the way such money has been made. The prophets remind us that sacrificing animals and grain while committing injustice will not please God. The prophets say the wealthy and powerful become covetous, have the power to take what they want (Mh 2:1–2), and use deception to pad their pockets by manipulating weights and measures (Mh 9–12). Covetousness motivates theft and violence, and acquisitive desire takes priority over equity and justice. An oil company's donation to the World Wildlife Fund won't clean up an oil spill.

Some scholars take great pains to distinguish kinds of wealth. The biblical scholar Luke T. Johnson specifies that the prophets condemn *ill-gotten wealth*, specifically wealth gained through oppression, stealing, or manipulating the justice system rather than *all* wealth. He emphasizes that the prophets' admonishing of those who substitute correct ritual behavior can atone for the exploitation of the poor. Right relationship, the exercise of mercy, is prior to sacrifices.[36]

The story of King Ahab and Naboth (1 Kings 21) tells how Ahab seeks to buy Naboth's land. He offers what seems like a fair exchange to him, but Naboth rejects the offer. In response, Ahab's wife, Jezebel, manipulates the legal system to invent charges of blasphemy against Naboth, resulting in the death penalty. Ahab is now able to seize the land.

The story raises central issues in market and social networks. One sort of network understands land as replicable, as exchangeable, and thus profitable. Property primarily has a value for its productivity. For Ahab, the value of a piece of land has little emotional content. For Naboth, however, the land illustrates a deeper connection that reflects generations of relationships. His ownership of property is embedded within the system of relationships, his family. The wealthy person desires to make the land productive, but the landowner may not see productivity as the measure of the land's worth. We now see through this story the ease with which people who have wealth will seek to acquire more, who have an interest in gaining wealth through theft or exploitation, as these mock the proper relationship of God and destroy the covenant of the community.

Scripture is particularly aware of how wealth intensifies envy and disrupts the minds of those who have more. While it also refers to the resentment of the poor, the avarice of the prosperous is pernicious because they set the rules of the network. When the acquisitive accumulate without restraint, the poor get crushed beneath their desires. Luke warns us, for example, to beware of the scribes: the honor received by them to the devouring of widow's houses. Beneath the prayers of the religious leaders is an acquisitiveness that conceals the exploitation of the poorest. The connection is implicit; the places of honor come upon the backs of those who cannot afford it (Luke 20:45–47).

On Abundance and Having Things

> "For the Lord your God is bringing you into a good land, a land with flowing streams, with springs and underground waters welling up in valleys and hills, a land of wheat and barley, of vines and fig trees and pomegranates, a land of olive trees and honey, a land where you may eat bread without scarcity, where you will lack nothing, a land whose stones are iron and from whose hills you may mine copper. You shall eat your fill and bless the Lord your God for the good land that he has given you. Take care that you do not forget the Lord your God, by failing to keep his commandments, his ordinances, and his statutes, which I am commanding you today. When you have eaten your fill and have built fine houses and live in them, and when your herds and flocks have multiplied, and your silver and gold is multiplied, and all that you have is multiplied, then do not exalt yourself, forgetting the Lord your God, who brought you out of the land of Egypt, out of the house of slavery, who led you through the great and terrible wilderness, an arid wasteland with poisonous snakes and scorpions. He made water flow for you from flint rock, and fed you in the wilderness with manna that your ancestors did not know, to humble

> you and to test you, and in the end to do you good. Do not say to yourself, "My power and the might of my own hand have gotten me this wealth." But remember the Lord your God, for it is he who gives you power to get wealth, so that he may confirm his covenant that he swore to your ancestors, as he is doing today." *Dt 8:7–18*

Central to the scriptural narrative is that the people of Israel will be led into a land of abundance. The Hebrew scriptures do not commend poverty for its own sake; poverty neither proves moral righteousness nor signifies moral turpitude. Wealth need not represent moral righteousness, but abundance is a good and a gift from God. Scripture suggests the land will provide for the people; it commends those who are industrious and faithful. While scripture condemns wealth that has been built through exploitation, wealth may benefit an entire nation. The impulse of austerity, frugality, scarcity, and miserliness arise from a fear of God's displeasure, that he will take away his promise.

However, individual ownership and abundance raises a tension. The importance of having property, of an individual making a claim to having a thing, highlights the roots of some of the internal and external challenges communities face. Differences in kinds or amounts of abundance between people creates envy, which in turn shapes our economic choices. People want what others have, including trinkets, land, and persons. Objects can have power; they reflect and shape perspectives and establish identities. Property can organize our life, claim our time, and direct behavior. Goods, land, and persons are exchanged and given. Stuff matters, and things like bread, a table, a stone, or money can convey an emotionally charged or religious experience. Also, giving things or property away, furthermore, can build relationships and reduce tension. One reason money heightens the emotional connection with property is that it facilitates how persons create, make, and allocate the goods they have.

Archbishop William Temple wrote, "The institution of property is regarded as rooted in sin; for if all men loved God with all their hearts and their neighbors as themselves, they would cheerfully labor for the common good and take for themselves no more than their fair share. But men are sinful, so property-rights are needed, not so much for the satisfaction of the rich as for the protection of the poor." The state should then protect both the property rights of those who have, as well as those who have less. In this way the idea of property rights can limit and curtail the economics of plunder and theft. As, in other words, "avarice created the rights of property," the desire to have more and the fear of losing what one has creates the need to build institutions that will protect having property.[37]

Property has several characteristics. For example, the biblical scholar Luke Johnson says persons perceive within their possessions a sense of the ultimate. Some possessions, as idols, control their worshippers; but then God "who calls humans out of such fearful, compulsive self-grasping into a new life of freedom that enables them to use things without being owned by them." He says that it is possible to relate to possessions with disinterest. Possessions are neutral, but they also reflect a concrete connection to the world, a sense of place and identity. Having things does not make one greedy or grasping.[38]

While Johnson takes a more individualistic view that deemphasizes the impact of one's possession upon the life of another, he recognizes that the relationship of a person to their property and possessions can be disordered. Even if property is a thing, it is possible to idolize or fetishize it, as it misdirects us away from God. Prioritizing God deprioritizes the ownership over a thing.

Honoring ownership, through custom and the rules of the state, mitigates the problem of envy. Therefore, institutions that protect the warrants of ownership, and prevent or prosecute theft, may seek to prevent envy from destabilizing a relationship. Such institutions include legal institutions, such as the state, that can enforce the rules around owning property. Having property rights therefore necessitates the power of establishing those rights.

The scriptures explained this bargain between ownership and coercion. The problem intensifies because money makes it easier to accumulate property and builds the larger bureaucracies of empire. Money provides several functions here; it reduces transaction costs, and allows bureaucrats and soldiers who protect property to be paid. It depends on the existence of these institutional relationships while also establishing different sorts of relationships and networks among a greater number of people. Money intensifies, therefore, while also rendering invisible the social relationships implicit in the exchange of property.

The doctrine of the incarnation may imply that property and self cannot be always neatly distinguished. If our materiality reflects the reality of God becoming a human, then in some way the material forces that shape our lives reflect our experience of God. It is the direction to which that pattern turns us which matters: does it turn us primarily toward the objects themselves, or toward God and our communities?

Scripture does not prohibit ownership or participation in an economy, but it does not assume an individual must own any good exclusively. The intuition of the Archbishop, however, that property reflects sin and avarice, deserves further clarification. Ownership implies more than the ability to use what is owned, that the object is somehow attached to a specific person apart from the actual use. The warrant for ownership, however, is not necessarily divine fiat, as all proceeds from God. The warrant to own goods is physically justified through claims backed by institutions that maintain titles or deeds and defend customs. While money may be directed by a person to purchase or share, it given the power of obligation by the state.

If I have a visitor, for example, and I was not in the house but they needed to drive my car or were thirsty for glass of wine, it would make sense that they would seek my permission because these objects are mine. But it is also plausible that there are some situations where ownership does not matter or its declaration would seem awkward, insensitive, taboo, or wrong. For example, if I have some friends over and I begin to eat, stating at the beginning of the meal that the food is mine would seem impolite and rude, even though I had bought the food with my own wealth. If I remind a visitor flipping through my library that the books were owned by me and repeatedly declare what is mine, and what the visitor can and cannot touch in my house, I might be breaking the unspoken custom between people that places a way of relating above ownership. Thus, common courtesies affirm "my house is your house" or other kinds of a shared life or values.

Furthermore, personal ownership can include both exclusive and shared ownership. Two people can have the same object. While possessions express significance about the self, practical ownership allows for sharing in familiar networks of kinship or affection.

The importance of individual property ownership introduces the problem of scarcity, as what makes the having of property relatively important is the idea that someone else does not have the same thing. If all people have the same kind and quality of a good, the importance of individual ownership diminishes. Alternately, scripture affirms an abundance that arises from what is held in common, what cannot be owned by any person.

In Deuteronomy, the writer says,

> "For the Lord your God is bringing you into a good land, a land with flowing streams, with springs and underground waters welling up in valleys and hills, a land of wheat and barley, of vines and fig trees and pomegranates, a land of olive trees and honey, a land where you may eat bread without scarcity, where you will lack nothing, a land whose stones are iron and from whose hills you may mine copper. You shall eat your fill and bless the Lord your God for the good land that he has given you." (Deut 8:7–10)

In this way, God does not want his people to lack. This does not deny that ownership is valuable, but that it cannot be central to the life of the people of Israel. All that is circulates among the people. While we each may have objects that we own, that we use, that we possess, God's economy arises from the abundance of the earth which we all share.

Individual property brings forth the problem of envy, which challenges the mechanics of establishing ownership in a community of persons. Scripture offers some clues as to how the people of God can understand envy. Jesus has something to say about envy and its connection with debt and empire, and ways for his followers to diminish their own propensity to covet.

Jesus: Envy, Debt, and Empire

In the story of the rich man and Lazarus (Luke 16:19–31) a wealthy man consumed by envy dies and is sent to hell; his envy made it impossible even to see Lazarus until after he dies. The wealthy man is always, implicitly, looking upward, to those who have more, whereas Lazarus is surrounded by comforting dogs.

One constituent element of envy is the desire to be seen by others. In contrast, Jesus commends not practicing piety in order to be seen, to give alms in secret, and to eschew praise (Mt 6:1–6). Instead, God rewards a piety where rivalry is diminished in favor of the act itself; comparison should not be the reason one engages in acts of charity or redemption, but the inclination to perform the act apart from needing to be seen. God removes us from a network where envy is the driving force.

In the parable of the guests (Lk 14:10), Jesus commends the disciples to take the lowest seat rather than the first. He critiques the seating arrangements that reflect the status of the members of the dinner party, exhorting a rearranging of the places, short-circuiting the immediate desire to be placed in the seat of honor.

Similarly, Jesus' response to the competition between the disciples (Mk 10:35–44) for his attention illustrates how Jesus manages rivalry, by rearranging the idea of status and questioning if it is an appropriate object of envy. Jesus diminishes the appeal of the objects desired, asserting that human forms of lordship and public displays of piety are not what God rewards.

This does not mean that fasting, charity, and acts of mercy are unimportant, but that who sees them is irrelevant. He limits the power of envy by illustrating that what we see is relativized by God's own omniscience. What matters is not that other people see us, but that God does. Therefore, Jesus destabilizes desire and envy by rearranging our instinctive need to be seen.

Jesus Exhorts the Forgiveness of Debts (Matthew 6:12)

In the central prayer that Jesus teaches the disciples, we read that we are to forgive debts. I assume that the Lord's prayer remains central to how Jesus prays and who he is. The biblical scholar Hans Deiter Betz writes that the language of debt "comes from law and commerce," but asserts that, "applied to the relationship between God and humanity, this language is used metaphorically." Even for one of the foremost scholars on the Sermon on the Mount, debt is a theological concern. While he describes debt as one fundamentally of relationship, he seeks to extricate the problem of debt away from the problem of markets. Because mutual obligations matter, and are often not reciprocal, justice has to manage the "unresolved obligations" in which we find ourselves. Betz does not discuss compulsion or money itself; instead, debt is a sin because we haven't fulfilled our obligations and we can never meet them, so we are asking for something: "Since human life as a whole consists of an interconnected web of obligations, the totality of all obligations constitutes human sinfulness."[39]

Betz shows that Jesus understood we are in debt to God. God knows the degree we are dependent upon him and each other, and this is reflected through the obligations in which we are embedded. We must approach God for a new accounting, a cancellation of our debts to him. Since others may not forgive our debts, so we appeal to God. And so upholding debts is both a part of divine justice, a description of our real dependence, but alone we cannot pay it back.

Betz hints at there is some tension: "That these debts are indebted to us means we can do something about their debts. Regardless of whether we know these debts personally or whether these debts are large or small, old or new, we are authorized legally to dispose of them either by claiming them or by forgiving them."[40] One on hand, this debt reflects the space between our limits and insufficiency and God's, but it remains a problem of justice, for the debt holder as well as the one indebted. Betz struggles with the fact that debt itself is not *mutual* obligation, but expresses a dynamic relationship of power; some people are in debt to others, and Jesus would have known that while there is a system of debts implicit, this forgiveness of debt is not merely a recalibration of mutual obligation, but a way of restoring the life force outside of market driven realities. Certainly we have a debt to God, but Jesus is also saying that the people here should forgive debts, and that we may be forgiven so that we can recalibrate the system upon which the market depends. Because Betz lacks a theory of money behind debt, he cannot see how Jesus seeks to remake the system. Scholars like Betz may correctly identify that we are parts of networks ("mutual obligation") but they do not identify how obligation actually is manifested. Practices of obligation aren't merely ones of sentiment, but also ones of force, and money is part of the physicality of mutual obligation. For as Gary Anderson writes, "According to the logic of the metaphor this prayer employs, we are in danger of becoming debt-slaves when we sin. Should the act go uncorrected, then one will have to "pay" for the "cost" of the misdeed through the "currency" of physical punishment. Fortunately God is merciful and will remit the debt we owe if we humbly beseech him."[41]

The mechanics of debt and sin show how a hearer would have understood Jesus' prayer. To remove one's debts is to put oneself in a different relationship with ownership and changes one's relationship with money and coin itself. The relationships between the person forgiving and the one being forgiven change because the tool that holds people in bondage, debt, and money is removed.

Jesus Critiques the Master to the Household

Jesus describes the relationship of the master and lord to explore the household economy. Jesus is not only prescribing behavior, but illustrating the nature of plunder at the heart of the economic relationships his hearers would have known. In Matthew 21:33–41, Jesus explains the relationship between the absentee landlord and the servants. In Matthew 22:1–14, a brutal master invites everyone to the party, and yet even one person dressed wrong is deposed of at the unrelenting hand of the king. The parable of the "foolish" maidens explores what happens when one set of maidens excludes another due to a false sense of scarcity; the parable of the talents (Matthew 25:14–30) may be a story about wise investing, but the third servant also exposes the rapaciousness of the master who holds him in complete bondage. The master is someone who does reap where they do not sow, and gathers where he has not winnowed. Other people have done the work for him, and because the truth has now been shown, the last servant is cast out. The master must always gain, and everyone else is bound to lose. In this sense, Jesus is critiquing the social or political arrangement that has arranged an economy that has created a false sense of scarcity. The problem is not merely the arrangement of resources but who gets to have a say.

Jesus Counts

Whereas the economy of the householder and market describes persons who are indebted to the master, Jesus relates parables about loss and gain, recasting the emotional content of worth. The experience of loss matters. The scholar Amy

Jill Levine notes, in Luke 15:4–32, various differences in experiencing loss: "the shepherd does not take responsibility for losing his shoe; the woman admits her fault; and the father doesn't even realize his elder son is lost."[42] Through these parables, Jesus provides a fuller explanation of what matters, lifting up emotional experiences outside the market network, ones that cannot be merely explained through a simple cost-benefit accounting. Instead, Jesus reminds us what matters in our reconciliation, in our reconnection, in our rediscovery after loss: "We need to take count not only of our blessings, but also of those in our families and in our communities. And once we count, we need to act. Finding the lost, whether they are sheep, coins, or people, takes work. It also requires our efforts and from those efforts there is the potential for wholeness and joy."[43] *We are loss averse, but remember what matters.*

Jesus offers a different framework of understanding worth and abundance. For when the son of man comes, compared to the previous master, the faithful are rewarded based on providing for the least of these. Jesus Christ or God is not identical to the masters. In the household of the market, worth is measured in monetary terms. But Jesus constantly resists this. Instead, Jesus looks to count what has not been counted, and what cannot be measured by money. Jesus asks us, what do we have to lose?

Jesus and Abundance

A market economy is mediated by money; some households are organized through a careful accounting and measuring that money provides. However, a market economy is also identified by scarcity, the possibility of not having enough. But Jesus hints at a deeper kind of abundance which describes the multiple other networks that make up a human life.

> He says, "Therefore I tell you, do not worry about your life, what you will eat or what you will drink, or about your body, what you will wear. Is not life more than food, and the body more than clothing? Look at the birds of the air; they neither sow nor reap nor gather into barns, and yet your heavenly Father feeds them. Are you not of more value than they? And can any of you by worrying add a single hour to your span of life? And why do you worry about clothing? Consider the lilies of the field, how they grow; they neither toil nor spin, yet I tell you, even Solomon in all his glory was not clothed like one of these. But if God so clothes the grass of the field, which is alive today and tomorrow is thrown into the oven, will he not much more clothe you—you of little faith? Therefore do not worry, saying, 'What will we eat?' or 'What will we drink?' or 'What will we wear?' For it is the Gentiles who strive for all these things; and indeed your heavenly Father knows that you need all these things. But strive first for the kingdom of God and

> his righteousness, and all these things will be given to you as well. So do not worry about tomorrow, for tomorrow will bring worries of its own. Today's trouble is enough for today. (Matt 6:25–34)

Jesus points to other sorts of abundance. The children of God have enough. When Jesus says that the Kingdom of Heaven is like yeast or a mustard seed, he describes an economy of abundance. The scholar Amy Jill Levine playfully suggests that "perhaps the parable tells us that despite all our images of golden slippers and harps and atolls, the kingdom is present at the communal oven when everyone has enough to eat. It is present, inchoate, in everything, and it is available to all, from the sourdough starter to the rain and the sunshine. It is something that works its way through our lives and we realize its import only when we do not have it."[44] This seems to describe a way of understanding networks differently, where we have a better understanding of an alternative form of how our social networks exist: God is more like yeast than money.

Similarly, Jill Levine interprets the parable of the mustard seed like so: "the kingdom is present when nature and humanity work together."[45] God works through other networks that map our environment. While the market system has the power to direct and organize the household and economy, there are many other ways the world connects, shapes, and gives life.

In contrast, the market, as described in scripture, drains the life force of individuals through debt, forcing the actions of tenants and servants into patterns of self-destruction. In the human economy, however, small actions that build a community are powerful. Levine suggests, "what we see now is potential, but that potential needs to be actualized. The yeast has to be placed into the dough, the seed has to be planted. Even small actions, or hidden actions, have the potential to produce great things." Furthermore, it may be that, as she says, "some things need to be left alone."[46] There's no need to presume we are the center of all activity. Money, because it intensifies and identifies specifically human power, invites us to feel like gods, as if our need to act is everything that matters.

Finally, the abundance Jesus values is illustrated by his anointing (Matt 26:7–11; Mark 14:3–7; Luke 7:36–50; John 12:1–8). It provides another clue of how Jesus understands the use of wealth even as his disciples are counting every penny. While disciples are displeased at the extravagance of the woman, carefully noting its expense, Jesus looks at the oil as a way he is relating to the woman in question. She is preparing for burial. The disciples still see the oil through the lens of dollar signs, whereas Jesus is taking in the physicality and the appreciation, the gratitude of the event itself. Luke describes (Lk 7:41–42) it precisely as a riposte to debt itself; in John it is held in contrast to Judas' zealotry. But in every case, *Jesus puts the relationship of himself with the woman outside whatever accounting the disciples require.*

In sum, Jesus refocuses his parables to highlight the impact of a monetary market-based way of organizing our networks, contrasting to the many other ways we create networks of relating. Jesus understands that individuals lose things and measure incorrectly. However, God values what people cannot or do not measure. The earth grows around us and our small actions make a difference. And even during rest is when one can get out of the way and enjoy the wholeness and joy known in the Sabbath. The call to love one's neighbor is not meant to be an impossible demand, or merely an eschatological description.

Putting this into practice in the early communities, however, is reflected in Paul, who has something to say about church networks in light of his understanding of the response to Jesus Christ.

Interdependence and Redemption

> For you know the generous act of our Lord Jesus Christ, that though he was rich, yet for your sakes he became poor, so that by his poverty you might become rich. And in this matter I am giving my advice: it is appropriate for you who began last year not only to do something but even to desire to do something—now finish doing it, so that your eagerness may be matched by completing it according to your means. For if the eagerness is there, the gift is acceptable according to what one has—not according to what one does not have. I do not mean that there should be relief for others and pressure on you, but it is a question of a fair balance between your present abundance and their need, so that their abundance may be for your need, in order that there may be a fair balance. As it is written,
> "The one who had much did not have too much, and the one who had little did not have too little."
>
> Now it is not necessary for me to write you about the ministry to the saints, for I know your eagerness, which is the subject of my boasting about you to the people of Macedonia, saying that Achaia has been ready since last year; and your zeal has stirred up most of them. But I am sending the brothers in order that our boasting about you may not prove to have been empty in this case, so that you may be ready, as I said you would be; otherwise, if some Macedonians come with me and find that you are not ready, we would be humiliated—to say nothing of you—in this undertaking. So I thought it necessary to urge the brothers to go on ahead to you, and arrange in advance for this bountiful gift that you have promised, so that it may be ready as a voluntary gift and not as an extortion.

> The point is this: the one who sows sparingly will also reap sparingly, and the one who sows bountifully will also reap bountifully. Each of you must give as you have made up your mind, not reluctantly or under compulsion, for God loves a cheerful giver. And God is able to provide you with every blessing in abundance, so that by always having enough of everything, you may share abundantly in every good work. As it is written, "He scatters abroad, he gives to the poor; his righteousness endures forever." He who supplies seed to the sower and bread for food will supply and multiply your seed for sowing and increase the harvest of your righteousness. You will be enriched in every way for your great generosity, which will produce thanksgiving to God through us; for the rendering of this ministry not only supplies the needs of the saints but also overflows with many thanksgivings to God. (2 Corinthians 8:7–15; 9:1–12)

Jesus critiques economics through telling stories about envy, governance, abundance, and loss. In response to Jesus, Paul commends how the early community organized its network responding to their experience with Christ. He connects wealth, both material and spiritual, contrasting the wealth of those in Corinth and Christ's poverty by exhorting a sacrificial gift from the wealthy that is also acceptable by the recipient. The exchange is neither extorted nor patronizing. Paul affirms instead an equality prior to an equality of wealth, one where the transfer and exchange of wealth will not be humiliating for either party. There is a willingness to give, and an exhortation, a reminder of the abundance that has been given through Christ. Implicitly, the economy of the church suggests a willingness to give all.

What matters to this equality is that *all get fed*, and there is neither surplus or a shortage. This equality contains a sense of a deeper, spiritual equality beyond wealth that undergirds peace; its opposite is acquisitive desire, greed. Secondly, this dynamic reflects a desire for unity and interdependence among different church communities. Unity, an understanding of shared values, is thus prior to economic distinctions.

In Paul's church economy, spiritual worth precedes economic value. What is valuable is not measured through money. Money cannot measure the particularity and concreteness of human relationships and identities. Therefore, wealth comes in different forms, not simply money. One may have an abundance of spiritual gifts, the other financial gifts. And one should not have too little of one and too much of the other; for this reason, a more unified church requires generosity that points to a richer sense of equality. This equality may mirror the relationship of the nature of the trinity—distinct, but equal, and always relating to each other. And fundamentally, this relationship is interdependent.

Consequently, early Christian communities engaged the poor. Bruce Longenecker, writing about Paul and Poverty in *Remembering the Poor,* affirms that the care of the poor was an integral and ubiquitous part of early Christian communities, a marker for Jesus' followers. It exemplified being transformed by the God of Israel. He writes, "For Paul, the notion of 'love' is grounded in the gritty realities of self-giving for the benefit of others... This kind of generous goodness to the needy exemplifies and characterizes precisely the 'faith working practically through love' by which the Mosaic law is fulfilled." In short, "remembrance of the poor seems to have been a prime attribute of the cruciform pattern of life."[47] This affirms that any understanding of Christian economics has always been marked by *some* transfer of wealth to the poor. An economy, either planned or free, cannot be understood as Christian unless it includes some stipulation that generosity is a prior social and institutional commitment, one that may require its own set of prohibitions and incentives. A Christian economics cannot treat such generosity toward the poor as an incidental lucky break in a free-market economy. If one is to support any institution that makes economic decisions, it must begin by asking what are the consequences for those who are not at the center of market networks. Certainly the shape of *how* may be specific to time and place, but excuses of bootstraps, self-help, self-reliance, and other misdirections cannot abdicate the responsibility of Christian disciples to be openly generous. At the heart of the faithful economy is a network of free-flowing abundance that offers grace and kindness to those who have the least.

The early Church communities allowed both a release from the constant pressure of seeking status and others more access to status. It mitigated the difference between economic classes, providing places for, as Bruce Longenecker notes, "the early Jesus-movement was able to balance both other-interestedness with self-interest, in what was perceived by many to be a win-win situation." In other words, providing help for others also meant helping oneself; a moderately prosperous person could receive some status in a small community outside the competitiveness for honor of the civic arena, while also rewards for being in a new community.[48]

Those who desire to experience God or reflect his will recognize that all wealth is dependent upon God, and not only the fruits of personal labor, and, correspondingly, the abundance of the community reflects its interdependence. This is both true and desirable. Individual accumulation of wealth corrodes social life and is therefore prescribed. Instead, the spirit encourages saying "enough," and taking joy in our shared abundance. The correction is to remember the call to be generous and to observe the Sabbath.

The Perils of Money

> Come now, you rich people, weep and wail for the miseries that are coming to you. Your riches have rotted, and your clothes are moth-eaten. Your gold and silver have rusted, and their rust will be evidence against you, and it will eat your flesh like fire. You have laid up treasure for the last days. Listen! The wages of the laborers who mowed your fields, which you kept back by fraud, cry out, and the cries of the harvesters have reached the ears of the Lord of hosts. You have lived on the earth in luxury and in pleasure; you have fattened your hearts in a day of slaughter. You have condemned and murdered the righteous one, who does not resist you. (James 5:1–6)
>
> "Let all who are under the yoke of slavery regard their masters as worthy of all honor, so that the name of God and the teaching may not be blasphemed. Those who have believing masters must not be disrespectful to them on the ground that they are members of the church; rather they must serve them all the more, since those who benefit by their service are believers and beloved. Teach and urge these duties. Whoever teaches otherwise and does not agree with the sound words of our Lord Jesus Christ and the teaching that is in accordance with godliness, is conceited, understanding nothing, and has a morbid craving for controversy and for disputes about words. From these come envy, dissension, slander, base suspicions, and wrangling among those who are depraved in mind and bereft of the truth, imagining that godliness is a means of gain. Of course, there is great gain in godliness combined with contentment; for we brought nothing into the world, so that we can take nothing out of it; but if we have food and clothing, we will be content with these. But those who want to be rich fall into temptation and are trapped by many senseless and harmful desires that plunge people into ruin and destruction. For the love of money is a root of all kinds of evil, and in their eagerness to be rich some have wandered away from the faith and pierced themselves with many pains. But as for you, man of God, shun all this; pursue righteousness, godliness, faith, love, endurance, gentleness. Fight the good fight of the faith; take hold of the eternal life, to which you were called and for which you made the good confession in the presence of many witnesses. In the presence of God, who gives life to all things, and of Christ Jesus, who in his testimony before Pontius Pilate made the good confession, I charge you to keep the commandment without spot or blame until the manifestation of our Lord Jesus Christ, which he will bring about at the right time—he who is the blessed and only Sovereign, the King of kings and Lord of lords. It is he alone who has immortality and dwells in unapproachable light, whom no one has ever seen or can see; to him be honor and eternal dominion. Amen. As for those who in the present age are rich, command them not to be haughty, or to set their hopes on the uncertainty of riches, but rather on God who richly provides us with everything for our enjoyment. They are to do good, to be rich in good works, generous, and ready to share, thus storing up for themselves the treasure of a good foundation for the future, so that they may take hold of the life that really is life." (1 Timothy 6)

Traditionally, there has been a distinction between ill-gotten wealth and having wealth itself. Money need not be corrupting, but even a wealthy person, with

God's help, can enter the kingdom (Mark 10:27; Mt 19:26). It is the love of money, not money as a thing, a tool, that is the problem. Such a view allows a pious wealthy person to have possessions, as long as they understand they are a blessing from God and they should have cheerful inclinations toward generosity. Timothy emphasizes contentment in contrast to the desire "to be rich." And since, to be rich is abstract, it is implicitly comparative, not connoting that one has general comforts, but that one is richer than someone else. Thus, we can have our rich friends with their yachts and apartments on Fifth Avenue as long as they invite us on board and bring us to their dinner parties and don't compare themselves to others. However, the above readings of James and Timothy question this understanding.

In an essay that begins his interpretation of the New Testament, David Bentley Hart challenges this view.[49] He argues that the epistles specifically condemn all acquisitive desire and seeking profit:[50] "It is almost as if, seen from the perspective of the Kingdom, all property is theft. Fair or not, the text does not distinguish good wealth from bad—any more than Christ did."[51] As he relates the sixth chapter of Timothy, "all who seek wealth—not simply all who procure it unjustly—have ensnared themselves in desires that will lead to their ruin."[52] And that the rich should actively redistribute their wealth and hold all of it in common. Only then can the rich be saved.[53]

The early Christians may have thought that Jesus' impending return meant that money had no real value. But over time, the church would have to hold in tension the view of wealth as inherently corrupting with the reality of Christians in the world. As long as there is a church, an empire, and markets, Christians would have to relate with money. It would have to seek a way to balance the different needs of the Christian community within the context of other networks that included the state. One of the main tensions within Christian economics therefore arises from the belief in Christ's impending return.

This was illustrated in the way the church transformed the relationship of the wealthy to the public. As Peter Brown notes, "The imaginative effect of Christian giving was to break down traditional boundaries that had been maintained by the ancient city. Gifts to the city gained fame in this world and in this world only. By contrast, gifts within the churches were thought to join this world to a boundless world beyond the stars. Furthermore, giving was not only for the rich. All believers of all classes were encouraged to contribute to the care of the poor and to the upkeep of the church and clergy. Furthermore, to give to the poor was very different from giving to a clearly defined core of fellow citizens. It was to reach out to a group that was imagined to be as immense and as silent as heaven itself."[54]

As the rhetoric of giving changed, giving became the duty of all members of the Christians community. They were called to give because such giving would not give rewards on this earth, but because there was a heavenly exchange in the process of giving. And so wealth became not a problem, but a way of redemption. Brown continues, "Rather than denouncing the evil origins of wealth and insisting on its total renunciation, writers of the fifth century came to emphasize how wealth could be used to consolidate the Christian community." Wealth need not be given up completely, but a rich person with spiritual discipline, who understood that wealth was a loan by which the heavenly kingdom would be the form of redemption, would share their prosperity with the poorest.[55]

The church understood that generosity, charity, or almsgiving, represented an exchange. It may have included the amelioration of the poor, the widow, and the orphan, but the rewards were also heavenly, and not merely for the status of the city or person. Instead, wealth could redeem, while strengthening the Christian community as a unified whole. This allowed for a greater variety of people to see themselves as responsible for giving. Not merely the prosperous publican, but any person who could give was responsible. And they were not merely responsible for the smaller class of persons within a city's geography, but because their giving had cosmic consequences.

Charity and Sharing Possessions / Trust, Hospitality, and Mercy

The Body of Christ, in light of what constitutes our nature, suggests an economy of generosity, a heavenly economy, erases our sins. Being generous is akin to offering a loan from God that will be paid back with greater rewards.[56] God has given everything, and the debt to him is erased through the payment the haves, the wealthy, the prosperous, make on behalf on the destitute.

The liturgy of the divine mass reflects this mercy, as the Eucharist symbolizes this exchange between Jesus and those receiving the body. As an act of mercy, the Eucharist liberates us from our debts. Although God maintains his sovereignty in rewarding the generous, our almsgiving and offering of our own gifts within the mass both reflects this relationship. A heavenly economy loves mercy and justifies charity and generosity.

Generous networks of charity facilitate the effectiveness of the larger economy. The network of the Body of Christ coordinates together persons of different conditions and therefore inculcates values of love in action. As such, it is intrinsic to the economy of redemption. God does not need our acts of charity himself, but generosity expresses redemption. Giving to the poor becomes a "sacramental" act.[57] Peter Brown, for example, notes that "The joining of generosity to the expiation of sin would become the prevailing breeze throughout the churches of the west."[58] Almsgiving expressed a divine economy where the exchange included eternity. The burden of sin, the temptations of idolatry and acquisitiveness, could be tempered, or even forgiven, through practices of giving.

Redemption means becoming unbound from another, becoming free (Lev 25:48–49). Although slavery is permitted, the owner and purchaser cannot solely determine what is owed by the slave (Lev 25:50–50). The Jubilee year guarantees that the intensity of exploitation is diminished and that bondage is not guaranteed in perpetuity. No just economic system bounds people in perpetuity. Redemption is thus ensured by the Jubilee year and, because the people of Israel are God (and thus cannot be any one else), this redemption is an essential part of who God is for the people (Lev 25:55). Redemption is thus not merely a spiritual consequence of turning toward God, but an economic condition that asserts a limitation to the degree one can own or be owned. Wealth cannot be used to penalize the hungry, and one cannot withhold one's wealth in the face of such conditions. We remain obligated to help one another. Gary Anderson notes that in Daniel, for example, "One way out of debt is physical punishment, but Daniel informs us that there is a second option: giving away one's money to the poor."[59]

Christians can overcome the inclination to acquire through giving: to share the fruits of our labor and their debts and burdens. Almsgiving represents a spiritual economy where debts are paid through generosity. It affirms a symmetry between the poor and the rich; the wealthy were dependent upon the poor so that their own spirituality would develop. The rich needed the poor as they were closer to Jesus; the poor needed the wealth of the prosperous. Almsgiving is a loan to God, where the interest is a reward in heaven. In some sense, a loan is an agent, a key lever, in creating an economy. The poor person, who understands their dependence upon others, is the guarantor who asks for blessings upon the lender, as they are closer to God.[60] This contrasts to the world the church entered where the rich were to be generous, the poor grateful, the relationships asymmetrical. Churches, now tax-exempt, become responsible for the benefit of the poor by administering the physical space and a range of services, including providing food and clothes to medical care. The state in this way incentivized almsgiving.

This reformulation of almsgiving as a loan had an impact in how the state understood its role as incentivizing charity. Loans enhanced productivity: "God has given wealth to some and not to others in order to ensure productivity on the part of everyone." Wealth could better flow within communities. The church fathers believed, for example, that "a healthy economy thrives on a diversity of employment… The wealthy sold their excess wealth to the marketplace, the church, for the love that the poor have from God, becoming richer. Instead of accumulating more money in the bank, it was spread into the economy, accumulating instead as eternity."[61]

This understanding of generosity and almsgiving affirms dependence upon God and the work of other people. As one writer notes, "The ability of an individual to labor and to produce goods at a profit is in due to God's granting of ideal climate conditions, access to land, and gift of life." Workers needed to have been trained *by others*; and tools to have been invented *by others*. No person's profit in a transaction solely belongs to them. Our gains are dependent upon previous generations, and society at large: "The Christian Person was taught that… the one who earns a profit is to be taught the virtue of beneficence; the one who does not is to be taught the virtues of patience and humility. Thus the private motive, such as it exists, has its telos in beneficence rather than personal or corporate enrichment."[62]

Other consequences follow. A coordinated, incentivized almsgiving creates a disinterested respect between two different parties, almost a precursor to capitalism. The idea that almsgiving is a loan softens divisions between the haves and the have-nots, which can reflect the conscience of each the giver and the receiver, rather than affirm solely a relationship where the power dynamic may be unbalanced. Both are receiving goods—one spiritual, one material. Furthermore, almsgiving fosters the idea that we can have *enough*, and puts limit on what would normally be a limitless desire. If money represents the debt to the body politic, then the wealthy owe more to all those impacted by money than do those impacted. The prosperous cannot silo themselves outside of their communities through accumulation. Wealth is not conceptualized as simply what one owns, but also what one stewards on behalf of God's creation.

Generosity and almsgiving connect us with broader networks. Acts of giving, charity, and generosity are future investments. They are examples of trust in God's rewards, both now and in the future. Our generosity, especially toward the poor, reflects God's true nature. It reflects a knowledge that God will give Himself to people. This reflects, in part, the Church's understanding of debt and obligation, for without God we have nothing; our act of giving what we have allows us to also reflect Christ, who became someone who had nothing by giving his life. This extends the scope of reciprocity, identifying especially the poor as the recipient of our exchange. This also extends our commitment to other persons, builds greater moral networks, and inculcates greater virtues in the prosperous.

Although there may be some calculation in justifying generosity, God remains sovereign. Giving does not guarantee God's approval nor his beneficence. Even while the market provides an exchange network that seems stable, God has the authority to establish worth outside the exchange between the donor and the receiver. For the poor are not merely the recipients of generosity, but they are the conduit through whom persons can sacramentally receive redemption. In God's world they are more than the worth calculated by an accountant or an insurance adjuster. This ultimate sovereignty, however, implies that God has only a secondary interest in the impact of money; instead, we may need to challenge the idea of sovereignty though exploring how the cross undergirds our relationship to the market, in which it is God's complete self-giving rather than his independence that matters.

Scholars such as Martin Hengel and Luke Johnson have eschewed radical conceptions of generosity that require communal ownership of possessions (Acts 4:32). While the apostles shared their wealth and Christian communities offered a critique of the wealthy, possessions by individuals themselves remain part of the world as it is. Nonetheless, it is impossible to ignore that for some early Christians, owning property represented the reality of human sin. The urge to possess, especially as intensified through money, was the root of evil, a powerful rival with God. To be wealthy was to own the fruits of exploitation through stealing the wealth of the desperate. As such, Basil and Ambrose both denounced property, because property reflected the greed that exploited the poor. Chrystostom, for example, was convinced that all wealth was ill-gained, as even someone who inherited it did so from someone who received it unjustly. The genealogy of any wealth could be traced to stealing or exploitation.

Nonetheless, the wealthy could participate in the divine economy. In another view, property was a gift from God and a gift for righteousness and prudence. God lends material things to his people, and they are now stewards, called to use them well, and share through the church. Covetousness and insatiable nature, however, creates more wants more than one really needs, while the individual is unaware of what stimulates desire. Others would argue that the shiny baubles, the goods themselves, are not evil, but the faith (or lack of it) one has or doesn't have deceives and distracts the human heart, letting greed and envy blossom. On one hand God is good because it's possible to have goods, but the goods require us also to have a willingness to be generous and share. This became an essential part of the Christian world view. As Peter Brown writes,

> The imaginative effect of Christian giving was to break down traditional boundaries that had been maintained by the ancient city. Gifts to the city gained fame in this world and in this world only. By contrast, gifts within the churches were thought to join this world to a boundless world beyond the stars. Furthermore, giving was not only for the rich. All believers of all classes were encouraged to contribute to the care of the poor and to the upkeep of the church and clergy. Furthermore, to give to the poor was very different from giving to a clearly defined core of fellow citizens. It was to reach out to a group that was imagined to be as immense and as silent as heaven itself.[63]

Giving became the duty of all members of the Christian community. They were called to give because such giving would not give rewards on this earth, but because there was a heavenly exchange in the process of giving. And so wealth became not a problem, but a way of redemption: "Rather than denouncing the evil origins of wealth and insisting on its total renunciation, writers of the fifth century came to emphasize how wealth could be used to consolidate the Christian community."[64] Wealth need not be given up completely, but a rich person of the right spiritual discipline, who understood that wealth was a loan by which the heavenly kingdom would be the form of redemption, would be thus directed to share their prosperity with the poorest.

The church understood that generosity, charity of almsgiving, represented an exchange. It may have included the amelioration of the poor, the widow, and the orphan, but the rewards would have also been heavenly, and not merely for the status of the city or person itself. Instead, wealth could redeem, while strengthening the Christian community as a unified whole. This allowed for a greater variety of people to see themselves as responsible for giving. Not merely the prosperous publican, but any person who could give was responsible. And they were not merely responsible for the smaller class of persons within a city's geography, but because their giving had cosmic consequences.

While we are commanded to share and be generous in our economy, it remains accurate to say the institutions that make our economy possible are distinct from what we see in scripture. Our technology distinguishes our experience of time and space from the first writers and readers of scripture. They might consider our world incomprehensible, our goods magical. We know how idolatry and envy work, but also that people matter. Consequently, we are to shape our personal lives, our networks, and our institutions to encourage a sort of economy within the market that diminishes our own envy, trains people to understand rivalry, and fosters generosity.

Scripture has a preference for the poor, but less clearly affirms centralized economic planning. We may make some theological generalizations about how we treat others or spend our money through the analogy of the cross, the grace bestowed by the Holy Spirit, or the ever-flowing perichoresis of the Holy Trinity. But it is not yet settled that such readings require more than a personal, or local, transformation. The empire, whether it seeks to own the means of production, or shape the commercial institutions within the market, may be beyond redemption. Nonetheless, the language that focuses solely on personal transformation, conversion, and responsibility wrongly assumes that individuals are self-creating and sustaining. It is such individualistic language that invites some of the confusion about individual relationship to any institutions, be it government, corporations, or churches. Therefore, I believe the language of "individualism," while useful, is imprecise. It can help us measure some sorts of values, but it will be incomplete. For this reason, we need to have a strong, robust exploration into how individuals are a part of networks and what this means for understanding the shape of a moral economy.

I believe scripture implicitly challenges the split between personal piety and institutional behavior; the institutions shape personal choices in order to create long-term stability. While scripture does not give detailed instructions about managing a corporation or a government, it implies expectations about generosity and challenges the powerful in their miserliness, and eschews envy by all. Scripture examines the relationship between desire, wealth, and sin, and therefore has an interest in putting money in its proper place in the structural order.

The mandate to love one's neighbor becomes concrete when accounting for how Jesus challenged the power of money in human networks. The ultimate sacrifice of Jesus can tame the dynamic power of markets and money by offering a liberation from both. He does this by forcing the listener to examine the roots of their own desire, from multiple perspectives—from the position of power, from loss, and from powerlessness.

The Sabbath

While the great commandment provides a structure to reorder actions individuals make in a network, the Sabbath provides the geography and the time for understanding its place. The Sabbath provides an internal reset that halts the frenetic intensification of desire. By establishing a space of rest that is separate from the necessity of work, especially to pay off one's debts, the Sabbath and the Jubilee year provide a setting to ensure that one's life is liberated. Acquisitive desire becomes impossible to initiate on the Sabbath, and envy is given a day off.

By being a space that diminishes the power of such desire, the Sabbath restructures the economy of idolatry, sin, and debt by limiting the power of the market. For one day, the use of time redirects away from acquisition toward rest and the cultivation of other sorts of networks, such as kinship. The Jubilee year, as an intensified period of Sabbath time, reestablishes the priority of networks not marked by inequality or slavery. Therefore, the Sabbath creates some internal limits around work and working for others. The desire to acquire, to hoard, to create surplus and money, or to create more work is limited by the command to rest and enjoy the fruits of our labor. It asserts that the purpose, *the telos*, of economic life is toward rest and the celebration of rest. Resting is a good in itself and not for the purpose of working more.

The Sabbath and the Jubilee year realign our relationship with money. They impose limits because they restrain the extent to which one can demand debts upon persons. By affirming a moratorium on debts, it gives space for freedom from work (Lev 25:10). This is one place where the indentured and the slave is now free, because the Sabbath asserts industriousness has no value apart from rest; working eighty-hour weeks is not merely exhausting, but unholy.

The centrality of the Sabbath invites consideration that leisure, reflection, and rest take priority over accumulation, counting, and busyness. Whereas desire shortens time with the immediacy of want, the Sabbath has a capacious, open-ended view of time, which challenges the allocation of our resources. It affirms a pace of time, where relationships, communities, and contexts have value. The scriptures, therefore, invites us into a correction of the impact of market forces on our other networks where time moves at a different pace. They challenge the priority of money over time by providing a space where the desire to acquire more is given no reward.

The insights of economics, the market, and a better accounting may allow us to have a richer way of experiencing rest. Although markets may help quantify and allocate desire, scripture offers constraints upon envy and want in order to sustain other networks worth having. Making money is fine, but being surrounded by kin, friends, and a body of people at rest and in celebration is better. Therefore, God seeks that the people of God create networks that diminish envy, limit debt-bondage, and allow for rest—true security for the Body of Christ.

Peace at the Heart of a Spiritual Economy

God calls us to be in relationship with one another and understands the people of Israel as a people that is bound together. They are dependent upon Him, and each other. The scriptures warn us about the impact of our envy, our acquisitive desire, by reminding the people that he has promised them plenty. As markets and financial networks spread, God warns that desire can be disordered away from God and the community of people toward an attachment to money and wealth itself, which is the root of social tension. This deepens our indebtedness and reflects a separation from God, whereas redemption can be found in our generosity toward others, and creates social conflict. The propensity of the institutions behind money and markets to foster debt-slavery and plunder are intended to be rearranged by networks that direct us to remember the Sabbath. Therefore, scripture establishes prohibitions against coveting, establishes space for leisure and rest, and mandates liberation from debts. This seeks to restore the right kind of interdependence among a people, reducing the conflict between them.

Money has power. It captivates the mind. It has the ability to make individuals act. These very real elements of its nature show why it has the capacity to replace. However, instead of understanding money as a tool that reflects God's grace, it can mislead into a belief that money measures our worth. Money deceives persons into thinking they are independent of others or God. Money can suggest that one can value one's own worth more than others, diminishing how others are also worthy of God's love and concern. The powerful may even use religious liturgies to excuse their obligation to others. But the purpose of money is to flow through the society so that it can be redemptive, reduce tension, and bring peace rather than accumulate, through interest and time, in one layer of society.

An alternative exists. In this alternative, the strict hierarchy between the rich and the poor is relaxed through a different sort of interdependence that limits debt relationships. The sharing of wealth, whether through personal relationships or within the coordination of the market, is the foundation for an economy that moves, affirms, and strengthens our mutual interdependence. The followers of Jesus and their networks remembered the poor and shared their resources as best they could. It was not a coercive sort of equalitarianism, but one where money was shorn of its power. While some scholars have been skeptical about deriving broader principles about economic behavior, establishing broad rules about organizing market institutions remains viable. It's not hard to argue that exploitation and plundering are wrong or that envy corrodes human relationships. But the scriptures clearly nudge, if not coerce, individuals to be more generous and create structures that redirect networks toward the love of God and neighbor.

Scripture affirms that our lives are interdependent and embedded in multiple sorts of networks. In the next chapter I will explore more deeply how economists understand market networks. In Ancient Israel, God wants the people to have abundance. The writers are realists, however, not imagining a world free of poverty, but requiring an open heart toward the poor and needy (Dt 15:11). The ancient *market* economy has been described as one of exploitation and plunder. Individual acquisition was intrinsically ill-gotten, reflective of our idolatrousness. For that reason, scripture critiques the power of money and constrains covetousness because they corrode the lives of the people of Israel. To that end, scripture provides an alternative shape that seeks to constrain the power of wealth and the desire for it so that peace can be found in Israel.

This is not how economists understand markets. For economists, economies describe relationships where people purposefully make exchanges. To measure and count, to weigh the cost and the benefits, is how we make such exchanges mutually beneficial. For an economist, counting is value-neutral and there are no moral restrictions on desire. Modern markets, because transaction costs of certain kinds have shrunk, can now be coordinated in a way where wealth can be allocated more quickly and broadly. I will discuss in the next chapter the benefits and limits of approaching some economic concepts without a value judgement.

The Body of Christ thus does not insist on radical equality of resources between people, but an equality where money flows through generosity and exchange. Therefore, the circulation of wealth matters for the people of Israel and the church. Some Christians, however, do affirm that the Christian community may own all in common, and that private ownership is to be eschewed in the truly Christian community. The tradition, however, does not affirm that the empire or state produces such abundance—it comes from what is naturally provided by God. In either case, Paul shows the wealthy and the poor have a dynamic relationship between them, a spiritual need for each other that is reflected in the Christian network where wealth and spirit are exchanged.

Currently, economics describe behavior with value neutral terms. While this was not always the case, it has refrained from judging power or desire. It has insisted that money is a fungible tool that assists coordinating exchanges. Sin, for example, is calculated as a rational sort of opportunism, limited knowledge, or other sorts of explainable behavior patterns. Desire is merely a behavior and counting allow individuals to calculate it.

The ancient economy and modern markets are distinct in some crucial ways. I presume that modern markets are identified by an intensified division of labor, of precise counting and measuring, as well as a decrease in transaction costs and expenses that arise in the act of exchange. Geography and time have been quantified and measured much more efficiently; time and space have shortened. The coordination of markets now can become a way for benevolence to be more accurately counted. Indifference in markets becomes an improvement to cronyism, and prices a way of limiting exploitation. Mechanisms that reduce transaction costs, regulate and promote trade, such as steady prices and contracts, distribute wealth to a greater class of persons, rewarding the entrepreneurship and resourcefulness of what was previously the permanent underclass.

Furthermore, the sophisticated systems of coordination and exchange facilitated by modern capitalism complicate almsgiving, charity, and sharing. As technological and organizational developments changed how people interact, capital enters into more spaces where counting and incentives had been invisible. Our current system of arrangements as found in the market seems to have little precedence in scripture, so making judgments about large-scale planned or commercial economies should be made cautiously.

Desire still remains the heart of the problem. In the next chapter I will examine how economists describe desire, networks, and communities. Scripture shows that envy, debt, and markets are connected in how they destabilize communities. Economists, however, may offer congruent ways of counting and measuring that reveal with greater precision the way models of human behavior work. This may help the members of the Body of Christ to understand how to align our desires more effectively. Now I will show how economists explain individual behavior, markets, and value.

Notes

1. Roland Boer, *The Sacred Economy of Ancient Israel* (Louisville: John Knox, 2015).
2. Boer, 88.
3. Boer, 94.
4. Boer, 95.
5. Boer, 101.
6. Boer, 103.
7. Boer, 152.
8. Boer, 172–3.
9. Boer, 176–181.

10. Gary Anderson, *Sin: A History* (New Haven: Yale, 2009).
11. Anderson, *Sin: A History* (Kindle Locations), 290–291.
12. David Graeber, *Debt* (New York: Melville, 2011), 391.
13. Graeber, 118–119.
14. Graeber, 122
15. Boer, 162.
16. Boer, 159.
17. Boer, 160.
18. Boer, 160.
19. Mark Taylor, *Confidence Games* (Chicago: University of Chicago, 2004), 66.
20. Richard Seaborn, *Money and the Early Greek Mind: Homer, Philosophy, Tragedy* (New York: Cambridge University Press, 2004), 16–20.
21. Seaborn, 6–9.
22. Devin Singh, *Divine Currency: The Theological Power of Money in the West* (Stanford: Stanford University Press, 2018), 5–6.
23. Boer, 144.
24. Boer, 144.
25. Boer, 187.
26. Graeber, 133.
27. Graeber, 136.
28. Taylor, 66.
29. Taylor, 67.
30. Patrick Miller, "Property and Possession," in *Having*, eds. William Schweiker and Charles Mathewes, (Grand Rapids: Eerdmans, 2004), 47.
31. Daniel Finn, *Christian Economic Ethics* (Minneapolis: Fortress, 2013), 48.
32. Finn, 70.
33. Miller, 47.
34. John Durham, *Word Biblical Commentary*: *Exodus* (Waco: Word, 1987), 298–9.
35. Bruce Longenecker, *Remember the Poor* (Grand Rapids: Eerdmans, 2010), Ch 2.
36. Luke Timothy Johnson, *Sharing Possessions* (Minneapolis: Fortress 1981), 91–97.
37. William Temple, *Christianity and Social Order* (London: Shepheard-Walwyn, 1976), 49.
38. Johnson, 79–80.
39. Hans Dieter Betz, *Hermeneia: 2 Corinthians 8 and 9* (Philadelphia: Fortress 1985), 401.
40. Betz, 404.
41. Anderson (Kindle Locations), 770–772.
42. Amy Jill-Levine, *Short Stories by Jesus* (San Francisco: HarperOne, 2014), 46.
43. Levine, 70.
44. Levine, 125.
45. Levine, 167.
46. Levine, 166
47. Longenecker, 217–8.

48. Longenecker, 276–8.
49. David Bentley Hart, *The New Testament* (New Haven: Yale, 2017).
50. Hart, xxix.
51. Hart, xxx.
52. Hart, xxxi.
53. Hart, xxxi.
54. Peter Brown, *Through the Eye of The Needle* (Princeton: Princeton, 2012), 528.
55. Brown, 529–530.
56. Anderson, *Charity* (New Haven: Yale, 2013), 184.
57. Anderson, 2–3.
58. Brown, 379.
59. Anderson (Kindle Locations), 328–329.
60. Brian Matz, "Early Christian Philosophy as a Marketplace," in *Distant Markets, Distant Harms*, ed. Daniel Finn (New York: Oxford, 2014).
61. Matz, 130.
62. Matz, 131.
63. Brown, 528.
64. Brown, 529–530

2

Engaging Economics

In the previous chapter I explored the connections between markets, money, debt, desire, and sin in scripture. In this chapter, I explain economists' view of markets and self-interest. By describing both markets and self-interest, I offer a general critique of some foundational assumptions within the discipline, such as of individual rationality, markets, and the good life.

Anglican theologians and economists have contributed to a conversation between both their disciplines. One issue is whether economics is a *neutral* discipline—that is, whether the discipline benefits by confessional, or a religious, perspective. A neutral view insists that the bible and our liturgical tradition *may* help us understand *why* study economics or what it is for, but it won't expand what economists know. Economics can describe the mechanics of markets, but it lacks the moral authority to prescribe behavior.

Anglicans hold a range of views about individual self-interest and the role of the state. Some believe in minimal government, while others believe the government should have an expansive role in managing the economy. This diversity of views is reflected by how a Christian view may not be easily distinguishable from a non-confessional perspective. Even though it is hard to distinguish a Christian and a non-Christian view on economics, a personal particular stance as a Christian and an Anglican can shape the conversation between the disciplines that has been framed by one's religious faith.

Faith dictates that economic concerns remain central to the people of God. Because of these concerns, Anglican priests and laypeople have long weighed in on the role of state in the market. They make judgments because the church does have wealth and expertise. And so, while there may be little unique about an *Anglican* voice, distinctiveness does not diminish the worth of Anglican reflection on such matters. Furthermore, as a Christian, I approach this project from the view that, at the very minimum, Christians act in the world purposefully rather than as disinterested, and that in church, acting together is possible, even though at times such work is circumscribed by our specific contexts and cultures. Individuals may have power, the capacity to act, to engage God through their surrounding environment, their relationships, and their institutions we manage. As disciples of Christ, *Anglicans should study economics through questions of meaning and virtue in the light of the Gospel's true ends.* This means to raise issues about the proper allocation of resources. We cannot *not* talk about economics.

Because the church has resources, it has a responsibility to understand its role in allocating these resources for the furthering of the kingdom. The church has land, endowments, and individuals who give to its mission. Although it may be ambivalent about understanding itself as a firm with economic interests or power, if it were to understand itself as a specific, peculiar sort of corporation or firm—one with Christian convictions—it might be more receptive to insights from economists that can help it make well-informed choices along the way, which enhance its ability to work in the world. A better understanding of economics will help us shape a responsive, yet well-ordered institution so that the church's wealth can be an asset that allows us to solve problems, rather than as a burdensome, blood-soaked inheritance. With greater clarity, it is possible to identify when to sell, rent, or renovate physical structures, reallocate our compensation structure, and provide more effective charity. A lack of alignment and a confusion of roles leads to a lack of clarity about how to implement our mission as a church, which hobbles our potential for managing our resources. Corporations, however, are effective because they have identified incentives to align people for their own purposes; some of those incentives could be tested by the church.

Anglicans participate in institutions that create, produce, and consume goods. Churches distribute and allocate resources, own land, employ staff, have pensions and engage the market. While what we say may overlap with claims made by other traditions, without any greater moral bearing than any other faith or the pretense that our word is final, we do have the tools, resources, and tradition of reflecting about capital, markets, and wealth, and arguments to offer.

Understanding Economics and Morality

Economics can be intimidating because of its pretense toward being a hard, rigorous science that requires a certain kind of mathematical competence. The subdisciplines within economics, including econometrics, mathematical finance, and neuroeconomics, create an aura of impenetrability, where the profession ordains a set of mystagogues who, through the magic of higher level mathematics, make their discipline a science. As one economist wrote, "Economics is not just any academic discipline. It is the theology of our age, the language that all interests, high and low, must speak if they are to win a respectful hearing in the courts of power."[1] If only theologians could recreate that aura of competence.[2]

This chapter, however, will review a narrow subset of economics that bridges micro and macroeconomics, introducing economic work of interest to churches such as irrational behavior and governance. This is in contrast with macroeconomic schools that look at patterns of aggregates of individuals, business cycles, or the impact of government intervention. This is, however, a fuzzy construction because individuals themselves are impacted by broader forces, and institutions shape individual behavior.

Economics is interested in the purposeful activity of individuals. The Episcopalian economist Paul Heyne wrote, "There is no economic order that can be distinguished from other forms or orders of social interaction. There are no economic goals, economic motives, or economic institutions. Economic action is simply *purposive* action, action that tries to use means to achieve ends. It is necessarily "individualistic.""[3] Economics is about intentional, purposeful, voluntary behavior that coordinates strangers.

Three assumptions pertain to the general framework that economists use. First, *the individual is the source of moral worth*, rather than traditions, cultures, or abstract ideas. Such a default individual has been given names such as "homo economicus" or "econ." This person is described as a self-interested, opportunity maximizing individual, a cost-benefit machine, who makes knowledgeable decisions about their desires from a position of rationality.

Second, economists believe their approach is value neutral. They refrain from making social judgments. What is important to the economist is that the *choice is voluntary*. An individual wants what she wants. The economist may not judge if the person wants to sell baseballs or babies, or buy a dozen yurts or yachts. The time spent learning to play Beethoven's violin concerto and the time spent making widgets are each equal depending on the incentives and desires of the self-interested person. Desires are desires, and what's best is to be free to have them at any particular time.

Finally, while economics was not always primarily concerned with mathematics, *counting matters*. Early economists were concerned with the nature of desire in society, seeking to describe human behavior and critique political institutions in economic life. From Bernard Mandeville's *Fable of the Bees* to the work of Thomas Malthus and Adam Smith, economists reflected about human nature, critiqued political institutions, and considered new worlds. But markets themselves relied on calculating debt, counting coin, and measuring one good against another.

Economics explores the nature of networks. The simplest economic network, *oikonomia*, considers the ordering of resources within a household, the relationship of the master and the slave, the husband and the wife, the parents and the children, and the family to their animals. It includes the house, the stuff and labor that made it, the garden, the livestock, and various possessions to make work viable. It includes the distribution of work within and without, the care of individuals and farm animals, the planning, ordering, and arranging of things and bodies in season. At its very inception, economics is a study of order.

While it is understood as a unit, *oikonomia* relates to other networks that include the relationship of one household to the community around it. Some of the spaces will be shared or integrated. The boundaries move. As counting becomes easier with the introduction of money, recording, accounting, and calculating income becomes possible. It becomes also possible to examine costs of social goods that reflect our dependence upon others, such as effective sanitation, good roads, and suitable schools, as well as our desire for private goods.

One tension that arises is the confusion between the descriptive from the prescriptive, or the empirical from the normative. The implicit values within economics articulate a way of behaving and a justification for designing economic networks. Networks impact, constrain, and direct the sorts of choices people make, leading people to make a variety of priorities, substitutions, and compromises. When economics studies the empirical evidence of human behavior using the insights of psychology, sociology, and even history, it has a *descriptive* role: it studies real behavior patterns. It may use math to describe its findings. This should be understood differently than asking how an idealized understanding of a person, as an "econ," works. A rational econ is therefore different than describing how people actually behave in markets.

Moral questions are implicit in deciding *what* is counted, not only the amount accumulated. To calculate worth itself reflects a moral stance: both the affirmation that the worth of some things can be calculated, and that *calculating itself is worth time*. To apply questions of cost and benefit, to purchase, or to save, presumes a value judgment that prescribes and directs our choices. Calling attention to a particular action gives an action meaning, and by ignoring another it signifies a lack of worth. This examining of the cost of buying services or goods such as cars, shoes, or health, but away from other expenses or costs in the environment, suggests a specific value system. What is chosen to describe in an economic model reflects the greater relative value assigned to it, and magnifies the decision to call attention to one thing above another. For this reason, the design of our choices is important. The descriptive influences the normative and prescriptive.

Three aspects of economics undergird this particular project. The first is a description of markets. Markets are a part of our social and communal life. The second is the relationship of the unit, the individual, within markets. Describing both with a degree of accuracy will reveal the depth of some of the problems involved. The third is what facilitates the transactions between individuals in market networks. These are transaction costs. Without some description of how individuals engage other individuals, and what allows such engagement, our analysis would be incomplete.

The three are intertwined. Markets coordinate individuals. Money, technology, and firms reduce the costs of making the coordination possible by making transactions easier. Markets are networks where people make choices, and those choices are possible when transactions are easy to make.

What Are Markets?

Markets are networks. The theologian Daniel Finn writes, "Markets are sets of relationships entered into by producers and consumers"[4]. Paul Heyne writes that a market is "a set of interrelationships."[5] Daniel Finn describes markets as a "set of relationships among preexisting social positions… This market relationship is complex and entails long chains of interactions,"[6] and geographer David Harvey writes that markets are "tentacles of trading networks intertwined and stretched onwards and outwards to infiltrate everywhere."[7]

Markets are systems of relating. Market networks include a variety of relationships; they may be complex or simple, between friends, families, colleagues, or strangers. The marketplace includes both social relationships as well as independent institutions that compete for attention. Social relationships and institutions overlap. Wall Street is not only a trading network, but a social one where its members are pulled from specific cultures, such as fraternities, universities, or other associations. Markets are systems where both social and monetary networks intertwine. Money, or other "signs," are exchanged and circulated through networks that are not defined by money, but by, for example, friendship, familiarity, habit, or convenience.

Markets coordinate and relate. For markets to be effective, parties must engage in trustworthy behavior, because coordination without the expense of enforcement mechanisms requires trust. Individuals cooperate with one another by adjusting and aligning their preferences with other individuals, especially if market activity must be replicated. Deception, on the other hand, because it inhibits transactions from being carried out, causes market failure. Even while deceptive and predatory tactics can have short-term benefits, commerce rewards trustworthiness and cooperation in the long run. When commerce is assumed to be voluntary, any of the parties can bow out at any time. Thus, trust is required in market networks, even when outside the state's legal mechanisms. Exchanges demand trust if the relationships are to be maintained. The extensive supply chains that get various transistors from their origin to my Honda require an enormous amount of coordination. These exchanges represent disinterested cooperative, coordinated sharing without the fear of being robbed or killed. As Paul Heyne once wrote, "economics mostly explains how cooperation occurs among people who don't know one another at all, but who nonetheless manage to work together with extraordinary effectiveness."[8]

Markets require extra-market institutions to function. Building trust requires institutions that can incentivize trust. The coordination of markets and the establishment of rules that make markets possible do not happen instantaneously. Market networks interact with other sorts of networks, such as a state body or a theoretically neutral or a superior infrastructure, that enforce agreements through courts or other neutral arbitration. While agreements may be habitual, based on a firm handshake, credit, or insurance, markets also rely on networks of administration and enforcement by governing institutions that establish rights.[9] Markets depend on institutions that protect them; they do not necessarily protect themselves. Operating within and around markets are other sorts of networks, such as the state or associations that regulate behavior.

These institutions, as the political scientist Elinor Ostrom explains, are defined as sets of "working rules" that determine actions and constraints that are monitored and enforced.[10] Commerce depends on customs, such as friendliness and benevolence, which maintain relationships. However, conflicts happen, rules get broken, and these instances require mediation by networks and institutions outside the market. *These extra-market institutions and actions are expenses or costs.*

Therefore, the market relies on other structured networks that can enforce the ownership of capital or otherwise regulate exchange. These networks include the state or informal networks outside of the market, such as the institutions that maintain and implement types of technology that include record-keeping, deeds, contracts, weights, and measures. These outside networks may operate not only with formal but also informal rules obscure to outside parties and dependent on embedded social relationships. Rules may consist of customs guided by social habits or technology regulated by a wider institution, such as moveable type.

One role of these extra-market networks is to help reduce conflict and enable agreement. In an efficient market, the role of outside authority is one of last resort, while the parties exchanging rely on a shared understanding of the rules of the game. That said, markets where haggling is part of the culture include a social transaction that is considered desirable, even though it may lengthen the time of the actual exchange. Haggling is a transaction expense, but it also serves as a way of building trust and providing non-monetary sorts of satisfaction, as well as more accurately determining the actual value of a good or service to both parties.

The institutions behind the coordination in a market have several roles. They make the rules to restrict and regulate participants, to open or close the market. They also ensure agreements can be renegotiated, especially in those cases where there might be market failure. Standardized regulations ensure that every person can be aware of the rules that shape the way the market works. Technology, such as record-keeping, documentation, and contracts, allows for individuals to predict and plan the future, which increases confidence in the market by smoothing over potential problems in advance and managing risk. In cases where the market extends the network beyond the immediate and familiar, institutions that set and enforce the rules in extended networks are expenses of coordination. This also illustrates how few networks are either fully private or public but vary in type and extent of entanglement. Some networks are more social and familiar with fewer strangers, and others may be bureaucratic. Some networks have a far greater geographic reach than others.

Cooperation may be more important than competition in making markets effective. While not all interests are mutually reinforcing—not only will people compete, they will have conflicting interests—*cooperation creates value.* That markets are *networks of cooperation* cannot be considered obvious. As explained in the previous chapter, scripture considers money and markets as connected to institutions of plunder and power, and the individuals who were engaged in market activity, such as the trading of preciosities or the handling of debt, as disruptive to the people of God.

It is important to note that the perspective that the market incentivizes virtue reflects a modern shift in understanding the beneficence of markets. In such a view, the commercial economy as a system of cooperation requires and develops virtuous habits, such as benevolence, fairness, prudence, and temperance. The energy used previously that had been fragmented into a series of competing emotions that were sinful and disordered, which led to wasteful projects such as war, is now focused into the virtuous building of resources. Markets now foster social bonds. In this world view, commerce must prefer peace to war, as war disrupts trade, so capitalists will emphasize prudence and self-restraint through identification of appropriate places to invest. Therefore, commerce is not about plunder but requires trust, or some element of faith in others to work. *In a modern economy, commerce follows rules that people agree to ahead of time.*

Markets are where capital flows. Capital includes the variety of sign-values that can be moved from one point to another. Without a system of coordination that facilitates the dynamic motion of capital, capital does not accumulate. Within the system of coordination, extensive supply networks develop that include institutions that have the capacity to change a physical object into a sign value such as money, and institutions that have the power to move geographically. Institutions that determine worth, such as banks, can transform money into land and vice versa by assessing future value. If capital can be moved, it can accumulate, it can be squandered, and it can move from one hand or person or place to another, through the Internet or through a deed. David Harvey explains, "Capital is not a thing but a process in which money is perpetually sent in search of more money."[11] Capital seeks to expand the market network. Capital must *move.*

Capital flows quickly with the reduction of transaction costs, caused or amplified through technology such as money, writing, or the wheel. Money, such as coin, conveys a sign-value that reduces the cost of exchange[12] because it is fungible, allowing a diversity of goods to be exchanged across time and space. When a government expands over a greater territory, money creates longer supply chains that allow people greater access to markets through offering a standard unit of exchange, while also enhancing mobility.

Money also reduces transaction costs when it assigns a precisely defined value to an object, a price. Combined with the principle of substitution, pricing eases the exchange so that it is possible to offer a clearer start from which to negotiate. It then becomes possible to exchange between strangers with relative ease.

Through pricing, money can express value, facilitating assessment and comparison, measuring costs and benefits, and substituting goods across a wide variety of individual desires. Pricing allows the possibility of comparing a car to college, or a smart phone to a dinner for six. Pricing also reduces the time haggling, which is also a transaction cost, to agree on a price. As theologian Paul Heyne writes, "Money provides a common denominator through which the relative advantage of innumerable options can be precisely compared."[13] It is a sign of measurement. That said, the power of this definition can conceal other attributes of money, such as its relationship to the state and its social power.

Faster capital flow incentivizes the division of labor. Innovations encouraged specialization and repetitive work. Compared to transportation costs in biblical societies, modern advancements have made transportation relatively cheap and reliable. Capital flows not just across the land, sea, or air, but now through light waves. These distribution networks coordinate networks by reducing the time and expenses, including those caused by human beings, of making exchanges. As efficiency increases, the need for human interference is reduced. As efficiency increases, time is itself reflected as a cost and therefore rewards speed.

Markets require trust. While there were technological reasons that made capital easier to move, networks expanded because people understood that commerce could be relatively virtuous, reliable, and trustworthy. Without a prior faith in flow and trust in networks, trading stops and becomes too expensive. As the theologian Mark Taylor writes, "Faith is a confidence game whose stakes are undeniably economic; there is an economy of faith that mirrors and is mirrored by a faith in economics. The speculum in which this play of mirrors is staged is the space of speculation."[14] Faith instills confidence to participate in making economic decisions; that we have made them allows us to continue participating. Without faith that capital will continue to flow, the flow would itself stop. Economics depends on this trust; it measures and counts activity in the world, the coordination of makers and consumers, with trust at the heart of its flow. Insofar as faith's central marker is trust in God who holds all our debts, without such faith, the economy could not hold together.

The technology behind markets allows individuals to compare and allocate goods and resources that are relatively scarce. Paul Heyne defines scarcity as a matter of sacrifice: one can only have as much as one's want of one thing if one sacrifices something else of value.[15] The fulfillment of desire is thus constrained by one's resources, forcing individuals to measure and compare, to calculate, our different needs and wants.

Although markets are voluntary, they remain bounded areas of freedom. Ideally, money disciplines choices, but there are some limits societies impose upon their extension. Selling children, hiring assassins, and selling organs or wives remains outside of legal market networks. Traffic signals are not auctioned to those who have fancier cars. Laws establish licensing of physicians, require procuring insurance, prohibit dumping, and restrict abusive behavior. It is desirable to enforce a fair playing field and exclude violence and fraud from market networks. Therefore, it would be hard to imagine an economy being limitlessly free, because total freedom or lawlessness will be exploited by the most aggressive, violent, or powerful. Furthermore, established customs for negotiation allow for more effective transactions because the state cannot negotiate every single voluntary transaction. As the economist and moral theologian Daniel Finn notes, "When speaking precisely, even the most energetic proponents of "free" markets want the government to enforce some limits on what people are allowed to do."[16]

The Market and the Usefulness of Firms

Coordination of markets can be clumsy because it is impossible to predict chance or fortune, or the variety of random events that occur in a life. Human beings will create and be impacted by events beyond their control. Out of this reality, groups such as firms arise to smooth coordination. The complexity in the market arises because individuals change their minds, their desires fluctuate, and outside pressures alter our priorities. Persons are hard to predict. Decisions are often only marginally rational, motivated by the immediate, and conflict with competing persons, firms, or authorities. A good description of markets should reflect this complexity, both by attempting to offer a model and by acknowledging that any model may also be incomplete.

Markets are effective when the cost of conducting the exchange is less than the profit from the exchange itself. A series of agreements precedes any market exchange, and aligning those agreements requires the coordination of people, another kind of network. This network is called a firm: an organized body of relationships.

The economist and political scientist Elinor Ostrom explains that firms (and states), including corporations and not-for-profits, exist according to interdependent relationships, defined by agreements between individuals to incentivize coordination and make organized activity efficient.[17] Economist R.H. Coase explains that firms arise when negotiating prices between individuals is time-consuming or expensive. A firm is the cost of doing business, which includes anticipating risk or reducing the variety of indeterminate factors in the market. A firm might include the organization that builds the actual market; it includes the individuals who do the counting and assess value or foster agreements. Markets themselves cost something to operate.[18]

The government may be a sort of firm, or an interlocking network of firms. It may be responsible for public safety, transportation systems, and the sorts of rule-making that build trust and bind, enable, and enhance other networks such as markets. Not-for-profit networks are institutions like firms, but sit in-between and engage other networks for their own tasks and interests, and most rely on institutions that manage trading or money. Each firm contains networks and sub-networks which shape behavior through their specific rules cultures.

Firms arise to create consistent, repetitive collaboration and managerial expertise to smooth out the difficulties that arise in life. Firms, thus, will create habits which develop and change over time. They cover the hidden expenses of research, negotiation, verification, and enforcement, even if they are hard to calculate. They govern relationships of groups within their body. When firms smooth out problems that arise in institutional life, they reduce the expense of doing the sort of business they engage in. In firms, people iron out the messiness of human engagement in relationship to other networks.

Firms also help coordinate when new problems or opportunities arise. They share and manage information, and align individuals with divergent interests. When unexpected events happen, circumstances change, and the complex network of coordination fails, people change agreements, settled negotiations are renegotiated, and time spent doing one thing means time not doing another. In these situations, the internal works of any organization are also transaction costs. Money is one way to diminish transaction costs, through incentivizing collaboration by paying salaries. Of course, there are other ways to incentivize aligning interests.

Coordinating Markets as a Transaction Cost

Exchanges do not typically happen instantaneously. Prices need to be set, agreements need to be made, and a network needs to be already in place. Before any exchange is made in a market, even before the price is set, individuals negotiate how the exchange will take place. Creating, designing or distributing capital or money from one place to another requires prior work. Firms attempt to mitigate the costs of any transaction that can slow or interrupt getting a good to a market. These costs are the root of *Transaction Cost Economics* (TCE), which examines the messy interactions of persons in institutional life from a neoclassical economic perspective. TCE explains how firms smooth out and diminish conflict so that individuals can make exchanges.

The study of transaction costs is how neoclassical economists address the challenges of persons in institutions, especially to diminish tensions so that work can be done. With a value free vocabulary, TCE abstracts the particularity, or "asset specificity," of the work of institutions that have a variety of challenges. It groups the distinct challenges in a diverse array of firms. Firms create customs, rules, and governance to anticipate interruptions so that their work can be brought to market.

Governance seeks to reduce tension and conflict within and between firms. The Nobel Prize-winning economist Oliver Williamson writes, "transaction costs are economized by assigning transactions to governance structures (the adaptive capacities and associated costs of which differ) in a discriminating way."[19] The cost of governance is, therefore, a transaction cost which reduces other transaction costs. It regulates behavior internally and anticipates occurrences that make it hard to accomplish tasks.

Governance is concerned with the behavior of persons in firms. Individuals alone lack knowledge and may not instinctively work together. Therefore, as Williamson writes, "any attempt to deal seriously with the study of economic organization must come to terms with the combined ramifications of bounded rationality and opportunism in conjunction with a condition of asset specificity."[20] In other words, individuals lack universal knowledge, and have individual desires outside of the firm—a title, more money, or happiness—desires that are specific to their particular context. Therefore, firms arise in order to manage the costs of unexpected, and unique, problems that arise because people do not have knowledge and have desires.

Because much of what mediates exchanges is local, particular, or specific, it will naturally require management over time.[21] No bureaucracy, whether commercial or not, can predict every possible event. Williamson says, "Even knowledge in particulars does not preclude surprises. The capacity for novelty in the human mind is rich beyond imagination."[22] Therefore, firms arise because exchanges happen over a period of time, and therefore require governance. TCE reveals governance is a part of economics, and seeks to measure its impact.

Transaction Cost Economics identifies the negotiations, conflicts, inconveniences and tensions in institutions and firms that are hard to measure, and all of these take time for different parties to come to agreement. Long-term and short-term interests, limited knowledge, instability, and changing desires complicate the coordination of markets because people have different knowledge, competing or conflicting interests, a lack of resources, or an ability to get things done. Firms can renegotiate the rules when there is a conflict, but this renegotiation is also a transaction cost. By identifying these expenses, firms can coordinate by assessing a value to the worth of coordination.

Transaction Cost Economics identifies a few central challenges that inhibit coordination. One is the expense of *insufficient knowledge* or *bounded rationality*. Individuals, despite their confidence, can't understand the complexity of reality. An individual, because they are not God, lacks access to the information necessary to make absolutely correct decisions; there may be technical, legal, or practical issues or unforeseen hiccoughs before any product comes to market. The supply chain, the regulatory framework, and the potential for new negotiations with purchasers or sellers make it hard to anticipate the future or plan. Therefore, institutions like firms manage bounded rationality by offering incentives such as a salary to incentivize individuals to share information, widen the bounds, and bring persons of different expertise together to manage complex problems. Firms find financial, emotional, or spiritual ways to incentivize collaboration, but this incentive is a cost.

Another specific problem that is addressed by TCE is *opportunism*. Opportunism is a kind of "self-interest" that includes the desire, for example, for some object valued by themselves and others: to gain advantage, a higher salary, or a new title. Opportunism explains why individuals are not always open or honest. They may want what another person has or sees their interests as opposed to another's. Firms cannot rely on self-denial, subordination or obedience.[23] Therefore firms may offer incentives, such as salaries, to collaborate. While the exact incentives to reward opportunism can be varied and sometimes hard to calculate, all types of firms, including the church, use some kind of tool to guide the obscure motivations for our choices. People seek opportunities for a variety of reasons from the perverse to the saintly, so firms harness the myriad ways opportunism drives and directs behavior. The challenge of management or governance is to align personal opportunism with the firm at large. Opportunism here is a purely descriptive, rather than a moral, judgment,[24] an element of economic life that makes economic transactions uncertain.

Transaction Cost Economics exposes that *decision-making has costs*. Changing contexts, conditions, and desires create additional costs of decision-making, as people reevaluate situations, renegotiate agreements, and spend mental energy enduring the stress of participating in a social organization. Management becomes an economic expense of uncertainty, dealing with the emotional and legal costs that may arise. Put another way, Williamson says that transaction costs "are the economic equivalent of friction in the physical systems," or the cost of doing business apart from what is produced: the costs of managing tension in a network. As we are not perfectly rational or transparent, we look for ways to account for the costs of skewed and changing relationships, as well as repeated interactions within their institutions. Governance minimizes the friction caused by the behaviors in life that create tension. TCE thus shows that paying for governance helps us calculate the *cost of doing business.*

Governance Matters

Transaction cost economics is a value-neutral way of calculating the cost of minimizing and smoothing out the various problems and challenges that arise. It includes the cost of governance, which is a way of aligning individuals to work together. Firms "organize transactions so as to economize on bounded rationality while simultaneously safe guarding them against the free hazards of opportunism."[25] In another way, because individuals are poor at planning for the future, are prone to rivalry, and are sinners, governance redirects toward the shared mission of the firm. TCE is a way of calculating the cost of working together to diminish the expenses of limited information and rivalry.

The cost of working together is *governance*—the work of managing irregularities, opportunism, and limited knowledge. It requires adaptability, skill, and time to practice. Limited rationality and knowledge prevents anticipating the future perfectly, but improved collaboration develops mechanisms to manage the unpredictable. The rules of governing in a firm thus relieve an individual from taking unwarranted or unreasonable risks. These rules manage the everyday work of people negotiating, going to meetings, making procedural decisions, and even renegotiating prices or time of payment that contribute to the cost of doing business. They are the habits and practices of getting work done.

The quality of administration matters. It includes transactions that cannot be easily quantified. In addition to technical checklists, administering includes understanding of the various sorts of motivations of individuals in any group. In addition, the skill of administering social interactions takes time to learn. This is the work of managing the subtle rivalries in any firm, negotiating the social rules where individuals need to manage their own sense of place, while also guiding people to do the work of collaborating. The skill and the time it takes to implement is an expense.

Economics reveals a few general tendencies in firms. For example, as organizations become larger and more effective, power becomes more oligarchic. Not every individual needs to attend every meeting; indeed, many meetings would not be effective if they required the participation of all persons in a firm. It reduces the time required when fewer people are responsible with coordinating networks. Williamson quotes, "who says organization, says oligarchy." Large institutions necessarily concentrate effective power in the hands of a few who have competencies to coordinate others.[26] As institutions become larger and more complex, power will become more concentrated.

Identifying the need for governance in complex firms does not mean firms will run perfectly or anticipate all possible futures. Not every crisis will be avoided or negotiated effectively, not every problem will be closed. It may be impossible to measure the effectiveness of every interaction. The skill of administering the emotional needs in a firm prohibits a degree of calculation. Counting every action can undervalue the dignity of persons because it treats individuals as numbers rather than as individuals. Measuring transaction costs does not eliminate the implicit problems inherent in quantifying individuals, but merely makes the challenge more precise. Effective firms recognize that individual interactions cannot be priced.

Williamson writes, "Economizing is a means, not an end."[27] Calculating the worth of others may also impede trust when it renders human interaction as purely utilitarian and functional, rather than familial. It diminishes how individuals live in and value other networks besides markets. While we need contracts to establish trust and trust enhances contracts, quoting Kenneth Arrow, *we are trustworthy even without being coerced to be so*. Trust, loyalty, honesty are not commodities that can be sold.[28] Not everything can be counted, and counting everything diminishes the ability—or the incentive—to trust. And trust is the most efficient way to diminish transaction costs. It need not cost anything.

Faith is what makes markets possible.

Churches as Firms

Churches are also firms. Individuals and groups have interests and negotiate with each other in Jesus' name to do the work of the gospel. While individual churches face unique challenges, the language of transaction costs may provide a neutral way of counting what congregations would identify as *sin*.

TCE reveals the emotional life within firms, offering a non-judgmental way to acknowledge the needs and perspectives of their members. Congregations, as firms, also do not have perfect knowledge (in spite, perhaps, of their belief system), are not solely inclined to altruism, and also have self-interested members. TCE reminds the church that it takes work to foster cooperation and coordination, and that this work has a cost. In short, *overcoming the sin of rivalry is an expense that requires payment.*

Just as TCE reinforces the importance of governance, churches can identify why shaping congregants matters. Parishioners can now be understood as individuals who are also persons who have limited knowledge, have self-interest, and need to learn how to collaborate. It also reinforces that people are still prior to economizing.

Firms create rules to harness opportunism and rivalry through sharing knowledge and interests. The rules harness desire for the greater good by building relationships. These relationships are the coordination of strangers. While churches have their own specific challenges and needs, the coordination of individuals remains central to any task of the gospel, however specific or idiosyncratic that work may be.

Churches make decisions based on transaction costs. Hiring an organist or a sexton or a regular employee conveys benefits, such as consistency, that volunteers might not fill. Churches measure the trade-offs between paid staff and unpaid work. In a congregation, there may be several tasks that happen repeatedly—baptisms, renting the parish hall, taking phone calls. To find new volunteers each day or week would create more work for the priest who manages them. It may make more sense to hire someone who will be consistent, who will learn tasks over time and do them well. Some tasks do not require a long-term contract: hiring trumpeters or a timpanist for the Easter Service only requires a single performance. But accounting for transaction costs is how we measure whether hiring steady employees is efficient. The economic reasons for hiring employees are not calculated by simply putting another line item in the budget, but by taking into account the opportunity costs of *not* hiring, as well.

TCE, however, also suggests that *non-monetary* values may add sufficient incentives for those participating in firms. Longer vacations, sabbaticals, parental leave, shorter work days, shorter commutes, are incentives that workers or members of firms value. Clergy may choose to have school debts forgiven for the opportunity of working in communities. The church, however, can recognize that acknowledging sorts of opportunism, such as reduced debt or steady housing, or self-interest, such as more sabbatical time, can reinforce the emotional capacity to spread the gospel. By measuring resources more fully, from individual skill to physical properties, it's possible to allocate most effectively.

Churches may identify how various non-monetary exchanges enhance the life of the church. This might reveal some of our strengths, such as the reasons why people stay in an institution that has non-monetary values. Perhaps examining our basic forms of governance can suggest how voluntary organizations can benefit from a wider set of incentives that make any sort of collaborative, corporate, firm-based activity useful for spreading the gospel.

More specifically, TCE explains *the cost of rivalry* through its neutral description of opportunism. Strong firms account for rivalry. Rivalry reflects the comparative nature of our choices and must be considered a regular part of organizing firms, including in the Body of Christ. It can be expressed by a multiplicity of personal desires, including non-financial ones, in any network. Rivalry does not only inspire competition for personal profit; it can also encourage the Body of Christ to strive for self-improvement and growth, and the improvement of our world. The structural, social, and economic challenge is to reveal, as best we can, the incentives that can alight people for the greater mission of the cause of the Kingdom. This requires recognizing how people frame the opportunities around them.

In congregations it is possible for congregants to compare congregations or with the priest; one cleric judges their parish against one that is more, or less, prosperous. And everyone compares themselves to bishops. Good governance will include practices that diminish or redirect rivalry.

The economic view is not the last word, but it may allow us some precision. Rearranging our relationships so churches can be more effective at their task will not replace the need for grace. It may, however, guide our communal life by helping identify what the church values. By identifying rivalry, it's possible to ask what a congregation can do to redirect and harness it for the sake of the gospel.

Limitations and Critiques of Economic Thinking

Transaction Cost Economics is a way of addressing the human problems that arise in markets and firms. It helps us understand the ways firms address human limitations and self-interest when collaborative work is required to get tasks accomplished. It uses a vocabulary that refrains from endorsing collaboration by merely noting that it exists.

Economics defines itself as value-neutral in its assessment of wants and desires. Its focus is on what incentivizes individuals to make choices. Its understanding of the economy and of money separates the market from political forces. An alternative view posits that political networks are prior to market networks, so that money reflects the social relations within society. The market requires an institution to back up, possibly through force, the fundamental claims that money makes.

One critique includes the use of money or other tools that seem neutral in their use but also shape social relationships. Money, for example, while facilitating use through its fungibility, depends upon the power of the state to enforce the value of such sign values. For this reason, money is not only a convenient way of reducing transaction costs but also reflects the location of power. As the geographer David Harvey writes, "Money is a form of social power that can be appropriated by private power that has no limit."[29]

The economist A.O. Hirschman also notes that money can be a threat to social order because consumption patterns reorganize society.[30] The habits of the landed and the aristocracy are displaced by the newly rich: "New material wealth is, then, placed in a double bind. If it filters down to the masses, the conservatives are aroused because it threatens the social order. If it does not filter down, the progressives are appalled by the widening disparity of consumption."[31]

Furthermore, individuals experience money differently, suggesting that individuals value money differently. A hedge fund manager treats a twenty dollar bill differently than someone poor; a billionaire experiences the first hundred thousand dollars differently than the last. The value of money is therefore relative, ill-suited to quantifying the value of relationships, sentiment, affection, or sympathy.

The notion that economics is value neutral conceals the mechanics of the power of market. Prices, for example, do not necessarily indicate an equal relationship between producers and consumers, especially when there is either only one buyer or one seller, especially when combined with political power, when there is no opportunity to negotiate the price mechanism. While set prices make transactions easier and faster, and allow for much more extensive coordination of the market, individuals can struggle to find a place in a world where TicketMaster and StubHub are able to corner markets. In our current context, algorithms can adjust prices in financial markets to adapt to supply and demand in nanoseconds.

The metaphor of the "invisible hand" seeks to provide a neutral way of explaining the imaginary way economies naturally coordinate peaceable, disinterested networks through self-interest. Without the interference of government, trust between individuals replaces deceit. The division of labor makes coordination of the market more viable, increasing dependence between individuals and therefore increasing peace. Cooperation arises because it is in each person's self-interest to trust his or her trading partner. In this way, individual competition—and coordination—benefits all of society.

However, individual interests may actually conflict. Individuals sometimes pursue their self-interest in such a way that corrodes the same institutions that *allow* them to pursue their interest. Their self-interest collides with the interest of the larger community. Competition can benefit individuals, but not necessarily their communities.

Lastly, there may be some social good to inefficient, clumsy, and awkward social engagements that are *not* smooth. Markets that remove human interactions by replacing haggling with set prices render exchanges so efficient that conversation, interaction, and familiarity become unnecessary. Highly efficient market choices also make it easy for individuals to make more people strangers, reducing our capacity to engage in the messiness and work through the discomfort of human interaction. An efficient market may allow us to have swift and easy interactions with strangers, but its stated benefits arise from a view that spending more time to engage the stranger is burdensome.

Critics of economism and economics question the logic of scarcity. They note scarcity is also a self-creating value, not merely about rare goods, but as an expression of social relations where some people will have the social benefit of status or goods that signal distinctiveness. Scarcity explains that not everyone gets to be king or can have the house on top of the mountain, but God, in contrast to scarcity, provides enough for what is necessary. One does not need a rare French Bordeaux from the right year, but can be satisfied with a roughly equivalent Cabernet from California that costs one three-hundredth of the price. Ranking itself creates a degree of scarcity, and to some extent, scarcity itself creates want. One may desire what is beyond one's reach precisely because it is beyond one's reach. Robert Frank notes "the dependence of reward on rank eliminates any presumption of harmony between individual and collective interests, and with it, the foundation of the libertarian's case for a completely unfettered market system."[32] Scarcity increases value because it increases desire. Desire and scarcity are intimately linked, although the market solves the problem of scarcity it creates, redirecting envy by providing satisfactory substitutes for scarce resources.

Lastly, in spite of the efforts of economists to conceal the political roots of allocating resources, a more thorough examination of the relationship between slavery and the market, for example, reveals the moral limits of economic freedom. The power of debt and money can constrain freedom within a market. With slavery in particular, White Supremacy limited the power of capital to whites, illustrating how market networks can be constrained by prior social relations and enforced by political institutions. Institutions within the market may still be organized around social relations that create and impoverish a specific class of persons. For not only is the market comprised of the set of exchanges at any given moment, it also includes competing social and political institutions that are made of people who assess costs and benefits within those institutions.[33]

The market coordinates strangers. It fosters neighborliness and allows for the possibility to respect other people's dignity and welcome the foreign and unknown through the coordination of the market. When someone enters a shop to purchase a product, the wise proprietor welcomes; they are engaging strangers without conflict. While the market described by economists is not a sentimental love, it benefits from a kind of neighborly love that religion demands. In the market, our neighbors include individuals who are like us but whom we perceive as different, and those who are unlike us. This love may have an indifferent quality, but it is relatively better than hostility. In markets, indifference can be positive, as it allows us to stay out of another person's way or desires.

The familiarity, trust, or "love" offered by the market may not compare, at first glance, to the sorts of love known by individuals who are familiar with one another, or the love in the Gospel that we know in Jesus. But exchanges allow for trust between strangers through offering spaces, such as markets, where it is possible to negotiate without violence. The indifference that is provided by the simple exchange of money—coin, paper, (or in our age, light)—is understood as relatively better than coercion or theft.

The Anglican economist Denys Munphy writes about the market that, "The market mechanism has to be understood and appraised for what it is worth; it is neither a monstrous impersonal force to be denounced, nor an idol which will serve all problems. It is a serviceable mechanism, which can serve men, if properly used and not abused. It provides no complete substitute for organized action, whether through institutions, or by means of government action and the central or local level. But the proper combination of organized action and reliance on market forces is a continuous test of statesmanship."[34]

Defining Self-Interest

In the previous section we described a traditional, neoclassical interpretation of the market. The market as a network smooths out transactions in several ways, using money and methods of organization called the firm. Transactions happen between individuals, the default unit. A key element that undergirds this is the idea that a market network consists of individuals who are *self-interested.*

Self-interest presumes that minds and bodies are individuated and separate. These prior metaphysical and epistemological positions are not self-evident. It may be that individual minds are not truly individual, or that the choices are merely perceptions in a highly determined universe. It is enough for now to assume that bodies *are* individuated, distinct from other persons, while parts of our consciousness are not. Furthermore, while the word "self-interest" can rankle if confused with selfishness, in this context self-interest is only the default unit of the economist. Self-interest is of central importance in the understanding of markets.[35]

In economics, self-interest is a morally neutral term, a description of our reality. It was not always considered a favorable sentiment. The economist Albert O. Hirschmann posits that self-interest became a virtue because it was superior to a desire for glory or inherited animosity,[36] since pursuing wealth was better than the alternative—fame through war and plunder. Instead, the many motivations that would inspire action could be distilled into a single one: self-interest. This made it possible to measure and quantify using neutral units such as money. The virtue of self-interest as plundering or winning for the sake of glory is replaced by the virtue of indifference, because the criteria for success could be measured in a simple fashion: money itself. The market was meant to inhibit precisely "human drives and proclivities and to fashion a less multifaceted, less unpredictable and more 'one-dimensional' human personality. The dangers of the destructive forces unleashed by passions with the exception of avarice."[37] Instead of a passion for glory in war, let it be a bank account. As the markets produce wealth, they produce a disciplined person who solves conflicts to make coordination easier.[38] More precisely, self-interest is the systemic evaluation of cost and benefit.[39]

The ethicist and Catholic economist Daniel Finn describes the economic understanding of self-interest as a type of egoism, where one's decisions are understood to benefit oneself. In such a view, all decisions, ranging from altruism to selfishness, arise from self-interest. However, while self-interest can be tautological, imprecise, confused with selfishness, or reduced to the default position of a European man, it allows a value-free way for economists to calculate patterns, using the individual as a fundamental unit to measure.[40]

The Calculator, or *Homo Economicus*

After J.S. Mill, I define the economic, self-interested, man as an individual who seeks the best opportunities for himself given the range of possibilities.[41] Self-interest can be measured by a person's desire to acquire wealth, a countable and measurable sum: a rational man always seeks a greater amount of some unit.[42] The presumption is that individuals are rational, they necessarily have knowledge about their choices, and they are self-maximizing in that they calculate costs and benefits.

Self-interest presumes that *the individual is the center of moral worth*. They make decisions and have purposes which should not morally be constrained except if they harm someone else. This is in contrast with a view that puts, for example, a family, community, a tradition, or an idea at the center of moral worth.

Individuals *desire*. They want. Thus, "*Homo Economicus*," the term coined for the self-interested person, is acquisitive. The desire to acquire is not given any moral weight; it is enough to say that individuals desire. As long as it does not harm another person, there is no moral reason to restrain the fulfillment of purposeful activity based on this desire. Defining *what harms* is contested.

Third, individuals engage in purposeful, *intentional* activity. Individuals decide. They are driven by incentives. Therefore, economics is concerned with *the purposeful intentional activity of individuals*. Purposeful activity is considered *rational* activity. Individuals have the capacity to make choices, to distinguish between different sorts of goods, to go down one fork in the road rather than another. Therefore, *incentives matter*. Incentives *compel* us to measure costs and benefits of engaging in specific purposeful activity. Incentives range. They may include a feeling of self-worth, security, satiety, pleasure, or even money.

Rational self-interest considers *cost and benefits*. An econ seeks to optimize his/her choices. This presumes however, the ability—and desire—to measure or count, which helps track and allocate resources, by comparing worth. The capacity to count and measure, to weigh costs and benefits, enables individuals to predict the results of their economic choices.

Defining self-interest helps clarify some assumptions about how individuals behave. Self-interest can include anything from a desire for psychological safety and protection to a desire for sleep or leisure or wealth. It can include worry about the future, whether it is about now, or tomorrow, or in five years. It can account for the fact that we are complex creatures, culturally bound, with contradictory wants and desires.

How People Make Decisions

Individuals make choices and act in their self-interest, but this tells relatively little. Assessing costs and benefits or maximizing resources doesn't indicate why someone makes one choice over another. Individuals behave, but what makes behavior rational requires definition. Spending twenty dollars on a donut seems irrational in one context, but makes perfect sense to someone who has decided to make that decision.

After the financial crash of 2008, the conservative economist Alan Greenspan wrote in Foreign Affairs, "No one is immune to the emotions of fear and euphoria, which are among the predominant drivers of speculative markets."[43] Echoing Keynes, Greenspan affirmed that the markets were wrong for three reasons. The "vast majority" do not rationally understand risk, including the business class. People invest when they think the markets are good and investment flourishes with the promise of future returns. Secondly, individuals prefer the now rather than the future. Individuals consume rather than save what they make. Lastly, our consumption patterns arise from comparing to peers rather than an absolute income, which contributes to a "herd mentality" that influences individuals.

Therefore, as long as there is betting and a game, people continue to bet—until there are suddenly no more chips.[44] Individuals make decisions based on limited comparisons and don't decide consistently. The alternative description of the default unit of the individual is the "rational" man who is self-interested. However, this person is either a psychopath or Spock—an emotionless calculator imagined by economists as an amoral agent. It is unclear whether this is meant to be an empirical observation or an aspiration by which the market helps constrain behavior.

While someone who is self-interested is purposeful, intentional, and driven by incentives, these ideas are remarkably expansive and flexible. "Interest" reflects, for example, a range of motivations; individuals are not necessarily rational in their pursuits, and our ability to be logical or calculate changes over the course of a day. The ability to count can be diminished by other factors[45]. Furthermore, there may be other interests than money. Therefore, individuals do not behave predictably or in self-maximizing ways.

Choices are often presentist and immediate because the future is unpredictable. There is a tension between what to do now and what to do later. I eat the bowl of nuts in front of me only because they are available, not because I am particularly hungry. My shopping choices are directed by the arrangement of cookies and cherries as I enter the grocery store. An awareness of immediate costs and benefits does not lead to an awareness of long-term benefits or an accurate judgment of uncertainty.

Explaining desire is fundamental to understanding incentives. Individuals, however, may not understand why they desire what they desire. Economics tries to put a number, a value, on what is desired, and therefore make comparisons between competing desires. The passions cannot be ignored. As A.O. Hirschman noted, "economics emptied the idea of self-interest from its psychological and moral origin."[46] By assuming it could be value-neutral, it neglected to explore the dimensions of our motivations. What follows are reasons people act in ways that seem irrational.

Comparing Ourselves to Others

It may seem obvious, but it is worth stating that individuals are interested in other people and relating to them. They are motivated by others. The default concept of the individual is incomplete unless there is a recognition of the influence of parents, peers, neighbors, and other institutions. Individuals evaluate their own goods next to their neighbors. They are influenced by other people having things—"keeping up with the Joneses" is empirically verifiable.

People desire to be seen by others. Clothes, cars, zip codes, and vacations shape and identify people. Attention creates a sense of being valued, and offers a sense of security. Certainly aspects of self-interest, or even "the self" are inherited or beyond our control. Values are inherited or influenced by one's culture. So individuals are driven by status, made anxious by the perception of their peers, and worry about the approval of others.

The comparison can take several forms. It may be status in an organization—having a title, or the keys to the supply cabinet. The closer the relationship, and the more similar the person compared, the more intense the comparison. I do not compare myself to a banker or a Gujarati rice farmer. These are *relative judgments*. As the economist J.M. Keynes noted, "What groups of workers really care about was their relative position."[47] Individuals are concerned not just with their income, but also with how it compares to others.

Individuals are more attentive to relative costs than absolute costs. One does not easily compare herself to others outside of immediate relationships or concrete contexts. I do not compare myself to individuals in the Sudan, but to my neighbors in Westchester; I make purchases in relationship to what is perceived as normal. What individuals consume and desire reflects a relationship to other people. Priests, for example, compare themselves to priests, academics, teachers, or nurses but not necessarily real estate developers; financiers compare themselves with other financiers. One would rather have a little more than one's peers than absolutely more than the greater of humanity. One can feel poor if they make less than their neighbor, in spite of being wealthier than the rest of the world. In short, happiness is more determined from relative advantage than by self love.

Risk, Loss Aversion, and Bounded Rationality

One aspect about making choices is that individuals tend to be *risk-averse.* More specifically, the fear of loss is a disincentive for taking risks. Repeated studies have shown that individuals are twice as sensitive to losing what is had to gaining something.[48] This is a principle known as *loss aversion.* Instead, individuals adapt to what they acquire. This may explain, for example, the power of sentiment or nostalgia. When fearing the loss or a tradition one can't take a risk.

This adaptation is called *an endowment*, when one prefers the certainty of keeping what is had to the possibility of risking loss for a greater payout, even when it may be a good bet.[49] Individuals choose to seek security at their rate of spending rather than to anticipate change, because downward mobility causes more intense anxiety. The inability to see the future creates an aversion to risks. Businesses are also risk-averse. Because they also cannot see the future, they examine what choices other people make before investing their own money. In short, an individual and investor will take risks when confident, but hoard when not.

Insufficient knowledge, as explained earlier, is one reason for this caution. This is called *bounded rationality*, the incapacity to solve complex problems due to incomplete information. While *homo economicus*, the self-interested optimizing man, assumes complete and comprehensive knowledge, the reality is different. Descriptively, individuals can be overconfident, uncertain, fickle, or wrong. Individuals pay different amounts for the same thing at different places—individuals will pay a higher price for a can of beer at a bodega near the beach than for one at a supermarket. Because it's hard to guarantee long-term assessments it's easier to make short-term decisions at the expense of the long-term. Unless coerced into depositing into a retirement account, it's easier to spend the money on more immediate gratification. It costs time and brainpower to count, measure, or judge so instead individuals take shortcuts and make guesses.[50] However, individuals lack knowledge, including knowledge of the self, as is reflected by the tendency to be overconfident about decision-making, including one's personal willpower. Self-discipline and hard thinking are limited mental resources that impact our decisions, explaining why an aversion to loss seems almost like a moral failure. It's hard to see the future when one lacks the energy to consider it.

This does not mean it's hard to explain. I generally choose to eat a chocolate chip cookie rather than an apple when it's offered. Over time, I will likely gain weight, and in the long run, I will remember the decision as impulsive and thoughtless. But what's also clear is that I consider the cookie delicious. I experience competing claims, and the immediate short-term reward outweighs the immediate reward I get from imagining the long-term benefit, so it is easy to make the more impulsive choice. The knowledge that the healthier choice is more beneficial in the long run is harder for our animalistic brains to grasp than the vivid certainty of enjoyment in the short-term. The critique does not necessarily diminish the use of "economic man" as a unit that is countable. But counting "happiness" or our desires remains elusive in part because there are divergent ways of expressing it. For this reason, over a lifetime one may reconsider valuing leisure over work, between spending time with family or in the office.

The Problem of Disappointment

The lack of awareness, overconfident knowledge, and fear of loss are all reflected in the feeling of disappointment.[51] The economist A.O. Hirschmann writes, "Acts of consumption, as well as acts of participation in public affairs, which are undertaken because they are expected to yield satisfaction, also yield disappointment and dissatisfaction. Any pattern of consumption or of time use carries within itself, to use the hallowed metaphor, 'the seeds of its own destruction.'"[52] The activities one pursues may lead to failure. Our decisions don't always lead to the results wanted: "We want one thing and then upon getting it, find out to their dismay that they don't want it nearly as much as they thought or don't want it at all and that something else, of which they were hardly aware, is what they really want."[53]

Hirschmann continues, "While a life filled with disappointment is a sad affair, a life without any disappointment may not be bearable at all. For disappointment is the natural counterpart of man's propensity to entertain magnificent vistas and aspirations. What would life be without the ever renewed production of such disappointment-yielding expectations and aspirations? The "cost" of disappointments may well be less than the "benefit" yielded by man's ability to entertain over and over again the ideal of bliss and happiness"[54]. In the end, our fear of loss is a natural part of a life; perhaps more loss just indicates a fuller life.

Why the Economic Model of Humanity Is Incomplete

The habit of counting raises its own problems. People do not calculate every moment or experience, nor would it be desirable to do so. Most of Christian history has tempered the desire of money, believing that the acquisition of wealth required exploitation, manipulation, and plunder. But as moneymaking replaced martial virtues, it was seen to promote self-control. On one hand, counting everything seems dull, inhuman, and utilitarian, but on the other hand, it leads away from the impulses of war or other passions. The market offers the possibility of acquiring wealth without violence or exploitation. It may create value, build relationships, and foster trust within the community. It may also foster speculation, encourage laziness, or teach us how to exploit others. Some argue that studying economics itself and valuing the process of counting makes us poorer at being humane.

Counting makes it easy to measure our desire. Through measuring, it is possible to compare difference in passions and the relative values assigned to different outcomes. Counting quantifies satisfaction, and dissatisfaction, by counting spending. It presumes that what is counted can be substituted, replicated, or is interchangeable because it makes persons and desires fungible and replaceable. It flattens and diminishes differences, such as the distinctiveness between persons and places. The abstraction inherent in the practice of counting renders the loveliness of specificity and concreteness into a commodity. Furthermore, even markets, while they facilitate the peaceful engagement of strangers, are not merely networks of the anonymous, and still take place in real communities with specific individuals. Markets *are* embodied, and even though we may trade numbers illuminated on a computer screen, networks of human relationships make the light upon the screen possible.

The implicit virtue of self-sufficiency, the idea of an acquisitive self as a suitable moral unit for creating a model of economic behavior, is limited. Even if people count, measure, and evaluate the cost and benefits of decisions, it may not model the variety of actual networks. The neoclassical conception of the individual therefore cannot explain the motivations within the networks people inhabit. While it helps discern what to count, it also exposes that most decisions aren't carefully considered. Instead, it is revealed that the impact of sentiment, of self-understanding, and environments must also be counted, because relationships with other people are what matter most to us. Individuals are more sensitive to loss than to gains, overvalue the present, and become paralyzed in a world of unlimited choice. And the act of counting itself contains hidden costs of time, effort, and desire.

It may also be that the concept of the individual self is unsatisfactory. Even the economist Adam Smith, in the *Theory of Moral Sentiments*, writes that individuals judge "in no other way than by endeavoring to view them with the eyes of other people."[55] The nature of our desires only makes sense in society. Although he hypothesizes that a man without society will have passions, he cannot avoid describing that our passions are impacted by other people. The idea of the self has a problem, that people are inherently part of larger networks; not only are they impacted by other groups of people with whom they identify, they also incorporate these groups into their own identities.

Further Critiques of the Market

I have previously described how markets try to smooth out transactions by reducing tension, and also described a fuller version of the self in markets. Human beings are rarely efficient or simple. Although we may be aggregate individuals to a state institution, individuals don't consider other people in their social networks as interchangeable. Using economics has limits when considering the values of specific, individual persons. In our daily life, some choices seem priceless or outside the market.

The assumption of value-neutrality conceals, ignores, and diminishes the group-oriented, social and political nature of human society, by hiding the social networks of power behind economic networks. The choice of what counts reflects values that economics denies having. For this reason, economics routinely overlooks costs and externalities by mistaking ideal models for descriptive ones. Its efforts to be value-neutral affirm values of maximization, hyper-rationality, and a narrow version of self-interest. These economic "virtues" are thus self-confirming. In its effort to be morally neutral and value-free, economics invents an idealized person and society that are not only inaccurate, but undesirable.

Furthermore, as the theologian and economist Daniel Finn notes, contemporary mainstream economists often "move from a descriptive economic model to normative conclusions about real constitutional and legislative life."[56] Economists may believe that the individuated, rational, optimizing *man* is a useful fiction, or an aspirational moral stance. However, by assuming that a rational, optimizing man is a reasonable default position to have, while ignoring the arbitrariness of such a unit, the descriptive and the normative, the actual and the hypothetical, become entangled. At different times moral agnosticism seems to desire moral conclusions, even though the model offered has no empirical basis in how decisions get made.

Time is one asset or value where "value neutral" analysis becomes clumsy because people value time differently for different reasons. Time is the ultimate scarce resource. For this reason, quantifying the value of one's time can become complicated because its actual worth for a person will change. Furthermore, counting itself implicitly requires surplus time outside of sustenance and merely exchanging, and the mental work of counting also counts itself, the benefits of surplus value, or time. Calculating the cost of doing business, or calculating the time one calculates, is an added cost.

Other challenges to economics include moral critiques of growth. Jean-Pierre Dupuy argues that economics, as a discipline, assumes perpetual growth, the continual expansion of the market and the production of goods.[57] Economism deceives us by assuming growth will be constant and beneficial, concealing how it relies upon a sense of an impending catastrophe. The gambling nature of international finance points to a dynamic where perpetual growth and catastrophe continually cycle.

Counting and measuring may help allocate resources more widely through noting how things are repeated and replicable. Markets are possible because of technological tools that duplicate and create substitutions of one good for another, and they can easily use money as a measuring unit, one that clarifies costs and benefits at any particular time. And yet, the various unique things and people in lives that give a specific identity defy measurement.

However, as Dupuy notes, "the valuations arrived at by the market are indifferent of merit, indifferent to moral worth, indifferent to human needs… It is as though economic agents are no more than marionettes, at the mercy of the whims of hidden divinities."[58] And this indifference toward human life, sentiment, or emotion provides its own moral problem. Consequently, the presumption that economics is value-free conceals the complexity of the desires that people have. The tools that facilitate commerce, such as money, pricing, or substitution, while greasing the circulation of capital, also signify power, the relationships that undergird that power, and intensify our personal desires. Money has the capacity to elevate the very human desire to be seen, and to have things that others see. Individuals count as valuable what other people count as valuable.

Money can orient, shape, and crowd out other values worth having. For economism, the primary value is liberty; it is indifferent to other values. It may seem that any constraint upon a market would then seem tyrannical and unjust. In economism, the liberty of the person who possesses money takes priority over those who depend on jobs for stability and their livelihood. As Dupuy notes, quoting Hayek, the loss of jobs, the abandonment of firms, the failure of products, going broke, and other failures cause humiliation, indignation and despair.[59] While liberty is a good, the question remains whether there are other values worth keeping.

In addition, while markets coordinate the behavior of strangers, they also make it easier for persons to avoid each other, "transformed into consuming zombies to protect ourselves from the evil that rises up from underground."[60] What has been useful in unmasking desires and allowing their immediate fulfillment renders persons both indistinct from others and mutually wary. Instead of deepening human interaction, it keeps people at a safe distance. It changes the direction and the sources of envy.

Why do individuals count? It makes it easy to compare one person to another. In short, individuals count because they want to know what to value, and they value what other people count. While economics is a study of voluntary behavior, and as such it prioritizes freedom and choice, it must also account for stronger and more accurate descriptions of desires and incentives. I will now show how economists specifically engage the problem of envy.

Economics and Envy

In *The Moral Ecology of Markets*, the theologian and economist Daniel Finn explores three central economists of the century: Milton Friedman, James Buchanan, and Friedrich Hayek. These particular economists represent one thread of the discipline that argues that economics is fundamentally value-free, prioritizing only individual freedom and choice above all other virtues.[61] What one chooses is not interesting to them, only the freedom to choose. They are agnostic about other values or any specific conception of the good life, as individuals have different passions.

With such a view, no person's desire can take priority over another's, except in the case of harm. The fundamental value remains freedom. Therefore, the organizing of social networks to orient and direct desire, whether in governments or firms, is incidental to the work of economists or to the economy. Envy, or the restriction of it, is not up to them; desire is not considered a contributor to irrationality, instead merely an incentive.

The mechanics of desire call into question the ideal of the rational, self-maximizing person. They insinuate that people are neither self-maximizing, in control, nor good calculators. However, economists have created their own vocabulary for describing the reasons people make their choices in the market, confirming what earlier sociologists such as Thorstein Veblen intuited, that not merely accumulation, but imitation, explains the choices of the wealthy. The wealthy do not act rationally in terms of maximizing their savings, but consume to call attention to themselves. While Veblen himself considered consumption irrational, reflective of barbaric, subconscious impulses, economists have generally been uninterested in *why* we consume, but merely *how much*.

Adam Smith

Adam Smith framed the fundamental ideas for the basis of a market economy:[62] the impact of the division of labor[63] and the role of self-interest in coordinating the market. His familiar quote explains the mechanics of how an economy functions: "It is not from the benevolence of the butcher, the brewer, or the baker, that we expect our dinner, but from their regard to their own interest. We address ourselves, not to their humanity but to their self-love, and never talk to them of our own necessities but of their advantages."[64] Through competing for services, each person's work benefits others. This would describe the invisible hand, the magic of market coordination of strangers.

The metaphor of the invisible hand, however, has its limits. While the theologian Mark Taylor duly explained its impact upon Darwin's theory of evolution, the economist Robert Frank writes that in collective action problems, advantages to the individual can conflict with an entire group as a whole: "Rewards that depend on relative performance spawn collective action problems that can cause markets to fail."[65] Individuals have limited knowledge about their impact on others, and because relative advantage or income matters more than absolute income,[66] coordination often fails.

Smith had a broader understanding of self-interest and human motivations in his *Theory of Moral Sentiments*,[67] where he describes the mechanics of moral intuitions. Anticipating modern behavioral economics, he theorizes that the root of sympathies arises from a sensitivity toward the experiences of others. People relate to their imagination of the interiority of others. They may not experience directly another person's broken foot or their feeling of despair or success, but they can imagine what their feeling is like. They empathize in accordance with our own capacity to imagine our own response. They see through the eyes of others. This intuition includes the capacity to imagine the gaze of an "impartial spectator," our conscience. This is how one learns how to become a moral person.[68]

Identification is linked to a desire for approval: "To be observed, to be attended to, to be taken notice of with sympathy, complacency, and appreciation, are all the advantages which we can propose to derive from it. It is the vanity, not the ease or the pleasure, which interests us."[69] Individuals want a place in the company of people. Not abstractly or imaginatively, but with the concrete relationships of the people they know. Because we are motivated by the desire for respect, status makes us rivals with others, and the market makes that a challenge to solve. Status is a position we hold relative to others.

The economist John Maynard Keynes understood how our human inclinations affected our decision-making in two important ways. The first is the idea of *Animal Spirits*, or the inclination of investors and businessmen to make a profit by taking a risk and displaying the initiative to create a business. However, when individuals are risk-averse, they stop investing, resulting in a cycle that leads into a depression. Thus, increasing demand returns people to the market again by making the risk more palatable.

The second influence Keynes affirmed is how people make decisions based on the opinions of others. Investors don't actually rely on a company's profitability but upon the judgment of other investors. Other investors provide a signal, or a shortcut, to discerning what is valuable. Because the value of a stock is dependent not on the soundness of a firm but upon the worth that other investors *thought* the company was worth, they sought to guess what other investors thought. Thus, investment decisions rely on a theory of mind rather than an objective valuation. Keynes compared this to a beauty contest, where men had to pick out the prettiest faces from a set of photographs but then tried to identify which the average person thought was prettiest, rather than select what they personally thought. As Richard Thaler describes, Keynes thought that money managers were easily influenced by the opinions of their peers, and that they play a guessing game where each one of them is trying to guess what the others think about stocks.[70] An individual's decisions depend on how others think.

The Elements of Envy

Some economists realize people make frequently irrational decisions in the market (they *misbehave*),[71] but use a different vocabulary to unpack its mechanics. Economists note individuals are motivated by *relative*, rather than absolute, position in networks. As I explained earlier in this chapter, people do not compare ourselves to an absolute standard, a single benchmark for an extended amount of time. An old joke describes this condition: *A bear chases two hikers. One takes off his boots and puts on running shoes. The other exclaims, "What difference will those shoes make? You'll never outrun the bear." He responds, "I don't need to outrun the bear. Just you."* He knows his survival is relative to the other hiker's[72].

People are more sensitive about their perceived relative income than their absolute income. They would rather live in a 3,000 square foot house in a neighborhood of 2,500 square foot houses than live in the same house in a neighborhood of 5,000 square foot houses. They build self-identity by comparing themselves to others. They care about how others think. So individuals purchase goods that make them like others, and they grow attached to our things because they shape their identity and self-worth. What they perceive they need and what is available depend on the choices of their neighbors and those to whom they compare.[73]

Relative position impacts the different networks, not just our financial status. As one economist notes, "people in each category are involved in their own competitions to move forward in local hierarchies."[74] Our market mentality merely puts a monetary number on how we rank. In part, this reflects our physical reactions to other people; mirror neurons, while giving us the ability to empathize and imitate, also illustrate how our minds are dependent upon the choices of others.[75] This is the physiological counterpart to mimetic behavior in the fourth chapter.

In an economy where income inequality is intensified, the rewards associated with relative performance are concentrated at the top.[76] While relative position expresses our desire for respect and connection with others, it also creates anxiety.[77] The constant barrage of goods in advertising, television, and social media portray constant use of positional signals that foster dissatisfaction by increasing our status anxiety. There is a structure to how this happens.

First, there is an *endowment*. Our endowment includes what one is used to having and what one expects: social position, inherited wealth wealth, cultural preferences, the size of one's childhood house, the education expected, and the possessions accumulated. One's endowment changes as one gets familiar with having more.

The evidence is that it is hard to lose what one has. The familiarity makes it painful for us to give up what makes us feel like a person. As Richard Thaler points out, loss aversion means that *losses hurt twice as much as equivalent gains feel good.*[78] And as life goes on, the impact of losses and gains diminishes over time. Therefore, individuals will refrain from making choices for unpredictable gains, but are willing to do much more to avoid losing.

Television and social media have had a pronounced effect in how people perceive their relative positions. As a result, the media now frames our expectations at least as much as our friends and extended networks, which becomes a further source of dissatisfaction.[79] The lower influence of friends and networks in a media-saturated age means there is less of a buffer against the influence of violence, sex, beauty, and wealth represented in the media. As materialism proves that it can't satisfy our inner yearnings, it's possible to withdraw from the world and spend more on our possessions, resulting in a lack of companionship as well as a feedback loop of buying more stuff and raising expectations, while also reducing satisfaction.

Market Problems

The problems of envy reflect some of the greater challenges in markets. Markets cannot provide a moral value and may crowd out other values worth having—including some of the positive ones markets can create. While markets, as financial networks, facilitate the flow of capital between both strangers and friends, their effectiveness has limits. Individuals have limited knowledge and overestimate their abilities. Public goods that benefit everyone, such as traffic control or a lighthouse,[80] are not equally paid for by all. The market does not necessarily guarantee or calculate security or stability for people, nor reward long-term investments. If markets naturally incline toward the centralization of wealth, civic institutions can be threatened. The economist Thomas Piketty and others note that the increase in inequality correlates to nationalism, identity politics, and less stable markets[81].

In *Capital*, Thomas Piketty shows that historically, wealth accumulates. In times of low economic growth, capital flows upward, because rents build wealth through interest rather than by individuals taking risks. Congruently, Robert Frank shows that newer technology and economies of scale make it easy to reproduce the top performers.[82] The consolidation of wealth, attention, and income intensify the anxieties that individuals have in the market. As Frank notes, on special occasions, one gives two ounces of Russian caviar, not forty pounds of whitefish caviar; a half carat diamond, not a 30 carat garnet. This is because not buying "the best" might invite a sense of loss, or regret, and a sense of inadequacy or failure.

A central correction to the belief in the perfection of the invisible hand is that the wants of individuals will inevitably conflict with the stability of a community or the needs of others. As Frank notes, "The conflict between individual and group is the single most important explanation of the imbalance in our current consumption patterns."[83] The consequence of these intense changes in the market has been an increase in depression, a decline in satisfaction. and fewer resources for the care of children. As people measure themselves to new standards, they become increasingly unhappy.[84]

Furthermore, in a winner-takes-all economy, the intensification of our awareness of social position and status anxiety amplifies dissatisfaction by encouraging consumption: "All of us are spending more time at the office and taking shorter vacations; we are spending less time with our families and friends and we have less time for sleep, exercise, travel, reading and other activities that help maintain body and soul… When our spending on luxury goods is growing four times as fast as overall spending, our public infrastructure… [is] deteriorating," the economist Robert Frank writes in *Luxury Fever*.[85]

What Are We Looking For?

Markets may coordinate exchanges, but they do not seek to answer the question of *why* people want. Money does provide happiness to some people, but it brings less happiness as income passes subsistence levels.[86] Our expectations for happiness rise, while having more things offers diminishing returns. Individuals remain concerned with respect—our status, security, and social trust[87]—which has little to do with absolute income, and more to do with our comparison with other people. When money is used to build relationships, it provides a useful function. When it corrodes social trust, its use diminishes.

The market has improved the number of choices we have. As the economist Denys Lawrence Munby writes, "An expanding economy is that it means an enlargement of choice, and an enlargement of choice in a variety of directions." This includes more goods and services, art, education, healthcare, and the possibility of leisure. However, he also notes that "this enlargement of itself increases the insecurity of life, and is not to be expected that everyone will want to bear the burden of decision. There is no greater security than is to be found in the womb or the prison, but both these environments are usually considered incompatible with the full development of personality. There is undoubtedly a price to be paid for the exercise of choice, but it is an inescapable corollary of something of greater value in itself."[88] There may be benefits to choose between a dozen different kinds of cereal, automobiles, and craft beers, but making decisions between them can be exhausting. Munby expressed a general hope about the benefits of markets, but he acknowledged that they don't provide much more than choice.

Some economists have sought to count the benefits of the market differently. For example, instead of simply measuring wealth, they seek to measure happiness or other kinds of goods. Richard Layard defines happiness differently than a momentary sense of gratification or satisfaction from a purchase, as not merely a state of pleasure, but joy and contentment.[89] While there are various sorts of lists that encapsulate what the good life entails, there is some consensus that it includes security, meaningful work, health, companionship, respect, and leisure.[90]

One of the fundamental building blocks for any of these is trust. As Daniel Finn writes, "Trust is an important lubricant of a social system. It is extremely efficient: it saves people a lot of trouble to have a fair degree of reliance on other people's word." Without trust, individuals must spend more to enforce and monitor.[91] Without trust, the costs of enforcement rise.

Trust has its conditions, and the market may undermine what makes it possible. There is some evidence that markets left on their own allow wealth to accumulate at the top, and that the corresponding income inequality intensifies social anxiety and correlates to economic and social precarity. The answer is not an equalitarianism that demands the flattening of outcomes or rewards. Equality, after all, is not merely measured financially, except when wealth becomes the primary way people measure success. Income inequality becomes a problem when a level of income allows one to manipulate the law, to segregate oneself from the rest of the public, and to buy politicians to change the rules: "Where the rich behave with lawless arrogance, the poor with impotent resentment and politicians with obeisance to money, inequality has exceeded the mark."[92] When the wealth of one person motivates other people to abdicate their own values or sense of worth, trust in our broader networks declines. And this trust is what makes markets possible.

The nature of equality has to do with a specific quality of relationships. Richard Wilkinson and Kate Pickett[93] show that *greater* equality, not absolute equality, leads to desirable social outcomes. Increased inequality arrests our self-worth, and makes status even more important to us, because that is where the power is. The top is where everyone looks.[94]

Addressing Our True Needs

Markets have the power to coordinate disparate needs and skills and make individuals richer. They do not relieve the need for the security or respect that position and status give us. Material goods make life easier, but can make individuals more dissatisfied. Rather than worry about needs, it becomes easier to worry about wants learned through the perceptions of and by others. It may be the role of religious institutions to remind people about the distinctions between needs and wants.

While it is beyond the scope of this book to suggest governmental policy, some economists and political scientists have suggested a solution: policies that improve education, offer meaningful work, and facilitate good relationships. Education would include opportunities for reflection on values, and address the sorts of work worth having; policies to facilitate good relationships would include fostering networks that allow for healthy families and opportunities for friendships. Robert Frank suggests sorts of "positional arms control agreements."[95] This means perhaps it's possible to create a culture that says the fourth family car need not always be a brand new Aston Martin, but rather a ten-year-old Lexus.

While others critique the need for economic growth, good reasons remain to support it. The need for economic growth, however, also remains relevant. The economist Ben Friedman notes that improvement in growth overall leads to better tolerance. He writes,

> By giving most people a sense of living better than they or their families had in the not very distant past, sustained economic growth reduces the intensity of their desire to live better than one another. Economic growth satisfies the form of people's aspiration for "more" that is possible for everyone to fulfill. In doing so it reduces the urgency that they attach to the form of aspiration that, while perfectly understandable for each person individually, is nonetheless an obvious impossibility for the society of as a whole. When an economy stagnates, however, the importance people attach to living better than others against whom they naturally compare themselves is more intense. The fact they cannot do so, or at least on average cannot, then takes on a heightened importance in their eyes. The resulting frustration generates intolerance, generosity, and resistance to greater openness to individual opportunity. It also erodes people's willingness to trust one another, which in turn is a key requisite for a successful democracy.[96]

When the economy is stagnant, people will feel as if they are falling behind, creating further anxiety.[97] This suggests the power of loss aversion; they are worried about losing more, especially if they feel that their context is precarious. As Robert Frank notes, "More wealth could be a good thing, provided we spent it in certain ways."[98] Spending on the sorts of policies that increase growth, through improving education and health, would likely go far in addressing these issues.

The data indicate that individualism has made it harder for us to create the sorts of agreements that this requires. The church, however, affirms a variety of networks and relationship building in addition to the market. It provides a place for companionship, for individuals to share culture, information, and art. It provides examples of the good life through rewarding commitment and inculcating values that allow individuals to exit the hedonic treadmill, giving them skills to manage anxiety and loss. The church can strengthen the resilience of those who eschew the sorts of materialism that creates stress. Most specifically, as Richard Lane suggests, it can be a network of friends, a shield from the various social threats of the market.[99]

Networks and Governance

Voluntary networks, such as churches, can provide the kind of community, networks, and support governments can't or won't. The market, although it coordinates exchanges, cannot replace the importance of people making decisions together. At the very least, teaching people how to make decisions without rivalry and through friendship is what the church can do in the name of Jesus Christ.

The market does not pretend to be the sole purveyor of human values, but is more like a platform for people to assess the kinds of values they have. But this platform still requires human management because it still requires individual trust and an agreement between people: "If it is true that the economy must be deferred to, then there is a case not only for constraining the imprudent actions of the prince, but for repressing those of the people, for limiting participation, in short, for crushing anything that could be interpreted by some economist-king as a threat to the proper functioning of the 'delicate watch.'"[100] The market cannot replace political activity, and when most citizens are absorbed with making money, fewer people have the time to participate in political life which in turn opens the door for tyranny.[101]

Good governance helps communities and firms manage the challenges of opportunism and bounded rationality. The political scientist Elinor Ostrom, who won the Nobel Prize in economics in 2009, illustrates in her book *Governing the Commons* concrete examples of how voluntary communities have effectively managed shared resources. She explores how groups and institutions have made decisions around shared resources. Not only large states, corporations, and individuals but institutions, as collective organizations, have the capacity to organize efficiently. Ostrom outlines empirical data of how collective organizations manage.

Good management of shared resources includes several characteristics. After studying organizations that have existed for as long as nearly a thousand years, Ostrom noted the following traits in common: easy participation, shared monitoring, graduated sanctions, conflict management, transparency, and reasonable oversight. These organizations have the capacity to redress people's complaints.[102] They foster commitment, build avenues of trust, and institute methods of shared accountability. The rules are clear and understood, and individuals are held accountable.

Other economists affirm the need for good management and the benefits of cooperation. Layard explains that people are willing to cooperate for a variety of reasons, even when individually selfishness might seem like a better choice. Selfishness seems to be immediately beneficial when the market does not reward commitment or accountability is applied inconsistently or obscurely, so the benefits of cooperation are not readily apparent. However, in Ostrom's examples, it is possible to build trust with intensive work knowing that *building relationships over time* facilitates the skills that allow people to work together, using consensus to build trust and reciprocity.[103]

The terms *relative position, status anxiety, positional goods*, and *loss aversion* amplify the biblical narratives of envy, honor, and loss. They identify the sources of social tension that create conflict. The instinct to compare is an essential element of envy and rivalry, and an unavoidable part of being human. It would be an enormous challenge to eliminate these sentiments as position and self-respect are difficult to disentangle. As Robert Frank notes, "Although positional concerns may often entail envy, we have seen that they would be strong even if in envy's absence. They can be mitigated, but not eliminated, by cultural conditioning."[104] In the next chapter we will discuss some theological responses to how economists address the world. But perhaps this reminder should warn the church that problems that arise with envy cannot be easily dispensed with through continual exhortation, but may be managed through honesty and a careful realigning of incentives.

The church still has motivations and motivated disciples of Christ. The sources of satisfaction or happiness for disciples, which may be the good life, such as health, security, leisure, and companionship, are hard to measure. Individuals typically don't bill their children for parenting costs, nor is it viable to ruminate over every loss or gained experiences. Thinking about why one gives or how much to give itself costs time, so some give without measurement. It is possible to give without calculating, trusting that eventually the shortfall will cover expenses. A church hall may be rented below market value and justified by calling it "faith-based economics" because it builds relationships. The church reduces the rent for the Pentecostal congregation in exchange for shoveling. In another year, the church will ask everyone to help shovel. While there is an exchange, it may be local, human, and harder to quantify, and quantifying it too precisely diminishes how our specific relationships are more important than money.

Notes

1. Skidelsky, *How Much is Enough*, 92.
2. Akin to Issac Asimov's Mathematical Sociologists in his *Foundation* series, the psycho-historians who could predict the rise and fall of empires through precise modeling.
3. Heyne, *Christian Social Thought and the Origination of Economic Order*, 234–5.
4. Daniel Finn, "Social Causality and Market Complicity," in *Distant Markets, Distant Harms*, 259.
5. Paul Heyne, *Economic Way of Thinking* (Prentice Hall, 1997), 163.
6. Daniel Finn, "Social Causality and Market Complicity," in *Distant Markets, Distant Harms* (Oxford, 2014), 255.
7. David Harvey, *The Enigma of Capital* (Oxford, 2010), 163.
8. Paul Heyne, *The Economic Way of Thinking*, Eighth Ed, 562.
9. Sunstein and Holmes, *The Cost of Rights* (1999).
10. Ostrom, *Governing the Commons: The Evolution of Institutions for Collective Action* (New York: Cambridge University Press, 2011), 51.
11. Harvey, *The Enigma of Capital*, 40.
12. Heyne, *The Economic Way of Thinking*, 75.
13. Heyne, "Economics and Ethics," in *Are Economists Immoral*, 25.
14. Mark Taylor, About Religion: Economies of Faith in Virtual Culture, (Chicago: University of Chicago, 1999), 7.
15. Heyne, *Economic Way of Thinking*, 82.
16. Finn, MEM, 117.
17. Elinor Ostrom, *Governing the Commons*, 40–41.
18. R.H. Coase, *The Firm, the Market, and the Law* (Chicago: University of Chicago, 1990), 40.
19. Williamson, EIC, 18–19.

20. Williamson, EIC, 42.
21. Williamson, EIC, 58.
22. Williamson, EIC, 58.
23. Williamson, EIC, 49.
24. Williamson, EIC, 44.
25. Williamson, EIC, 32.
26. Williamson, EIC, 264.
27. Williamson, EIC, 405.
28. Williamson, EIC, 405.
29. Harvey, *The Enigma of Capital*, 45.
30. Hirschmann, *Shifting Involvements*, 55.
31. Hirschmann, *Shifting Involvements*, 57.
32. Robert Frank, The Darwin Economy, 11
33. Edward Baptist, *This Half Has Never Been Told.*
34. Munphy, GRS, 176–7.
35. Finn, *Moral Ecology of Markets*, chapters 3–4, 33.
36. Finn, *Moral Ecology of Markets*, 109.
37. Hirschmann, *Passions and the Interests* (Princeton, 1977) 132.
38. A. O Hirschmann, *The Essential Hirschmann*, ed. Jeremy Adelman (Princeton, 2015), 197.
39. A. O Hirschmann, *The Essential Hirschmann*, 197.
40. Finn, *Moral Ecology of Markets*, 55–59.
41. By "man" I do mean *male*. Especially one that considers himself to be a logical person who models a reasonable, default position. This is not meant to indicate a preferable or empirically accurate position. It may be considered also a "white straight man" although there are certainly non-white straight male persons who may hold such views about the status of the individual.
42. Mill, *On the Definition of Political Economy.*
43. Alan Greenspan, "Never Saw it Coming," *Foreign Affairs* (Nov/Dec 2013).
44. Greenspan, "Never Saw it Coming," *Foreign Affairs* (Nov/Dec 2013).
45. Ariely, *The Honest Truth About Dishonesty*, 81.
46. Hirschmann, *The Essential*, 209.
47. Sidelsky, 149.
    https://pubs.aeaweb.org/doi/pdfplus/10.1257/jep.5.1.193
48. Daniel Kahneman, Jack L. Knetsch, and Richard H. Thaler. "Anomalies: The Endowment Effect, Loss Aversion, and Status Quo Bias," *Journal of Economic Perspectives* 5, no. 1 (1991): 193–206.
49. Sunstein, *Nudge*, 34.
50. Richard Thaler, *Misbehaving: The Making of Behavioral Economics* (New York: Norton, 2015), 22.

51. Albert O. Hirschmann, *Shifting Involvements: Private Interest and Public Action* (Princeton: Princeton, 1982).
52. Hirschmann, *Shifting Involvements*, 10.
53. Hirschmann, *Shifting Involvements*, 21.
54. Hirschmann, *Shifting Involvements*, 23.
55. Adam Smith, TMS, III.1.2.
56. Daniel Finn, *The Moral Ecology of Markets* (New York: Cambridge, 2006), 21.
57. Jean-Pierre Dupuy, *Economy and the Future: A Crisis of Faith* (East Lansing, MI: Michigan State, 2014).
58. Dupuy, *Economy and the Future*, 8.
59. Dupuy, *Economy and the Future*, 17.
60. Dupuy, *Economy and the Future*, 20.
61. Daniel Finn, *The Moral Ecology of Markets* (New York: Cambridge, 2006).
62. Adam Smith, *The Wealth of Nations* (New York: Modern Library, 2000).
63. Smith, i.1.
64. Smith, ii.
65. Robert Frank, *The Darwin Economy: Liberty, Competition, and the Common Good* (Princeton: Princeton, 2011), 300 ;306–307.
66. Robert Frank, *The Darwin Economy* (Kindle Locations), 519–522.
67. Adam Smith, *The Theory of Moral Sentiments*, ed. Knud Haakonssen (Cambridge: Cambridge, 2002).
68. Christina McRorie, *The Emptiness of Modern Economics: Why the Dismal Science Needs a Richer Moral Anthropology,* Hedgehog Review 16, no. 3 (Fall 2014).
69. Smith, *The Theory of Moral Sentiments*, 1.III.2, 61.
70. Thaler, *Misbehaving*, 210–11.
71. Thaler, *Misbehaving*, 302–5.
72. Layard, *Happiness,* 51.
73. Frank, *Luxury Fever*, 11.
74. Frank, *Luxury Fever*, 137.
75. Wilkinson and Pickett, *Spirit Level*, 213.
76. Robert Frank and Philip Cook, *The Winner Take All Society* (New York: The Free Press, 1995), 23–24.
77. Frank, *Luxury Fever*, 121.
78. Richard Thaler, *Misbehaving*, 33–34.
79. Layard, *Happiness*, 85–9.
80. Charles E. Lindblom, *"Politics and Markets": The World's Political-Economic Systems Basic Books* (New York, 1977), 76–89.
81. Piketty, *Capital*, 539.
82. Frank and Cook, WTAS, 32–3.
83. Frank, *Luxury Fever*, 158.
84. Robert Lane, *The Loss of Happiness in Market Democracies* (New Haven: Yale, 2000).

85. Robert Frank, *Luxury Fever: Weighing the Cost of Excess* (Princeton: Princeton University, 1999).
86. Lane, *The Loss of Happiness*, 63, 75.
87. Layard, *Happiness*, 7.
88. Munby, *God and the Rich Society*, 42.
89. Layard, *Happiness*, 21.
90. Layard, *Happiness*, 63; Skidelsky, *How Much is Enough*, chapter 6.
91. Finn, *Moral Ecology of Markets*, 137.
92. Skidelsky, *How Much is Enough*, 160.
93. Richard Wilkinson and Kate Pickett, *The Spirit Level: Why Equality Makes Society Stronger* (New York: Bloomsbury, 2011).
94. Wilkinson and Pickett, *Spirit Level*, 43.
95. Frank and Cook, WTAS, chapter 9.
96. Benjamin Friedman, *The Moral Consequences of Economic Growth* (Vintage, 2005), 92.
97. Benjamin Friedman, *The Moral Consequences of Economic Growth* (Vintage, 2005), 92.
98. Frank, *Luxury Fever*, 75.
99. Wilkinson and Pickett, *Spirit Level*, 39. This is also the conflation of Robert Lane, *The Loss of Happiness in Market Democracies* (New Haven: Yale, 2000).
100. Albert O. Hirschmann, *The Passions and the Interests, Political Arguments for Capitalism Before its Triumph* (Princeton: Princeton, 1977), 124.
101. Hirschmann, *Passions and Interests*, 125.
102. Ostrom, *Governing the Commons*, 90.
103. Ostrom, *Governing the Commons*, 172.
104. Frank, *Luxury Fever*, 145.

3 Theological Responses

The link between religion and economics has a long provenance. The French Philosopher Jean-Pierre Dupuy writes, "Economy cannot be explained without reference to religion… Economy occupies the place emptied out by the sacralization of the world, itself an eminently religious phenomenon."[1] The theologian Mark Taylor also shows how religion explains economics, while W. Douglas Meeks illustrates how economics can help explain religion.

While economic analysis helps explain the allocation of resources, its separation from ethical or religious issues has caused a reaction among theologians who find the lack of concern about meaning troublesome. To restore the link between meaning or faith and economic analysis, theologians address the assumptions economists make by exploring the congruence and compatibility between theological and economic explanations of value and behavior. These explanations include understanding the relationship between scarcity and coordination, substitution and sacrifice, and sin and redemption, and also illustrate how incentives, opportunism, knowledge, and trust shape any sort of decision. Theological concepts such as sin and envy are sharpened by economic models, which can further help identify how theologians could better address the church's task.[2]

The congruence between economics and theology is reflected both in homologies, such as debt, and the compatibility between different values, such as market coordination and reciprocity. Trust, for example, remains central. Economics and theological ethics affirm that trust makes markets and communities possible. Without trust, coordination becomes too expensive, as it requires costly monitoring and enforcement mechanisms. Trust in markets mirrors trust in God. And trust exemplifies individual faith.

The list of theologians who reflect on economics is long, and by no means is my list here complete. I've decided to address the philosophies of the theologians whom I think are most important to our discussion. They are the liberationist perspectives of Timothy Gorringe, the Radical Orthodoxy of David Long, the "free-market" view of Michael Novak, and Katherine Tanner's and Daniel Bell's theological explorations of economics through the perspective of theological vocabulary of grace and desire.

Theological anthropology can accommodate both theological concerns about desire, sin, and redemption, while also incorporating the insights of neoclassical economics. Behavioral economics converges well with critiques of our rationality and knowledge as understood by moral theologians. Even though, for example, Michael Novak does not challenge the value-neutrality implied within markets, as most other theologians implicitly do, his defense of markets and his affirmation of personal and institutional governance remain useful explanations of desire.

Theologians are fundamentally concerned, in most of the literature, with our common life. These concerns include equality, work, rest, abundance, the common good, justice, and authority. They are concerned with the impact of poverty and the relationship between disparate sections of society. The gospel relates to communities and politics, not only the allocation of goods. Furthermore, they understand that some choices and inclinations are disordered. Sin impacts our desire. Individuals often want things that negatively impact the needs of others. And so, it is important to understand the critiques of theologians and explore how they might address the concerns of the church and economics.

David Long: Restoring Meaning to the Market

The project of the theologian David Long is to unpack the nature of value-neutral presuppositions within economics. He delves into the intellectual history of economics and governance and describes the shortcomings of libertarian and Marxist anthropology, as both are inaccurate representations of actual behavior. He critiques how Max Weber relates grace to practice and charisma to rationality. Long shows both how rationality has its own tradition and how Weber's abstract propositions attempt to render Christian ethics irrelevant.[3] Rationality diminishes the apparent need for a separate Christian ethic.

Long does this by describing economic thought as *marginalist*. This is the point where individuals are concerned with calculation, where decisions about scarcity need to be made. He writes, "marginalist rationality assumes that goods are not intrinsic to forms of life, and therefore it does not question whether certain goods might be incommensurable. For a marginalist rationality all goods are subject to the overarching law of value. All goods are potential objects of human choice, and thus through a person's choices, she gives value to that which is." The economist thus *measures choices*.[4] Choosing happens when different values or calculations conflict with one another. And then, when choices made become part of our endowment and become part of a person's identity, the nature and design of those choices by the market does not guarantee that the choices will be satisfying or fulfilling.

Long shows how markets take persons out of inherited traditions and remove them from the question of what being a person is. Rather than having an identity rooted in a community or a culture, the concept of the individual implies there is no embedded thing specifically that one can say has inherent value. The market is unchained from any specific, concrete claims about what should matter to persons. The moral and ethical consequences of the economic principle of substitutability, the calculus behind marginal costs, and the counting implicit, hide that most of what makes a life is not quantifiable.

Long restores the telos, the sense of meaning, of the human person, emphasizing the possibility of local control over common life. The principle of subsidiarity, the practice that embedded, concrete concerns should be the foundation of making economic decisions, implies limits to the hand of the market.[5] His description of the work of Bernard Dempsey is particularly fruitful. Dempsey offered the Functional Economy as way of bringing together justice and economics, where individuals can be directed towards an end that fits one's inclinations—where individual work, family and community can thrive. Long exposes how modern economics instead put groups of individuals in conflict, mistakenly presumes vices can be transformed into virtues, and inhibits the development of virtues through free associations apart from the bureaucracy of the state.[6] Long argues that economics should allow for the development of networks outside both the market and the state.

Long shows that an economy has a role to restore virtues—that "a laborer's work is in the common good of a corporate community," and not merely quantified by creating new wealth.[7] Long affirms the theology of radical orthodoxy, in particular, John Milbank, who put the values of the true, good, and beautiful, historically embedded and relational, above the heresy of the market, which reduces God to a privatized, meaningless sphere. Instead of presuming relationships have no intrinsic value, the Christian should direct the market toward valuing the true, good, and beautiful—the common life. The market should submit to it, instead of persons submitting to the market.

Long's work is an extensive and comprehensive intellectual history that provides a well researched resource for relating economics to the theological tradition. What is missing, however, is a more thorough description of desire and governance. While Dempsey's rejection of conflict as a necessary part of the market tradition recognizes that firms and markets can coordinate shared interests within a community, our desires remain hard to satisfy. The mechanics of creating virtues, of implementing governance, and of inculcating restraint remain unclear. I suggest that the church as a network, independent of the state or corporations, can create a non-competitive arena that avoids the financialization of all human relationships. It may be that some degree of organization and hierarchy is how to lead people into a more fruitful life, one that directs people to use money and markets for the purpose of building stronger communities.

We can, however, press further. Long writes, "to teach us to desire the infinite with an infinite desire and the finite with a finite desire—that is the mission of the theologian and the role of the church. To teach us to desire… that is the role of the contemporary market."[8] Long hints the crucial problem of desire.

The Radical: Timothy Gorringe Chooses Life

In the *Capital and the Kingdom*, Timothy Gorringe emphasizes why church teachings must broadly reject market economics, in particular, capitalist economics. Marx and the socialist tradition remain Gorringe's primary interlocutor. Like Long, Gorringe seeks to restore a sense of ethics to the economic, calling the perfect freedom of professional economists, as demonstrated through capitalism, fictive and coercive. The voluntary cooperation within markets that economists proclaim is a falsehood; instead, the market "disintegrates our fragile solidarities."[9] Gorringe argues that the markets create income inequality which results in worse health and educational outcomes for the poor. Inequality misdirects our resources, but equality creates a more cooperative society, and is better for the environment. Inequality results in comparisons that are degrading, whereas equality is what creates liberty. In markets, the liberty of one includes diminishing the liberty of another, which explains why the market is inherently exploitative.[10]

Gorringe argues that economics incorrectly measures wealth apart from other sorts of goods, such as unity and solidarity. He writes, "Class, patriarchy, and racism are of ethical concern because they destroy people. They are fetishes which diminish and devour life."[11] We must measure life through other means, not through GDP, which sets aside these other social concerns. Instead of simply a monetary value, work should have a sense of purpose, with leisure affirmed as an end in itself.

Gorringe argues that the market system is a form of social control implemented by management techniques: "Management is about control, getting things done through people,"[12] meaning management is fundamentally coercive. Managerial practices and expertise, "disguises the tyranny of arbitrary private preference,"[13] reflect hierarchy, and require submission. The market system therefore corrodes work and labor as it requires an anti-democratic managerial culture: "The conflict of corporations… is impelled by greed, fear and pride, self-interest, opportunism, and a desire for security. The creative manager is marked by egotism, vanity, selfishness, desire for recognition, and speed at taking offense."[14] It's a severe condemnation of both the market and of the private firms that smooth the market out. Governance, or management, is spelled out as merely ways for capitalists to destroy humanity.

Gorringe offers hope that the church can endorse cooperation rather than competition, emphasizing egalitarianism over hierarchy: "Egalitarianism follows from believing we are all one in Christ.… It is a revolution of grace, not of merit and deserving, or of parity and weighing out between individuals. This revolution of sharing is signified each time we celebrate the Eucharist, which is itself a practice of quality that is a very small first step towards the realization of a new society."[15] The Eucharist symbolizes the primordial, revolutionary corporation that the church constructs.

Gorringe offers an especially harsh critique of the Biblical scholars Martin Hengel and Luke Timothy Johnson, both of whom assert that scripture does not offer any particular insight about modern economic thought. Even though the scholars correctly note a contempt for societies driven by money among early Christians, he critiques Johnson's understanding of the individual and implies that their realism is a concession to idolatry. Gorringe goes forward to make some broad proposals. He proposes redefining work, the value of economics, and money, as well as abolishing usury, affirming decentralization, and implementing a basic income. He tells us that none of these ideas are utopian.

To be sure, some places may experiment along these lines. But Gorringe paints economics with too broad a brush and needs a little more surgical discussion of "management." While Gorringe does note that the markets do change human behavior and diminish some aspects of our relationships, he seems unaware of how the market also corrodes relationships that are hierarchical. The market destabilizes some relationships and reforms others because people want those changes. His discussion of management, furthermore, is limited in its scope. There may, after all, be good reasons why types of management matter, and focusing on a very narrow understanding of markets ignores the importance of governing.[16]

While Gorringe rightly corrects the general view of economists on the self, he doesn't offer a suitable, viable description of who the self is in a more just economy. The logic of capitalism is that it provides a useful direction for sin, redirecting greed into purposeful activity. This may be wrong, but a much more precise and explanatory view of the self would be helpful as people invent the sorts of institutions that would make his description of the world plausible.

He could have had a more robust description of sin that might have complicated his earnest proposals. Furthermore, he provides little instruction for how churches might help individuals become better at creating the economy he so desires. The mechanics of a just society remain elusive.

The Market and the Power of Creativity

Michael Novak was Catholic theologian and economist who believed the market harnesses the creative power of the individual against the state. He writes: "The debate is about the nature of the state and the degree of independence best left up to economic agents"[17]. For him, creativity and growth represent the work of God.

In his view, capitalism and markets express *freedom*: it allows people to exchange labor for what they desire and direct their impulses apart from the state. The market rewards reason, not merely in an abstract fashion, but through embodying and responding to the concrete needs of a particular environment. Novak defines markets in capitalism as both a framework and culture: capitalism is forward looking, "a continuous," technological enterprise[18]. Unfettered entrepreneurs, motivated by the best part of self-interest to be a part of public society, are unleashed to be creative agents. These agents are led into ethical behavior in a democratic society.

Novak affirms that capitalism requires competent management. He argues, |successful management in a large firm depends upon an ability to understand people, to inspire, and to draw the best out of them."[19] Capitalism becomes a social network where a manager cannot rule only by fiat, but by a sense of empathy, a way to align interests through persuasion rather than coercion. Novak notes such talents are uncommon: "Such forms of insight are difficult to teach and some individuals are more highly endowed with them than others. Managerial talent is rare."[20] In this way Novak implicitly reminds us that capitalism requires cooperation, and that cooperation within firms is a skill. Democratic capitalism protects both cooperation and the inviolability of the individual. Through the corporation, individuals in the market work for a common purpose voluntarily. It requires managers who have the competence to coordinate behavior and have the tools to organize.

Novak persuasively argues that management is important in describing the market economy. He may be too strong in asserting that managerial talent is rare. Such talent would require, at the very least, an ability to manage expectations, understand the limits of one's knowledge, and the capacity to manage the different sorts of rivalry that happen in any institution. But what is not convincing is how he distinguishes one firm from another, be it the church, the state, or a corporation, or why the virtues inherent in the capitalist firm can't be extended beyond capital.

Managing the government merely requires a different understanding of the stakeholders than running a business. But these have not been explored. Instead, management matters, and that perhaps its broader term, *governing*, might help direct where the church should put its attention.

While Novak's view of public goods is contestable, capitalism and corporations do help us coordinate effective voluntary actions. But by asserting that institutions and governance matter to creativity, Novak implies that it matters how we govern our desires, manage our expectations, and regulate the tensions that inevitably arise between rivals. Restraining and governing desire, broadly defined, remains a central problem for anyone administering work or participating in the market. In this way, Novak hints that the mechanics of desire matter, and that this is the role of churches. How this is done, however, remains unclear.

Tanner: Grace and God's Generosity

Kathryn Tanner's *Economy of Grace* shows how Christian thinking is, itself, deeply economic: "Every theological category and topic is of direct economic import, how every Christian idea about God and the world is directly and from the first and economic doctrine."[21]

Grace, for example, becomes a way of describing a concrete state of freedom that money provides. She writes,

> "Grace, (by which I mean God's favor and all the ways God's favor is expressed…) and on the other money (wealth and success). Grace and Money have everything to do with one another here, because from the viewpoint of Christianity the one means the other. Money means grace—it means one has grace; it is an indication of one's graced state. And grace means money- it means one has money; the grace one has, one's religious standing, is an indication of one's economic status. In short, the two have a direct semantic relationship as sign and meaning, signifier and signified."[22]

Having money means more breathing space, more of an ability to create meaning. This is not meant to be a moral view, but a descriptive one. Having money seems like a blessing.

Grace expresses, to some extent, what money promises. But they are distinct. The economy of God, through grace, reflects abundance; money inhabits the world of scarcity.[23] Christianity, rather than the market, keeps the world moving, by offering its love gratuitously: "What is noticeable about Christianity as a field… is its attempt to institute a circulation of goods to be possessed by all in the same fullness of degree without diminution or loss, a distribution that in its prodigal promiscuity calls forth neither the pride of superior position nor rivalrous envy among its recipients. The good is distributed by God and is to be distributed by us in imitation of God, in an indiscriminate, profligate fashion that fails to reflect the differences in worthiness and status that rule the arrangements of a sinful world."[24] It's not because we deserve these gifts that God gives them. God is both generous to those who have merit and those who don't, to the rich and the poor.

Because God's economy is abundant, it renders position and rivalry unimportant. Consequently, a Christian economics must incline disciples to be generous. Unconditional giving becomes the bedrock of an economy of grace.[25] Motives and merit are unimportant; instead "God does not give us gifts because we deserve them. They are not payments for services rendered."[26] The measured reciprocity of the market is one thing, but God's economy is much more fertile.

Tanner explains how ownership need not exclude others from also having—without rivalry, we can enjoy our life without withholding the possessions we have from others.[27] One can own property without being competitive or possessive. A thing can be my property *and somebody else's.* My having is not at anyone else's expense. I can have a thing without it being in my hands: "Our lives participate in that divine mission and thereby realize the shape of God's own economy by giving that follows the same principle: self-sharing for the good of others."[28]

Tanner's critique of capitalism is, in part, that it conceals the human decisions that remain at the heart of markets. Markets do not operate for their own sake, but are directed by human decisions. Politics matters.[29] She suggests some structural reforms: forgive international debt, offer land reform and social insurance, and emphasize principles of non-competition and mutual benefit. The market can be managed without abandoning some market principles. These values can cohere with an interest in equilibrium.[30]

Tanner outlines a way to flesh out a more human-centered market network. Within a capitalist market, the principle of non-competitiveness can still coordinate interests through pricing and incentives. It allows for the possibility that owners may compensate workers well or that well-made products can provide enough, rather than maximal, profits. Public institutions can therefore intervene in a voluntary system of commerce for the greater good, such as assisting places at a perpetual disadvantage.

Through non-competitiveness, Tanner recognizes that religions are interested in overcoming rivalry and restraining unfettered, acquisitive desire. In this book, she focuses on the structural consequences of the macroeconomy, rather than offering a more concrete way for people to extricate themselves from it. While she believes that religions seek to overcome the rivalrous impact of the market, her grounding in an economy of grace focuses her argument on the Trinitarian notion of God, who overflows in non-competitive love.

Tanner, like Gorringe, draws us to a closer understanding of what a more just market looks like, and what our place in that market is. But the specific strategies they offer seem politically fraught. There is also little that suggests how personal transformation is a fundamental part of economic transformation. Unfettered, unrestrained, misdirected desire impacts the economy. How is desire formed, and what are the ways we can govern and align our desires in accordance with the Gospel?

Tanner convincingly argues that economic thinking and theological thinking have important analogues. I add that when we talk about networks, whether personal, physical, or financial, it is difficult to truly disengage one from the other.

Tanner recognizes how the many dimensions of desire, such as needing connection and meaning, might allow us a more concrete way to allocate our resources in a more just fashion, and she hints that we can reorganize our institutions in such a way that informs our economic and political institutions and the many networks that undergird them. Grace may help us enter an economy that liberates us from scarcity and leads us into true abundance. Tanner's project, however, does not include examining the mechanics of desire, even though she also recognizes the importance of managing it. The question is, how does grace make managing desire possible?

Daniel Bell and the Problem of Desire

Daniel Bell has a much more intensive critique of desire. Through French philosophers, he seeks to examine "the practices, habits, and institutions that constitute our economic lives and shape our desire."[31] Bell asserts that Christianity offers an alternative framework for desire, and that theology frames the moral parameters of the market. The market should be subordinate to and reinforce the virtuous life.[32]

Bell first places desire in a broader context of networks. Quoting the philosopher Gilles Deleuze, he writes a "micropolitics of desire" precedes what is economic—a web of relationships and networks. Desire is central in any organization, and the way this is managed is through politics, the work of organizing a community, which precedes being. One's being cannot be disentangled from the context or the relationships in which one thinks, lives, and breathes:[33] "Every organization, every social formation, every subjectivity is a contingent, unstable assemblage of desire, whose duration is always uncertain, lasting a day, a year, a life, and order is nothing but a temporary check on disorder."[34] Things fall apart.

The market perverts this. It unleashes desire and offers no way to constrain it. In contrast, "Christianity developed technologies of the self for the sake of renouncing and repressing desire."[35] Economics, on the other hand, and neoliberal capitalism, offers little when understanding the morality or theology of desire. It only requires that money generate money and desire generate desire. The movement of the market is dependent upon this self-generation. However, in this task, the market further stokes human desire, not for any sense of fulfillment or meaning, but for the ends of the market itself: "The market is deeply implicated in forming and shaping human desire such that economy does not so much serve human ends as subdues and shapes human desire in service of capital ends."[36] The unfinished business of desire is to create more—just as money seeks more money.

Bell, like other theologians, notes that the liberal agnosticism about the purpose of human ends can diminish or crowd out other values that Christians find worthy. Capitalism privatizes virtues and goods and holds that public spaces have no necessary or intrinsic value. But more concretely, while Bell offers a critique along the same line as other theologians, the question of *how* we might govern desire remains a future task. He correctly notes that capitalism and money have unleashed a desire that is directed differently than how Christians would direct desire.

Harvey Cox: How the Market Is like a God[37]

Harvey Cox describes the market as a religious faith, rather than as system of purposeful, voluntary coordination. Finance and economics are its theology, with self-referential concepts based on its own circular logic. It has its own prophets and theologians, such as Adam Smith, and its own liturgical holidays, like Black Friday and Mother's Day. It assesses the worth of persons; through market research, it is omniscient. Because it seeks efficiency, it seeks to render all places interchangeable, uniform, and smooth. It seeks predictability and consistency. It tells us to buy and be happy.[38] Like religion, the market is evangelistic. It requires movement and growth. It seeks to know our inner desires and link them to commodities that will satisfy us for a short time.[39] But unlike the religion of Christianity, it prefers uniformity. Like the market, Christianity has a God that seeks abundance, but God also favors the poor.

Cox argues that the market is distinct from Christianity, which is not fundamentally based on amassing wealth. While it creates persons—through the corporation—the persons the market creates do not die, they shape shift, allowing them to avoid accountability.[40] Unlike actual persons, they are not necessarily accountable or able to relate to others as persons. Human beings, however, do die and one aspect of being a human being is being accountable for one's actions. The consequence is that, as Cox writes, "The market that has encouraged habits of creativity, risk-taking, and entrepreneurship, has also inspired wastefulness, cupidity and avarice."[41] He reminds us the market should be our servant, not our master.

Cox is concerned with the impact of the market. He worries that financial values will cause the loss of reflection and deliberation.[42] While the market has a way of entering other areas of life through its relentless and seductive power,

Cox ends his book by referring to the Catholic theologian Teilhard de Chardin's understanding that more complex networks help us explain God's consciousness, so that the God as the market is understood only as one sort of entangled network among many.[43] But in order to put the market in its proper place, perhaps we have to deal with the disease of acquisitiveness, "for which there is no cure."[44] Cox is right that networks and acquisitiveness hint at elements of a solution. While he suggests the need for decentralization and democratization of the economy, clarifying the root of that acquisitiveness will help explain why the God of the market is such a powerful alternative to the God of Jesus, and perhaps *why* governance of desire matters.

Mark Taylor: Religion as a Network and Our Need to Slow Down

While Harvey Cox writes about the market as a God, the theologian Mark Taylor takes a slightly different approach. Religion, for him, is everywhere. In *Confidence Games*, for example, he assembles a broader picture of the religious roots of money; its relationship to gods was there from the beginning. The use of money began as a substitute for the sacrifice, a tool for the transaction between God and his followers, which now quantifies personal sacrifice in the market.

Cox and Taylor agree that market networks harness a faith. Faith ensures a confidence that one can trust that *capital moves*. It moves because individuals can make exchanges with a tool—money—that can substitute one value for another. Taylor illustrates how the market creates its own motion because it incentivizes people to participate perpetually. He compares playing in markets to a poker game: "For the canny player, life is not a crapshoot but a game of poker. Since one can never be sure the chips can be redeemed, the best strategy is to keep the game going as long as possible."[45] As Cox intuits, there is no redemption in the market; faith keeps participation in the market going.

Using a genealogical history of ideas, Taylor relates how the ideas of Adam Smith, such as the Invisible Hand, can be understood as, themselves, religious. Taylor's point is slightly different than Cox's—he wants to show that religion is everywhere, even in evolutionary theory. But the point is clear: "Theology, it seems, is often most influential when it is least obvious."[46] A market is like a god, even though we don't call economists priests or theologians. And so, everyone is seduced by its church.

By detailing the relationship, for example, of money to religion, Taylor explains the mechanics of market religion. Describing market exchange, he writes, "All economic relations are in some sense sacrificial. At the most basic level, both parties in an exchange give up something but expect something in return. The expected return must be equal or greater than the value of what is sacrificed."[47] The connection to ancient sacrifice becomes apparent—in a similar way, money is related to an exchange between persons and their God. A worshipper sacrifices for God's protection, and money is a substitute for what is being sacrificed.

Taylor shows that "Markets are network phenomena."[48] They are one kind of network. He identifies four sorts of networks that impact us: nature, society, culture, and technology, of which religion and economics are but one part.[49] In his book, *After God*, he writes that religion is a complex adaptive network of symbols, myths, and rituals that lend life meaning.[50]

Taylor commends, in the light of constant destabilization, that we build a *relational* culture that embraces complexity, promotes cooperation, and *accepts* volatility and creativity between order and chaos.[51] It is impossible to get out of networks or to simplify them. Instead, in a world that is being destabilized by the interchange of different sorts of networks, it becomes more important to develop some spaces that allow for creativity to happen, where there is both order and chaos. Taylor suggests that the way to allow this to happen is counter-intuitive: to go slow.

Taylor provides a useful way of describing the many sorts of networks people inhabit. While he does not address the subject of desire as directly, his understanding of motion, connectedness, and activity reveals that a more accurate understanding of the mechanics of desire are necessary. Perhaps then we can better understand how and why we connect into these different networks, and begin to explore how better to *go slow*. It seems like a hint towards the Sabbath.

Catholic Social Teaching

Catholic social teaching has had a long interest in modern economics. While it shares, broadly, with neo-classical economics the view of possession as an intrinsic human good, it also believes that the market is naturally subordinate to other values. The market does not direct people to itself, but to other ends. Catholic social teaching endorses neither state planning nor an unfettered market. Instead, the church takes an agnostic, non-rivalrous view of both by acknowledging the benefits of the market, while affirming that public institutions, such as the government, have a role in helping the poor and the common good.[52]

Compared to an economic logic that sees the individual as central, the church understands that the person in relationship with others, like the family, is the fundamental moral unit. Individuals, as persons, must be understood spiritually and metaphysically, as relational.[53] *Pace* Marx, it also believes that there is no *necessary* conflict between the owner and the laborer.[54] It neither praises wealth as a good for its own sake, nor condemns the poor for their condition.[55]

Catholic social teaching asserts that to be truly effective for society and people, the market requires a prior ethic. While commercial logic and contracts have benefits, they cannot operate without prior forms of trust and mutual concern—solidarity.[56] Markets fail without other sorts of network trust. Markets have two related ends: *the common good*, and *the Sabbath*. The common good includes the widest range of persons in a community. The Sabbath includes rest, joy, festivity, and contemplation. Therefore, governments, through politics, may direct people to the common good. The church affirms that the economic network does exist within other kinds of networks and is to be directed so that the strong do not dominate. The market does not exist just to accumulate wealth, but for a people-centered ethic grounded in the Sabbath.[57]

Catholic social teaching distinguishes markets, governments, and charities, recognizing each has a different role. Human activity, activity between friends, is conducted within economic activity; economic activity is neither opposed to the common good nor inherently exploitative, but neither is it ethically neutral. It need not diminish friendship, solidarity, and reciprocity, but it considers these sorts of relationships to be secondary to economic activity. However, while the economic sphere is neither ethically neutral, nor inherently inhuman, since it is a part of human activity, it must be structured and governed so that it promotes *transparency, honesty, and responsibility,* and especially *generosity and solidarity.* The public justly governs market networks with *just laws* and *forms of redistribution* that should not disincentivize generosity.

Laudato Si frames the Eucharist as a representation, a real expression of God's economy. The Church's symbol of our cosmic network, which represents, affirms, and makes real God's intention and reflects the end purpose for humanity is the *Eucharist.* This sacrament is an act of cosmic love that permeates all of creation—the natural economy. Our celebration of the divine feast, through rest, reflects the true purpose of our economic life. It protects us from acquisitive desire, isolation, and empty activism. Rest puts our lives in perspective and motivates us for the true purpose of our ends: concern for each other.[58]

Catholic social teaching suggests a way of exploring the tensions that arise in a necessarily complex set of interactive institutions. It recognizes the different interests in the broader community and the difficulty of aligning all these institutions along the same ethic. It offers gestures, grounded in the symbol of the Eucharist, to provide for the well-being of all people. It works to redirect desire through its own spiritual, ecclesial, and economic practices. For this reason, Catholic teaching may help us understand the mechanics of desire.

Markets, Networks, and Institutions

Theologians question the value neutral stance that economics presumes. There is some implicit acknowledgement that markets express relationships in motion, and that human interactions are rarely neat, fully voluntary, or replicable. Theologians are concerned with the quality of human relationships and the impact of diminished transaction costs through the division of labor, money, record-keeping, and other cultural and technological changes that make markets viable. They are also interested in desire.

Several issues remain. One is the relationship of freedom to social constraints. While economists understand the market as being fundamentally free, theologians offer a couple of critiques. The first is that markets are actually coercive. William Cavanaugh, in *Being Consumed: Economics and Christian Desire*,[59] shows how the market consists of powerful institutions that direct and guide us to participate in the market. Advertisers create desire and dissatisfaction,[60] and study how to part us from our money. Freedom is not only the ability to consume, but to have other wants difficult to quantify. Without freedom of healthcare or to have friendships or a family, the freedoms the markets provide will be unsatisfactory. Theologians thus seek to flesh out what freedom feels like by identifying the ends of free activity. The proper end of what is owned should be directed toward the common good, or to our true ends.[61]

Secondly, the market is coercive in some aspects of the supply chain. Our global economy requires an enormous amount of coordination to move objects across great distances. Consequently, satisfying the desires of people in one part of the world will require hundreds of decisions that will move various materials from place to place. The cravings of one part of the world direct the behavior in other parts of the world.

These issues are of moral concern to those who worry about the people of God and God's creation. As Daniel Finn writes, "When the harms caused to others are sufficiently threatening to their well-being, they require redress. The moral character of my clothing purchase depends not simply on how the department store clerk and I treated each other but also on the moral character of the long chain of relationships connecting me to the Asian seamstress who sewed the shirt I am wearing." Markets disperse money, and thus conceal their coercive power in relatively poorer parts of the world that have enormous resources.[62]

Money diminishes misery because it can help moderate precarity and give individuals more choices. It is effective in creating happiness, to a point. It is possible for markets, as voluntary networks which include strangers, to circulate wealth when some transaction costs, such as distribution and the work of counting, are already diminished.

Wealth, however, does not provide clarity or guidance in how to use resources. It may inhibit allocating resources well for sensible reasons: people are naturally averse to loss because the loss of wealth may make them feel diminished and therefore disinclined toward generosity. It becomes easier to ignore the needs of the poor. Those on the margins who lack access to the sort of labor that can be exchanged for money may be coerced into selling their own (or even another's) body parts for money, or commit other social transgressions to settle a debt or survive.

Having access to wealth offers another, wider set of choices. Without access to food or health, markets cannot be considered absolutely voluntary. They may also conceal aspects of social power implicit in the use of money. Along the supply chain, some individuals may not be choosing freely, given the paucity of real time alternatives. Markets and money lift up some sorts of freedom, but some sorts of freedom, such as security, health, stability, or friendships, may take priority over accumulating wealth.

In another way, the financialization of choices pushes out the other values in other non-financial networks worth having. Our networks of family, friends, and associations are held together through non-quantifiable virtues such as kindness, restraint, prudence, and cooperation. As the philosopher Michael Sandel notes, money cannot buy friendship, an Olympic medal, or an Academy Award. One does not sell babies to redistribute children to better parents; using money to pay for sex changes the nature of the interaction from one of mutual pleasure to one of economic power.[63]

More precisely, additional choices may increase our freedom, but the inclination to measure diminishes it. The time allocated to measuring our activities financially degrades our willingness to do work for other reasons, such as loyalty, love, or out of principle. Financial incentives, instead, crowd out public-oriented behavior by diminishing the willingness of people to act without the promise of compensation. Instead, Sandel reminds us that "Altruism, generosity, solidarity, and civic spirit are not like commodities that are depleted with use. They are more like muscles that develop and grow stronger with exercise."[64]

Desire

The church has a role in framing what is the good life, and allocating resources to make such a life possible. Following Jesus offers one way to do this. While markets amplify and exploit desire, the church can be held in contrast by offering ways to have Jesus as our non-rivalrous model. Lives can then better flourish by being more clearly directed by the religious wisdom that is revealed through Christ. Scripture imposes a variety of limits, prohibitions, and exhortations, to redirect and diminish the intensity of acquisitive desire, and offers some clues to what sort of justice God seeks. The desire to acquire more is contrasted with the desire for the good, the true, and the beautiful, and for this reason theologians highlight conflicting desires, as well as reasons for restraint and correction.

Jesus teaches a way of responding to desire by revealing its spiritual impact. A better understanding of the mechanics of desire may identify the rules and governance that will guide our resources more effectively. Understanding desire and identifying the way markets create emotional engagement will help in identifying the reasons people consume. It may also reveal the stumbling blocks that prevent the church from harnessing money effectively to help congregations and communities flourish.

If the church had the capacity to inculcate individuals with the emotional capacity to handle tension and rivalry, its members would effectively serve other institutions and shape collective lives for the common good in the name of Jesus. This emotional capacity includes understanding the nature of desire and how it shapes our decisions. And so what is desire, and how does it work in the economy?

Notes

1. Jean-Pierre Dupuy, *Economy and the Future* (E. Lansing: MSU, 2014), 6.
2. I will discuss how this impacts the churches and communities.
3. D. Stephen Long, *The Divine Economy* (New York: Routledge, 2000), 69–71.
4. Long, 73–74.
5. Long, 208.

6. Long, 210–211.
7. Long, 231.
8. Long, 270.
9. Gorringe, *Capital and the Kingdom*, 38–39; Gorringe, *Capital and the Kingdom: Theological Ethics and Economic Order* (Maryknoll: Orbis, 1994).
10. Gorringe, 51–52.
11. Gorringe, 55
12. Gorringe, 79.
13. Gorringe, op cit.
14. Gorringe, op cit.
15. Gorringe, 112.
16. Gorringe, 125–6.
17. Michael Novak, *The Spirit of Democratic Capitalism* (New York: Simon and Schuster, 1982), 26.
18. Novak, *SDC*, 44.
19. Novak, *SDC*, 47.
20. Novak, *SDC*, 47
21. Kathryn Tanner, *Economy of Grace* (Minneapolis: Augsburg, 2005), 1.
22. Tanner, 5.
23. Tanner, 29.
24. Tanner, 25.
25. Tanner, 62.
26. Tanner, 63.
27. Tanner, 73.
28. Tanner, 85.
29. Tanner, 90.
30. Tanner, 108.
31. Bell, *Economy of Desire*, 22; Bell, *The Economy of Desire: Christianity and Capitalism in a Postmodern World* (Grand Rapids: Baker, 2012).
32. Bell, 27.
33. Bell, 40–42.
34. Bell, 46.
35. Bell, 70.
36. Bell, 79.
37. Harvey Cox, *The Market as God* (Cambridge: Harvard University Press, 2016).
38. Cox, *The Market as God*, 193.
39. Cox, 233.
40. Cox, 50–52, referring to the story of the Bhopal Union Carbide and Dow Chimical.
41. Cox, 242.
42. Cox, 198.
43. Cox, 271.

44. Cox, 278.
45. Mark Taylor, *Confidence Games: Money and Markets in a World Without Redemption* (Chicago, 2004) 331.
46. Mark Taylor, *The Moment of Complexity: Emerging Network Culture* (Chicago: Chicago, 2003), 180.
47. Taylor, *Confidence Games*, 65.
48. Taylor, *Confidence Games*, 284.
49. Taylor, *After God* (Chicago: Chicago, 2007), 31.
50. Taylor, *After God*, 42.
51. Taylor, *After God*, 356–7.
52. Leo XIII, *Rerum Novarum* (Vatican City: Vatican Website, 1891), 32.
53. Benedict XVI, *Caritatis in Veritate* (Vatican City: Vatican Website, 2009), 5.55.
54. Rerum Novarum, 19.
55. Rerum Novarum, 22.
56. Caritas in Veritate, 3.35.
57. Caritas in Veritate, 4.45.
58. Francis, *Encyclical letter Laudato si' of the Holy Father Francis.* 1st ed. (Vatican City: Vatican Web Site, 2015), 236–7.
59. William Cavanaugh, *Being Consumed: Economics and Christian Desire* (Grand Rapids: Eerdmans, 2008).
60. Cavanaugh, 18.
61. Cavanaugh, 25–26.
62. Daniel Finn, "Social Causality and Market Complicity," in *Distant Markets Distant Harms* (New York: Oxford, 2014), 259.
63. Michael Sandel, *What Money Can't Buy: The Moral Limits of Markets* (New York: Farrar Strauss and Giroux, 2012).
64. Sandel, 130.

4

Learning to Desire

In the first chapter, I described scripture's understanding of markets by connecting sin, debt, money, idolatry, redemption and the Sabbath. Sin is not only a spiritual problem, but an economic one. The God of Israel calls us to redemption by reminding us of an abundance that reflects the people's interdependence with each other and God. Envy and acquisitive desire corrodes a relationship with Him, but generosity redeems it. The Israelites managed tension through restricting covetousness, the misdirection of desire that is intensified by money in markets. Envy is intensified when money becomes an idol that rivals for our attention to God, leading to systems where debt organizes human relationships.

In the second chapter, I examined how economists framed individual behavior, concentrating on voluntary, purposeful agreements between individuals in networks mediated by tools, such as money and firms, which reduce transaction costs. Through more recent readings on behavioral and transaction cost economics, I described how economists empirically accounted for how individuals behaved. I showed how economists also engage desire with a different vocabulary. They break down envy into a series of discrete elements that are possible to calculate. I then defined markets and self-interest, affirming that they were also relational concepts, ending with a need to recognize that desire and governance remain central to understanding how markets and societies are managed.

In the third chapter, I reviewed a subsection of the literature on economic thought in theology, showing how many theologians themselves understand the problem of envy and desire in structuring the economy. It is now to the mechanics of desire that I turn.

The mechanics of desire are explained by the philosopher and literary critic René Girard through his work on mimetic theory. He engaged a wide range of disciplines, from literature to anthropology to biblical studies. Mimetic theory has proven to be a powerful way of understanding society. While I will not address all of the implications of Girard's framework or review the vast literature that engages his thinking, this chapter will explain how he breaks down the mechanics of desire, and its relationship to economics.

Girard has written on how scripture exposes the relationship of desire to sin and sacrifice. He connects the fall of Adam and Eve, the murder of Abel, the attempted murder of Joseph, and the crucifixion of Christ by revealing how mimeticism appears throughout the sacred story and leads the characters of scripture to act. He notes that acquisitive desire, as well as other sorts of crises, corrodes community, and that attempts to manage that desire through sacrifice explains how persons seek to worship God. Methods of managing desire include prescriptions, distinctions, or taboos that center around the sacrifice to a God who needs to be placated, the rules of how sacrifice is governed, and who is in charge of that sacrifice.

Mimetic Theory

Mimetic Theory (MT) explains the mechanics of desire. It helps understand the persistence of envy, and is congruent with economic insights on endowment, loss-aversion, and the inclination for persons to compare. MT offers a way of showing how the concerns of scripture and the description of economic behavior relate. It also implicitly suggests a way of connecting the atonement to our economic life.

"There is next to nothing in human behavior that is not learned, and all learning is based on imitation."[1] So begins René Girard in *Things Hidden Since the Foundation of the World*. Imitation is the root of culture, learning, and the collective activity that constructs human society. *Mimesis* is how we learn to behave in the world. The eyes see what other people see; people pay attention to the sight lines of others. It is the central element of child's play and a fundamental method of social formation. It orients our sociability and creates the complexities of our relationships. Two babies surrounded by a room full of toys are captivated by what fascinates another child. Individuals inculcate the desires and tastes of parents and peers, and through them acquire intuitions, habits, preferences, language, and traditions. The instinct to imitate is what guides the advertiser and the stock market trader. It is the root of cultural appropriation and assimilation. Virtually all of art and music centers around imitation, development, and transformation of earlier ideas. Scientifically, the evidence for mimetic behavior has been strengthening with the discovery of mirror neurons. But the central point bears repeating: aside from the basic needs for survival, such as for warmth, food, and sex, *desires begin outside of the person*. They originate in other people's desires.

Models

Desires are learned from models. Models include, but are not necessarily limited to, parents, peers, authority figures, and institutions—any person deemed worth imitating. Even while there will be contrasting and differentiating models over the course of a life, the actions individuals take will arise from what they have seen and experienced before. Models are not a unique, distinctive group; society is not clearly divided into leaders and followers. Anyone can be a model, and any model can be an imitator. A model is simply anyone who others imitate. People model each other.

Learning to imitate by doing can also be learning to imitate by doing the opposite. An individual can decide not to be like another person and be defined by not only being in a group but by being outside another group. One person might learn to love classical music because they are the sort of person who does not want to imitate people who listen to Justin Bieber. Some people may drive Ford trucks because that is what their peer group drives, eschewing purchasing a Prius because owning a Prius signifies membership in a different tribe.

In an individualistic culture, adults try to imitate in a fashion that attempts to conceal the extent of imitation. Adults will become uncomfortable with obvious forms of imitation because it seems either insulting or childish. If you are out to eat with a friend, trying to decide between ordering the steak or the fish, you might feel an urge to order the steak if your friend orders the fish, so as not to overtly imitate him. A model, however, is one who is not easily influenced, independent, if not unique. Modeling "individuality" *becomes the value worth imitating*. The impact of modeling individuality is that the adult *experiences* desire as independent and from the self, even though that experience has been modeled after someone who believes being an individual has value. One's mimetic nature becomes hidden to the self.

Desire

Imitation forms desire. The psychoanalyst Jean-Michel Oghourlian defines desire as a positive psychological movement that humanizes people by connecting them with each other. Through connection, desire leads a person to seek the company and approval of others. This desire creates emotional energy. It arouses love. It gives us a sense of self. The theologian James Alison writes, "Desire is what we call the movement by which mimesis gives autonomy and individuality to humans." While desire seems to be an individual experience, however, it is imitative.[2]

Put another way, desires are copied from others, transmitted from person to person. Desire is contagious. An individual initially does not know how or what to desire, so they learn by observing the desires of a model; social cues from models inform desires and set trends. The desire is not only about the object of desire, but also about a desire to connect with, and be seen by, the model. This desire is also *acquisitive*. A person will desire to have the same object as the model. This creates a rivalry.

The functioning of society requires some way of ensuring that the rivalry does not intensify, using various practices to reduce social tension. The imposition of social prohibitions, the division of roles, and even renunciation, are ways to diminish rivalry among persons.

Girard writes, "To untie the knot of desire, we have only to concede that everything begins in rivalry for the object. The object acquires the status of a disputed object and thus the envy that it arouses in all quarters, becomes more and more heated."[3] Our model desires an object, a rank, a good, an experience, and we want the same as what our model wants.

Outside interference, found in customs, rules, and taboos, constrains desire. This can chafe once an individual becomes aware of a desire they had not previously experienced. Then an individual may believe that once restrictions are lifted, desire will "be able to blossom forth," and be satisfied once the desire is fulfilled; however, the individual still remains dissatisfied.[4] The desire has merely shifted or changed. This mirrors the recent work that economists have illustrated: it's great when one has the first Mercedes in the block, but once everyone has one, satisfaction plummets. Unless one has the capacity to remember to compare with people who have far less, they might as well be Hondas. While distinguishing between satisfying a need and a want is one way to be satisfied, it's instinctively easier to compare to one's immediate network and neighbors.[5]

The origins of our desires may be obscure to ourselves, and the benefits of desire—to connect with others—also arouses rivalry. Because desires are framed by relationships with people, and people want to be connected, noticed, and seen, they desire what others have in order to demonstrate or to invite a relationship. It is a mistake to think one desires an object for itself, when it is the desires of another that one imitates. Individuals seek to desire the desires of others.

These relationships may amplify a variety of emotions, not simply affection. Desire has the capacity to intensify in such a way that it reduces self-control. As this desire intensifies, a series of emotional chain reactions can lead to both euphoria and violence, which may be the consequence of a crisis. Prohibitions, such as the Ten Commandments, seek to prevent those chains from intensifying. They seek to identify the specific links in the chain as misdirected and sinful. In these cases, sin is defined as an individual desire harming the community. One of these chains includes moments of envy, when one seeks to compare themselves to others or to God. Rivalry begins when one seeks to become like another.[6] Rivalry shows the way individuals are bound up in the desires of other people, not seeing them as fallen human beings, but as competition for God's attention. Sin says, *if God loves me, he'd make me have more than that other person.*[7]

Desire complicates the way economists understand the rational economic man. One can seek to discipline desire to be completely rational, calculating the financial benefit for every action. However, in such a view, one presumes the capacity and desire to be godlike, as a being with perfect knowledge. A confidence in one's own rationality replaces a more accurate understanding of personal decision-making, which will be often arbitrary and fickle, with an idealized perception of the self. This idealized perception, a rational person, *homo economicus*, however, ignores how dissatisfaction motivates our wants, while elevating its own moral worth and capacity for judgment. Furthermore, by removing the prohibitions upon desire, when the market unchains desires by liberating them from outside judgment, it conceals how the desire is intensified by rivalry and that desire does not originate within the self.

Rivalry

Mimetic theory illustrates how social tensions arise from desire, causing two or more persons to experience rivalry.[8] Rivalry arises from acquisitive mimetic desire. If the rivalry is not managed, such desire may lead to jealousy and envy, and eventually violence.[9] For example, one of my friends has twins. She always buys two of the identical toy, sweet, or clothing for them in order to prevent a potential conflict. Buying two of the exact same object means avoiding the headache of two equally matched children fighting over one object. It does not matter what the toy is, or whether there are other easily substitutable toys available. If they are not the same and not shareable, the parent must be a perpetual referee if the children do not have alternative models.

However, rivalry cannot be easily diminished, because it also expresses a fascination, a desire to relate, with other people. This desire for connection may also result in the tendency to compare ourselves to the person with whom one desires to connect. One person has an experience, thing, or a way of being that becomes a criterion to which we compare ourselves. The child's toy becomes, for an adult, beauty, status, a trip on a cruise, a new car, or the full head of hair of another. The person who has the object, experience, or title itself, does not want to lose what they have, while the person who is modeling the desire wants some sort of relationship with the model reflected by the possession of the experience.

Rivalry is ubiquitous. It occurs in many kinds of relationships—between siblings, parents, sexual partners, teachers and students, and institutions. In the church, each congregations, priests and lay people can be rivals. Parishioners complain that priests get sabbaticals and have rectories when nobody else does; priests compare their jobs to vocations that may pay slightly more with similar work. Everyone might compare themselves to bishops.

Scarcity also may intensify desire and, hence, rivalry. During Christmas or Black Friday, for example, we see how rivalry can erupt when people compete to purchase the most popular toy when only a few remain in stock. Advertisers stoke, shape, and align rivalry through intensifying a need for social proof, which includes a desire to be seen and acknowledged, to be loved. However, the intensification of rivalry becomes a threat to social order and security when competing parties begin to perceive each other as obstacles, enemies, or opposites, even as they imitate one another. They see the other as inhuman, as monsters, even when the differences seem minor. A crisis will escalate into a potentially explosive situation, heightened by quickening mimetic responses. These responses reach their pinnacle in times of mass hysteria or outrage. Girard hypothesizes that at the outset of civilization, mimetic crises led to a universal chaos of violence,[10] and religions arose to mitigate and prevent these occasions from occurring.

Mimetic behavior generates a powerful emotional state where individuals become caught up in a stronger feeling that arises through the imitation, the emotional entanglement, with other persons. When combined with rivalry it may become dangerous, so there are social cues and structures that allow us to avoid rivalry itself. Social structures create and enforce rules to prevent or redirect this emotional energy, by making distinctions, setting prohibitions, or governing in order diminish the impact of such emotions. In sports, for example, we construct rules to ensure that rivalries don't get out of hand: boxers must be of the same weight class; the rounds are limited in length; and the game stops when a person stops fighting. Pageantry and rituals of courtesy and politeness ensure the rivals are aware of each other, and ensure that winning and losing don't result in violence. Customs, rules, and rituals prevent rivalries from becoming uncontrollable. The occasional violence between rival football fans in the UK demonstrates the need for these structures, and the risk that even harmless rivalries can devolve into tribal violence.

There are many ways institutions manage rivalry. One is by setting boundaries. Marriage sets a boundary that takes people out of the arena where people are rivals for partnership. Another way is to refuse to participate, or to abdicate an investment in winning or losing. One can refrain from comparing to others. One can refuse to play a game in order to avoid being seduced by its mimetic intensity.

Rivalry remains difficult to diminish because its constituent elements are also beneficial. Distinguishing allows for clarity. Connecting with others provides pleasure. Furthermore, rivalry, once applied outward, may simply be redirected in other indirect ways. Even a refusal to participate in rivalrous culture can harness the emotional energy of being a rival with the rivalrous culture. For example, the common mantra of inclusivity, which is an attempt to diminish comparison and rivalry, can be understood as itself a rival to rivalry. Instead of acknowledging rivalry as a part of our condition, a consequence of human desire, it becomes important to *insist* that inclusivity *must* be a better way, when it may be more effective to train people to understand how they become rivals. In other words, inclusivity remains dependent upon being compared to the alternative "exclusivity" rather than in tension with, or merely as part of, a dynamic that begins with questions about building a healthy, self-aware, prayerful community.

Rivalry is a source of concern for any community. Scripture illustrates that rivalry exists in our closest relationships: Adam and Eve; Cain and Abel; Joseph and his brothers; or between ourselves and God. It's easy to compare ourselves to those who are familiar, with whom we connect, especially in our close relationships, which include tension of various kinds.

Individualism, Interindividuality, and the Experience of Freedom

Mimetic theory complicates the liberal, possessive, individualist conception of the self and the individual's experience of freedom. As the theologian James Alison writes, "there is no 'real me' at the bottom of it all when I scraped away all I've learned, all the influences I've undergone." An individual person is not self-contained or independent but interacts through a sense of desire with others. When an individual is influenced and shaped, they forget how that desire was produced.[11]

In mimetic theory, human consciousness is therefore *interindividual.* While a person may perceive being individuated, or separate from other people, their consciousness cannot be neatly disentangled from the outside influences of other people. Desires are not invented internally from a blank slate, but learned. A person's tastes and a worldview arise out of family, community, and culture. The interindividual is the individual as seen by others, a person who needs to see and to be seen.

Liberalism and neoclassical economics emphasize the distinctiveness between bodies, and articulate an integrity of the self. They attribute moral worth and agency to individual persons. In such a context, individuals have measurable amounts of agency and responsibility, and can be assigned or denied credit for their action. Mimetic theory posits, however, that our perception of individuality conceals why individuals behave the way they do. A liberal conception of the self underestimates how easily persons are influenced by models.

Interindividuality frames consciousness as constructed through relating to others. These relationships are designed. One's identity is formed in networks including one's environment or institutions or political life. These institutions shape choices, redirect desire, and align rivalry to reduce anxiety and manage tension. Rather than falsely assuming an individual can create their own identity, or that they alone have the capacity to restrain their own desires, affirming interindividuality lifts up a more accurate understanding of the person, suggesting how networks can foster intentionality and a greater capacity for creativity.

The theory of mimesis reframes the experience of personal individuality by describing individuality itself as imitative. Although the experience of individuality may seem more intense when it arises out a clear desire not to imitate, the desire not to imitate is itself modeled by another person who gave that desire value. Mimetic theory does not imply that imitation necessarily has moral content, but is merely descriptive in that it shows that our mimetic experience is not necessarily an experience of God, but of our desire to be connected. Instead, the Gospel responds to mimetic behavior by revealing the confusion between God and other persons, or God and wealth.

Imitation does not necessarily require uniformity or coercion. It may be uncomfortable because it implies a limited view of individual responsibility and agency.[12] A coherent understanding of mimetic theory, however, can help point to why and when individuality is understood as important. More importantly, it describes the mechanics of sociability, and explains why a pattern for the customs, prohibitions, and cues that both create and diminish anxiety make sense. It allows us to understand how the establishment of specific roles, patterns of civility, and rules of politeness all arise out of the dangers of mimetic rivalry.

Mimetic Theory and Individual Freedom

Mimetic theory provides a description of freedom. Freedom is the experience of being able to direct one's own choices without coercion. While philosophers and theologians may critique such a view confirming that individuals are socially and historically embedded, or determined by our physicality, individuals still have the experience of being able to make decisions and have some guidance control.[13]

Mimetic theory can still be congruent with a philosophy of free agency. In *The Metaphysics of Free Will*, John Martin Fischer describes freedom as a series of forking paths. I suggest that forking paths become apparent when individuals are faced with different models. A person can have several models that may manage a crisis differently. One parent may respond to anxiety with anger, another may respond with a sense of equanimity. One model may choose to take an interest in NASCAR, and another in the Tour de France. The person who follows these models can decide to test one, two, or many of the different models they are exposed to. Therefore, mimetic theory is compatible with certain understandings of freedom.

Mimetic theory is also compatible with the view that to be free is to want what God wants. In this case, God is considered the model. A person can acknowledge their dependence upon seeing as God sees, and creates a practice whereby they work to imitate God. With such a view, to be overwhelmed by one's own desires and passions is to be profoundly unfree, directed by a false sense of self, rather than God, who is to shape our actions. A truly holy desire cannot be addictive or corrode a relationship with God.

Mimetic theory therefore suggests a way to increase a *capacity* for freedom. Increasing freedom means one should develop more forks in the road, finding a greater number of models to imitate. This could allow for multiple and contradictory desires to be present. The ability to choose well could be fostered by a practice of discerning, the process by which one can intentionally let oneself be shaped. This discerning may be part of the process of identifying how God works, and is homologous to a process of prayer. In this way, understanding interindividuality can create a better experience of individuality, and can identify what kinds of individuality are worth having.

Mimesis does also imply that compulsion, redirection, hypnotism, and suggestion work, because it explains that our emotional life is dependent upon others. It also explains why religions are interested in prohibition, to prevent emotional chain reactions cause by mimesis that lead to violence. Religious practices, such as prayer, create the capacity for self-awareness so we can more effectively redirect how we are influenced by others. Governance and multiple mediating structures direct what legitimate models are created, formed, and shaped to structure human freedom and manage our anxiety.

The church seeks to govern behavior in order to manage the tension between a desire for security and liberty. Through its own mimetic activity, it reconstructs our freedom by fostering habits of reflection and connection. Our "voluntary" choices are guided by habits, customs, and restrictions—in short, governance.

The reality of governance is how mimetic theory links religious and economic behavior. Religious sacrifice arose as a way to restrain rivalry before it went awry. The rules and prohibitions that arose out of religion restrained emotional chain reactions through identifying God with violence. Out of the sacrifice, money becomes a way of sharing the God, distributing the sacrifice among the believers.

Religious prohibition, often illustrated during sacrifices, sought to prevent and diminish violence after a crisis. An event, an unexplained death, a plague, a flood, a famine, would destabilize a community. The community seeks a reason for the crisis. To prevent anarchy or a civil war, a vulnerable member of the community is identified, blamed for the crisis, and murdered. The community avoids destruction and elevates the victim to divinity. The resulting peace proves that death of the sacrificial victim was necessary. The violence of the sacrifice casts out the violence caused by the precipitating event.

Rituals are the patterned behavior around the sacrifice designed to prevent a crisis and placate God. Rules and prohibitions around who sacrifices and what gets sacrificed ensure the integrity of the ritual. Something precious or distinctive is offered as a scapegoat to prevent conflict and its escalation. At heart was also the origin of the market: an exchange between God and a community for order. A person or animal was sacrificed in exchange for stability. Violence in exchange for peace.

For Girard, the gospels undermined this exchange. The crucifixion revealed that it is not God who is responsible for violence, but human desire. Through Jesus' innocence, the story exposes how the process of scapegoating is human, rather than divine. It shows how group cohesion can depend on a sacrificial element to the hearers of the story, even if they do not quite see themselves as immediately susceptible. It begins to loosen the justification of religious ritual, and then begins to loosen the obligations that kept communities tight.

It should also be noted that Jesus taught several ways for his disciples to avoid mimetic rivalry: praying in secret; eschewing the need to be seen; rejecting status and power. Jesus thus invites us into a different understanding of who God is and what God wants by eliminating the need to make God and human beings rivals. To see through the eyes of Jesus means willingness to forgo the urge to compare; not abandoning how the law limits our rivalry, but to make living without rivalry a way of life. By doing so, the roots of religious sacrifice become unnecessary. The impact is that social obligations loosen. The market then fills the void now emptied of religious commitment.

When a person seeks to purchase goods or build an institution, they will be in networks that are mimetic. Rituals of sacrifice and prohibition sought to restrain desire, rivalry, and violence. As the obligations of religion loosened, however, the market redirected desire for the purposes of consuming relatively attainable goods, made possible through the reduction of transaction costs. In both highly structured societies and in looser market networks, however, governance remains crucial.

Girard suggests that the intensity of mimetic behavior is best prevented through creative renunciation, the surrendering to the rival. If there is rivalry for the same object, simply removing oneself from the game is the best way to go. Practically speaking, it means being comfortable with having second place, with losing, with not having what the model has. It does not mean desire is denied, but instead shaped by the model of Jesus, who doesn't need to be first or to be seen. To boast in Christ means to boast in the one who was vulnerable, naked crucified, the one whose prayers were not answered.

Original sin is related to the universal inclination to mimetic rivalry. It is based on the misunderstanding of the origins of desire. It is exemplified by comparing to others and feeling that one is lacking. Sin, therefore encompasses each overconfidence, fear, ignorance, and pride. It is both about not acknowledging our limits, and dislocating our power. It is not desire itself, but the illusions that conceal its reality.

Mimetic Theory and Economics

Previously, I explained how regulation theory, the idea that the laws and prohibitions in the Old Testament, explains how biblical society sought to minimize conflict and tension. Religious prohibitions about envy, and descriptions of state and financial power explored the coercive aspects of market networks. By and large, markets were seen as exploitative, where money was one way of extorting wealth from the agricultural class. However, as transaction costs decreased, the market could be redefined as a voluntary system of coordination, by which individuals could exchange a greater number of goods.

Mimetic theory explains how envy gets out of control and becomes an emotion that needs to be regulated. Our ability to mirror others explains how we learn to desire through the emotional chain reactions that arise in our social and economic networks. Mimetic theory also explains how in a market network, individual persons experience fascination with a model, and begin to desire that which the model desires. This includes both the lack and satisfaction of desires. A person can then imitate a model, with whom the person compares, through purchasing substitute goods, rather than acquiring the same exact object. The market is able to do this because lower transaction costs, reduced by money, technology, and the division of labor, allow the market to coordinate resources and labor through facilitating measurement and providing substitute goods with a fungible tool.

Like religious sacrifice, markets rely on reciprocity, which still implicitly requires restraint. However, in markets, the importance of social rules and relationships attached to exchange are concealed. Social prohibitions make way for market prohibitions—in markets, individuals are incentivized not to break contracts or steal property. The market has its own way of creating distinctions and substitutions. A person can buy an identical car as their rival, for example. The diversity of substitutable options keep rivalry to a simmer, as long as some options are satisfying, preventing a mimetic crisis.

Mimetic theory explains several elements of why individuals make purchases. Social proof, for example, demonstrates the desire to be recognized and identified through what one purchases. These positional goods are symbols, objects, and habits that can be acknowledged by others. They identify a person as worth envying or modeling, even as such a person is dependent upon previous models. Having social proof feels better. Making these purchases demonstrates the heart of wanting to be a model, to be worth imitating. Consequently, it is why Girard writes that "all you require for success is to give the impression that you have it already." It is not what one has, but what one is perceived to have.

The market economy creates a sense of lack, but because it also provides a way to satisfy our desires, it also can diminish the intensity of our rivalry. Because the objects of desire are now multiplied through technology, they are either easily available or substitutable. Satisfying desire becomes easy to do through the purchasing of replicas. The market network provides a constant series of different objects to desire, which distracts from being focused upon any person or object for too long. Commodities, objects produced by the market, because of their ubiquity, become discardable objects that redirect our sense of rivalry. The production of commodities replaces the ancient obligations of sacrifice, through substitution. Both obligation and rivalry become diminished.

The market conceals how it frees itself from the regulations that religion and politics provide, while it begins to foster its own system of worship. Usury and debt could once be regulated by religious fiat; markets could be managed by political regulation. But now the market has its own power and religious authority, creating firms that seek to smooth out human interaction so that agreements can be made and products produced, even when crises occur.

The Market and Its Impact on Social Solidarity

Mimetic theory explains the snowballing intensity of desire. Sacrifice, like the market, sought to redirect that intensity of desire. However, while sacrificial society used social obligations to limit desire, the market shreds those obligations, dispersing desire more widely across a greater variety of goods.

In a world where religious rituals have more power than markets and social bonds are more intense, self-interest is not easily calculated as of economic value, because the economy is not distinguished from other sorts of networks. In premarket societies, rules around social solidarity and group activity organize our behavior through obligation and need. As traditional moral concerns diminish, however, the market promises to provide peace, reducing the need for intensified group politics by providing instant satisfaction for immediate desires. It might not be able to fulfill such a promise.

The market diminishes the emotional intensity within tight group bonds by providing more opportunities to imitate through commerce. Whereas social obligations, such as those imposed by religion, restricted mimetic desire through various constraints, capitalism expends with prior restraints.[14] This includes the restraints that presumed greater familiarity with people, and dictated how individuals would behave. Through counting, the market abstracts persons and justifies violence, not through exerting the physical embodied power of one person over another, but through the networks of state power which uphold the broader market network.

The freedom from restraint allowed a freedom from engaging persons as intimates, permitting the possibility of indifference. Indifference frees us from emotional intensity of resentment and immediate envy, but it also allows us to treat individuals as instruments. Indifference allows us to be free from society, as efficiency dispatches obligation. As this efficiency allows for the networks of the market to expend, it makes it easier to be detached from the places where the earth is exploited, communities are displaced, and traditional networks of solidarity dispersed. Mutual indifference allows us to avoid the intensity of being rivals with our neighbor.

The market prioritizes expanding liberty, as defined by the ability to make choices. While envy, jealousy, and resentment may direct the choices people make, the market distinguishes between hostile emotions and physical violence. Alternatively, however, it also diminishes the practices of conversation and friendship. The market creates freedom, but in order for us to manage our feelings of rivalry we become slaves to consumption, connecting freedom only to commodities, choosing to relate to strangers, crowding out the possibility of intimacy and friendship.[15] The risk of emotional intensity is now replaced by the risk of disappointment.

By emphasizing the individual rational actor, the market conceals how individuals are still economically interdependent upon others and influenced by other people's desires. The market instead seeks to hide its mimetic roots, fooling people into thinking they are the source of their own desire, an elaborate hoax.[16] The market rearranges mimetic dynamics in a society through its trends, fads, and economic panics, but it cannot eliminate them.

Consequently, because individuals believe they are rational and independent, they are less equipped to recognize their social and future needs, such as friendships, or a secure, sustainable, environment. Individuals become less able to predict their future interests and will find it difficult to avoid fads of various kinds. The constraints and the discipline of the market have the unintended effect of regulating people away from building networks of social obligation.

The market, through its brutal and efficient discipline, is clumsy when calculating our need for deeper networks of trust and affection. Its global efficiency makes every place the same and replicable by eliminating the transaction costs implicit in culture and connection. The bonds that make a community distinctive, such as the obligations of loyalty and tenacity, are priced out to reduce their inefficiency. The market weakens other sorts of social solidarity, by allowing for one place to be easily substituted for another.

While markets may diminish the intensity of rivalry by providing numerous substitutions of models and rivals, it also weakens the solidarity to previous generations. It does not reward the emotional capacities of the non-financial virtues that develop over time, such as hard work, tenacity and or solidarity. These emotional capacities arose as a counterbalance to the vices of unfettered desire, such as envy, lust, and greed. Liberty is expensive because it costs the emotional value of social unity, the product of these same capacities.

Furthermore, beyond a certain level of wealth, accumulating additional possessions offers diminishing returns of happiness, while crowding out questions of the good life and the common good. It also reduces the power of groups to have control over their own lives through the rules of politics, which include some rules of restraint. The market, however, arises out of a lack of restraints made possible by exposing the true source of religious prohibitions. The market liberates desires and rids us of prohibitions, but by doing so reframes moral restraint as repression, when restraint is an antidote to the consequences of desire, envy, and greed.[17]"

The market's ability to substitute through reducing the costs implied in obligation, however, can also seem coercive, shifting the violence away from more obvious forms of power more diffusely. The market network harnesses the bureaucratic power of the state network, which includes the police, to enforce the obligations that money imposes. The indifference it encourages results in a lack of concern for the loser, fostering instead a continuous seduction into the next momentary fascination. Indifference can be understood as a series of fleeting fascinations, as no one single thing such as human relationships, maintains attention. It becomes more difficult to maintain bonds of solidarity because even some kinds of group commitments, such as a commitment to a brand or an identity, are also a more easily discardable commodity.

The importance of fascination illustrates how wealth is not only about individual success but about impressing other people. Dupuy quotes Adam Smith, "Wealth attracts the envious notice of others, because they wish to be wealthy themselves; and if they desire wealth it is so that they themselves may be noticed in their turn. The poor man suffers less from being poor than from the fact that no one pays attention to him."[18]

As Dumochel writes, "The moral asymmetry between the envious agent and his or her victim is not essential but a transient accidental characteristic.... Envy is but a moment in a process of mimetic conflict, a process in which we all participate at times. It is a shifting position that anyone can occupy rather than an essence. In consequence, the clear and final distribution of moral responsibilities is impossible."[19]

The sentiments of resentment and envy that arise out of our mimetic behavior can incentivize commerce and create a market. The market fosters a solution to envy by establishing a distance that diminishes the experience of a shared connection with others. As the feeling of connection with others declines, the sense of responsibility for others declines as well. Freedom means a freedom from responsibility. While the freedoms that markets provide to fulfill immediate desires remain powerfully seductive, those freedoms crowd out the virtues which provide a more sustainable sense of happiness, stability and order.

By understanding mimetic behavior, even when one lacks of feeling of being mimetic in a network, one can more easily recognize the context of one's decisions. When one is aware of how mimetic behavior explains a desire to compare oneself with others, it can help identify and distinguish between one's absolute wealth and relative wealth. Understanding the self as interindividual, as imitative, can equip persons because it clarifies how individuals need governance to better shape our social instincts, and can offer guidance on how to create environments that foster relationships where solidarity and mutual aid are central to a conception of the good life. These institutions will elevate a different sort of rivalry—a rivalry that encourages mutual joy, and reward, especially for those who seek no reward at all.

As the market creates more things, the intensity of our desire is both quickly satisfied and then dissatisfied. Scarcity generates desire, the desire is satisfied, and dissatisfaction begins again. Things become less infused with sacred meaning because they are easily attainable. Substitution and replicability, therefore, imply disposability. The ability to consume and purchase, substitute, and replace, desacralizes the world. Efficiency in our transactions means many of the things that can be purchased are less dear. The objects that are hard to have, that are the most scarce, that require highly intensive human labor have a higher value and become precious, holy, sacred.

The desacralizing dimension of the market does create another substitute for violence: trash. The appeal of convenience makes more things that are both replaceable and disposable. While the feeling of purchase distinct, while replicated, things may seem to create a sense of personal uniqueness, it is made possible through the replication that also makes things and relationships easy to discard. On hand it frees from the obligations of religion and the inconvenient sacred; but on the other hand in disassembles and exposes persons as replaceable.

Even though the market has the power to diminish some sorts of rivalry that are solved by cash and duplication of things, individuals still compete for prestige and status. Even though "fighting over prestige is literally fighting over nothing," and the market makes it easier be concerned with rank among other people. It becomes much easier to compare because everything in the market can be compared, and when the market triumphs over every sort of network, rivalry is also everywhere. And so, "the 'nothing' of prestige appears to be everything—not only from an adversary's point of view, but in the eyes of all."[20]

Girard notes, "Everything that brings me up brings down my competitors; everything that brings them up brings me down. In a society where the place of individuals is not determined in advance and hierarchies have been obliterated, people are endlessly preoccupied with making a destiny for themselves, with 'imposing' themselves on others, 'distinguishing' themselves from the common herd—in a word, with "making a career." At one time societies did not presume that any particular person could be anything, like a prince, or everything, but now everyone can compare themselves with others. The market makes people into *anybody,* where they compete with *everybody* so that they all can be *somebody*. In contrast, Jesus offers the possibility of being nobody and still be loved.

Girard notes that the intensification of rivalry has consequences. "The price for all of this is perhaps not invariably the aggravation beyond all bounds, but certainly the democratization and vulgarization, of what we call neuroses, which are always linked, in my view, to reinforcement of mimetic competition and the 'metaphysical' aspect of the related tensions." Because competition is now omnipresent, individuals do not find it easy to establish a place where they can be secure. Where the constant fluidity hinders a sense of integrity and the rules seem to be continually changing, people will experience less control in their world. They may become more anxious and depressed without that stability because they are now comparing themselves to more people, unsure of their roots.

In an economy where everyone is a rival, people are incentivized to elevate their own selfishness above others. However, as the philosopher Dupuy says, when self-interest becomes selfishness it impoverishes our world. He remarks that "interest, as Hannah Arendt reminds us, is that which, in coming between people, 'gathers us together and yet prevents our falling over each other,'" It relates and separates men at the same time."[21] It is a process rather than a static finality. This does not mean individuals are meant to become a unanimous political blob, become ascetics, or seek to become masters of the universe. There is no universal single choice in a single moment where every person must choose to sell everything and become nobody or play the game of seeking to accumulate everything and become the lord of their domain. "The alternative of either benevolence or self-interest is a false alternative."[22] The alternative to a world of rivalry does not require becoming rivals with it.

The market seems to offer a solution. The market can prevent conflictual mimesis. If purchasing is an exchange related to a modest, indifferent kind of sacrifice, then the act of shopping is a non-violent way to manage a crisis of rivalry. When someone feels like a rival to another, participating in an economy is one way to temporarily satisfy that desire. Workers now become consumers. However, the nature of consumerism keeps people in debt, obscuring the possibility of being liberated from perpetually working. The Sabbath becomes diminished because the perpetual need to purchase feels like the best way to manage rivalry. The time for us to be with God which expresses our freedom apart from the market, even as we are freed from the proximity of violence through the market, is too much of an expense to bear.

The mimetic distancing of persons in the market implicitly rewards isolation and indifference. In this way, it corrodes what it needs the most: trust. Without trust we cannot engage our models, or relate to our peers, or negotiate with strangers. A lack creates chronic stress through status anxiety,[23] and intensifies our envy and resentment.

Market economies redirect violence into a perpetual simmer of covetousness that fosters both liberty and indifference, including the liberty to be indifferent. The liberty to be indifferent is made possible because violence and coercion is exported to the end of the supply chain physically distant from one's specific physical neighbor. My Iphone, for example, does not immediately invite me to think of the Chinese workers assembling it or the strip mining required to develop the materials to make its battery. The question remains: should Christians extend their concern as far as the international economy reaches?

Sacrifice was the original exchange between the community, the victim, and God. Money substitutes for what was sacrificed. However, substitution loosens the bonds within the community by diminishing the emotional costs implicit in the immediate sacrifice and the rules surrounding sacrificial behavior. Markets arise out of this change because money provided a substitutable script that could be used for other goods, backed by the state. Now, while the market has replaced sacrifices for providing social order, it does so through a different sort of coordination which prevents rivalry from intensifying, unless a single person begins to hoard all the chits.

In my next chapter I will show how Jesus exposes that the costs of rivalry, even in markets that extend beyond our immediate sphere. He has shown how rivalry is an expense. Being liberated from sin and accepting the freedom of God includes the freedom of renunciation. This freedom is not for everyone. It is not mandatory. But it is as available as the cross, which makes the options before us crystal clear. The cost of rivalry has been paid by a death.

Notes

1. René Girard, J-M Oughourlian, G Lefort, S Bann, and ML Metteer. *Things Hidden Since the Foundation of the World.* London: Continuum, 2003, 7.
2. James Alison, *The Joy of Being Wrong: Original Sin Through Easter Eyes.* New York: Crossroad, 1998, 29.
3. René Girard, J-M Oughourlian, G Lefort, S Bann, and ML Metteer. *Things Hidden Since the Foundation of the World.* London: Continuum, 2003, 294.
4. Girard, *Things Hidden,* 294.
5. Girard, *Things Hidden*, 294.
6. S. Mark Heim. *Saved from Sacrifice: a theology of the cross.* Grand Rapids: Eerdmans, 2006, 322.
7. James Alison, *Undergoing God: dispatches from the scene of a break-in.* New York: Continuum, 2006, 63.
8. J-MichelOghourlian, *The Genesis of Desire.* Trans by E Webb. E. Lansing: MSU, 2010, 12.
9. Oghourlian, *Genesis of Desire*, 11.
10. Girard, *Things Hidden*, 149–50.
11. Alison, *JBW*, 31.
12. Girard, *Things Hidden*, 7.
13. Unless, however, they are in some sort of prison or being manipulated by an outside force where the person is more like a marionette. The project of this current book is not to examine the metaphysics of free will, but it is congruent with one type of argument of Guidance Control as described by John Martin Fischer, *The Metaphysics of Free Will.* Cambridge, MA: Blackwell, 1997.
14. Girard, *Things Hidden*, 295.
15. Jean-Pierre Dupuy, *Economy and the Future: A Crisis of Faith.* E. Lansing: MSU, 2014, 124.
16. Dupuy, *Economy,* xvii.
17. Girard, *I See Satan Fall Like Lightning*. Maryknoll: Orbis, 2004, 181.

18. Dupuy, *Economy of the Future*, xviii–xx.
19. Paul Dumouchel, *The Ambivalence of Scarcity and Other Essays*. E. Lansing: MSU, 2014, 125.
20. Girard, *Things Hidden*, 305.
21. Dupuy, *The Mark of the Sacred*, Stanford, 2013, p 168.
22. Dumouchel, *Ambivalence*, 130.
23. Kate Pickett, and Wilkinson, Richard. *The Spirit Level: Why Greater Equality Makes Societies Stronger*. New York: Bloomsbury, 2011, 69.

5 How Jesus Saves

Jesus saves. The contours of the Christian faith may be wide, but one central assertion of the church is *the death and resurrection of Jesus matters.* His resurrection changes how individuals understand their salvation. The mechanics of salvation have been explained or justified by others in a variety of ways: Jesus has saved us from hell; he overcomes the devil, creating a universal path to heaven; after Jesus, God refuses to participate in violence; now the spirit of Jesus moves everywhere in history; Jesus died for our sins and became the source of liberation of the oppressed; he is the root of how people reassemble ourselves anew upon this realization; because of Jesus, the world, and those who follow him, have changed. But the point all share is that somehow the cross and resurrection matters in the world. Following Jesus involves a difference in understanding and acting. Once saved, our relationship with God and the world changes.

Therefore, because Jesus changes our relationship with God, following Jesus may mean rearranging our economic choices. His atonement matters economically. Because followers of Jesus participate in the market and recognize their own rivalry through prayer and action, they organize in ways that align the church to form disciples who can manage a non-rivalrous institution.

The mechanics of rivalry are explained by mimetic theory, which shows how rivalry is an expression of reflecting the desires of another. The atonement offers a mechanism for reorienting that desire. Not only may the atonement save one from hell and lead to a closer relationship with God, but it will also change how individuals relate to each other in the market. Jesus exposes the power of unfettered desire and offers a solution to the problem of debt by illustrating a new way to be free.

The Economic Consequences of Being Saved

A distinctly Christian approach to economics has a variety of threads. Some Christians have approached economics by asserting that markets intrinsically diminish the human person, exploiting the many for the benefit of the few. In such a view, markets are necessarily controlled by people who have power and gain resources through practices that move money from less prosperous people into their coffers. As an alternative, Christians are guided by the clear command to share, to offer one's cloak, to feed the hungry and the naked. However, even if Christians are called to share their resources, the challenge remains, "but how?" One person can take up a call and be generous, but it seems unlikely that millions of others can be mandated to give away their wealth.

Another perspective of markets presumes they include exchanges that are mutually beneficial. By minimizing cost transactions, markets clothe and feed by harnessing self-interest. Even though the unleashed power of the market may accumulate at the top, it still improves lives by giving strangers freedom to exchange. The expansion of markets among strangers allocates resources more broadly and rewards the expansion of virtues of trust and fairness.

Others present that economic life is a representation of the Trinity. The Trinity demonstrates movement, generosity, and abundance, exemplifying how God shares himself in community. It is an economic analogue to a dynamic relationship with others and the flow of money. Therefore, a Christian economy should mirror the economy of the Trinity—just as God circulates within herself to generate love, a properly Christian economy is to do the same.

The doctrine of the Trinity and the atonement are interrelated. The Trinity implicitly contains the atonement through the relationship between the Son and the Father. The Trinity implies a soteriological answer that says Jesus saves by bringing us into that relationship with the triune God. While our economy should move in its generous self-giving essence like the Trinity, the salvation of Jesus points to the mechanics of that movement. Knowing Jesus saves from the intensity of our own desire and creates the capacity for generosity.

Deriving an economic framework from the atonement need not replace a Trinitarian explanation of a Christian economy. However, any economy that identifies as Christian must engage the distinctive position of Jesus. When one says that "Jesus saves," one makes a concrete, incarnational assertion that impacts how followers live in the world. It shapes discipleship. It transforms a life. Jesus becomes the primary model for Christians. While the specifics may be varied for each person, Christ's death and resurrection remain decisive.

Recognizing sin as rooted in mimetic rivalry suggests that mimesis can also be redirected for cooperation and encouragement. Mimeticism itself arises from an initial desire to connect with others before it makes individuals rivals. Desires arise because individuals are concerned about other people. As a model, Jesus defines how those relationships are governed. As a model, the salvific Jesus reorients the person who has affirmed Jesus as the Son of God. While the world instead models pride, inattention, carelessness, and envy—sin—Jesus offers a mechanics for economic redemption distinct from those models.

In scripture, Jesus, as the governor of desire, demonstrates techniques that illustrate how individuals can govern their hearts. The tradition around him points to the capacity to build institutions that can fulfill the needs of the gospel. While there may not be a single style that works, modeling Jesus has broad implications for how firms operate. Such institutions may seem countercultural because they may not emphasize individual status or finishing first. A person who intentionally eschews rivalry, because they have a non-rivalrous model in Jesus, will have different priorities regarding their work.

Reorienting rivalry does not require dispensing with it completely. It does not mean becoming a rival with rivalry. Instead, disciples of Jesus can recognize, understand, and redirect rivalry toward a shared conception of the good life toward the Sabbath, a life of rest and joy. Because rivalry also contains a desire to relate and connect, it cannot be eliminated, but with God's grace it may be directed it so that it aligns toward a life that flourishes.

Understanding rivalry clarifies how to build firms that inculcate virtues that arise from the salvific nature of Christ. It may include directing the practices of economic systems generally, such as counting, keeping records, or using various kinds of technology to diminish the transaction costs of rivalry. It may be possible to account for ways rivalry can be diminished and the Christian virtues rewarded, even though the market does not deliberately cultivate virtues that Christians take seriously. It may be able to help redirect an accounting of desire by including a shared vision of the good life as a value rather than rendering such choices private and thereby crowding out a shared vision as worthwhile.

The church may have the legitimate capacity to manage capital and money matters. If it can recognize how to direct rivalry, it may allocate resources to better increase the abundance for the good of ourselves and our neighbors. The meaning of "liberation" in the Christian context means redirecting desire away from accumulation for its own sake by exposing the subtle way resentment, jealousy, covetousness, and pride have shaped participation in the market. It seeks to provide individuals with enough, rather than everything. It does not shy away from luxury, but understands that luxury doesn't solve the problems of human emptiness.

Churches and other institutions create rituals and establish rules in order to diminish the impulse to compare. This includes prohibitions and traditions about authority and role, or who is responsible for specific tasks. It should be remembered that these rituals are not always universally replicable, practical, or effective. For example, insisting on uniformity may initially allow people to resist comparison, even though it may also intensify the desire for distinction or individuality. In practice, there may need to be continual shifts in how such policies are implemented, as rivalry cannot be eliminated, as it merely shifts because its constituent elements are also an inescapable part of individuality. While making things the same seems to solve some problems, the desire to be distinct or noticed is not easily suppressed.

However, Jesus offered some techniques for cultivating a non-rivalrous self. Jesus commands, for example, to pray privately and to fast without being noticed. His practice to engage all sorts of persons indicates how he redirected the need to be compared to others. He was vindicated not through the might of political power or status, but instead through the embarrassing nature of being a political loser.

Holiness is therefore neither connected to being either a conformist or an individual. Individuals are called to inspire and encourage each other to do good deeds, but the need for the approval of others to be holy is consistently deemphasized. This is how Jesus saves: he saves us from believing rivalry will save us.

The theologian S. Mark Heim describes the impact of the resurrection and Jesus' saving grace like so: "His purpose is to do the will of a God who vindicates victims, forgives without vengeance, stops the crowd's first stone. We live without scapegoating."[1] The insight is that the lives of victims matter, and our ability to kill innocent victims has now been revealed. The need for sacrifice to appease God has now been revealed to be a mistake.

The atonement then reorients our lives away from sacrifice toward praise. Being saved means one needs not be victorious over another person, or first in honor except in acts of charity. Taking up the cross does not replace Jesus's work or resurrection, nor does it affirm suffering is meaningful. The slaughter of innocents and breast-beating after a natural disaster does not require us to look for God's hand. As Heim notes, "The cross does not endow all suffering with meaning; otherwise, his life would have only been pain; rather, it was peculiar because he was innocent and unjust. The cross seeks to end suffering, not idolize it—but ending suffering requires knowing when one has suffered, when a victim has suffered."[2]

If Jesus does not end suffering nor guarantee a just reward for a good life, the experience of God nonetheless suggests a reordering of values and priorities. An experience of God as the salvation of the love of Christ may require different choices after seeing the world differently. That an "experience of the reality of God in one or more of its modes can well alter the purposes and directions which actions take... The basic orientation of one's activity can be directed by experiences which have religious dimensions, and by the beliefs which inform and express the significance of those experiences. There can be reordering of the intentions, of those things one values, and these reorderings can deeply affect the choices one makes without transforming the 'subconscious'" factors involved in the choices." That Jesus saves means it is possible to reorder a life and rearrange an endowment, using what has been inherited or given.[3]

The market already arises from a changed understanding of sacrifice. As markets are made possible through fungible substitutes, such as money, they redirect the energy of desire away from direct violence or sacrifice toward creating the possibility of exchange. Exchange among strangers becomes preferable to sacrificial violence designed to appease the violence of God.

So while Jesus has revealed himself as the perfect substitute for sacrifice by being a non-rival, he helps diminish rivalry by being a model that does not require comparison. A disciple is reformed by modeling Jesus, who still cannot be modeled perfectly and does not require the follower to be a rival with Him. Desire need be not diminished, but redirected when a disciple becomes aware of how models influence. As a model, Jesus reorders because he relativizes the other models in the networks individuals inhabit, allowing for a greater capacity to redirect our desire, even if it is neither perfect or identical to him. No other model will therefore be permanent or satisfactory, allowing the intensity of rivalry to be self-limiting. Being saved means being open to a new model in Jesus, but also recognizing that all other models are impermanent. This changes the way one engages both financial and non-financial networks, including geography, art, neighborhoods, associations, firms, close friends, and extended families. Furthermore, Jesus models making the market a non-rival to other institutions, altering it by reassembling it as merely one part of the network and not the most important one.

The mechanism of the atonement, or salvation, includes modeling. In these mechanics, one learns to need to not be ultimately seen by others, except God, as meaning can arise from God, not solely from other persons. Meaning is not a matter solely of self-invention or that which arises from within the self. Instead it rises through one's interindividuality, which is entwined with who God and Jesus is within other people. The model—the person one desires to imitate—is therefore not meant to be a source of frustration, but can possess the power of Jesus—someone in whom we cannot, and need not, compare. The model of Jesus liberates us from needing to have any other permanent model. Therefore, because it is impossible to compare to Jesus or God, our model, our enemy, can be who they are without needing a rival. To see Jesus in another is to eschew rivalry with that person.

Eschewing rivalry as a model has economic consequences. It implies a liberation from being connected to others through the obligations imposed by accumulating money as a sign of absolute value: "The cross saves us from the consequences of a debt economy by canceling it"[4]. Because the engine of the debt economy is envy, renouncing it makes it easier to cancel debts and restore a degree of equality between the creditor and lender. Liberation from envy, through cancelling debt, creates financial—and therefore spiritual—freedom. It liberates from spiritual slavery because debt enslaves and prevents us from the rest (i.e. Sabbath) required to live creatively and with joy.

Eschewing rivalry requires grace because it is never perfect or final. "The idolatrous impulse never sleeps,"[5] says Luke Timothy Johnson, as a nod to one of rivalry's elemental aspects. Any place of worth, such as money, status, education, looks, or even spirituality, will be a location of mimetic rivalry. Mimetic rivalry is a fundamental source of idolatry, and even when one desire is overcome, another will rise. It rises because individuals desire to be seen.

The desire to be seen, of course, has its extremes. Being seen and respected by the people one loves seems like a different category than wanting to have a million Instagram likes. The love of celebrity, or the desire to be a celebrity, is distinct from the love of the familiar. But the church equips disciples to trust that God's sight is most important, and in this way it helps form an antidote for envy, by fostering love in any network.

How Sin Gets in the Way

The mechanics of salvation requires a more thorough discussion of sin. I define sin as at least having the following properties. Sin includes our limited ability to know, especially other minds; our desire for a future that is secure and dependable above other desires; and for immediate satisfaction of our desires. Sin includes an incapacity to be satisfied; and an inability to recognize being dependent upon God and others. It enables and justifies selfishness and corrodes networks of relationships that allow the community to flourish. It is about a broken relationship with God and others.

Sin is reflected in materialism, a concern with one's status by possessing goods apart from a respectful and equitable relationship with others and a worshipful relationship with God. Such a condition seeks material wealth as a way to compare oneself to others. Economic materialists are concerned with winning and losing. They want to win, but feel as if they are losers.[6] Materialists of this sort are less able to defer gratification, which is reflected with an obsession with celebrities.[7] It is especially exacerbated through models of rivalry shown on television, a technology that effectively stimulates desire. Television, a highly atomized activity where several people each have their own entertainment device, is consumed in environments where other constructive kinds of mimesis are often absent. This sort of materialism is distinguished from understanding God as working through materiality, a view that the incarnation enchants or pulls our attention to God in the physical world.

Materialism makes rivals of persons, setting the desire of one person against another. Mimesis describes the mechanics of this desire. A person wants what another has, in part to become like them; our peers therefore become rivals.[8] When bound up in other people's desires, instead of recognizing others as also equally fallen human beings, they compete for each other's, and God's, attention. Sin says if God loves me, she'd make me have more than that other person.[9]

Economists use value neutral language to describe the impact of sin. Sin can be found in the economic language of bounded knowledge, opportunism, relative advantage, the endowment effect, loss-aversion, and other characteristics reflective of human behavior in markets. It is sin which conceals our limits and our capacities, rendering us unaware of what truly creates happiness, stability, and health. It is not desire itself, as desire connects people with each other and God. Sin is the fig leaf that conceals the source of that desire.

The Impact of the Atonement

I have described how the atonement has consequences for individual behavior. It gives us a stance, a model through Jesus to reorient how we are rivals in a network. However, the consequences of the atonement are not singular. One response is to abdicate any participation in markets or eschew the use of money altogether. While this view is suggestive and powerful, it remains perfectionistic, one that itself invokes a comparison, a rivalry, with those who refuse this path. Another view is the atonement requires that money has ends other than accumulation of itself. As Christ desires for people an abundance that the world can already provide, having more is unnecessary.

Because individual desires shift, as there are a variety of objects and persons with which to compare and contrast, one is unlikely to be inoculated from making absolutely non-rivalrous choices. If Christianity is to matter, it must account for the way individuals live in this world. If it can be possible to make relative choices through discipleship by accepting the model of Jesus, which allows for both absolute non-rivalry, as well as relative non-rivalry, one can sell everything, but also dine with the prosperous. One can give the second tunic, while also accept the generosity of a bowl of expensive perfume. One can renounce everything and walk everywhere, or one can buy the used ten-year-old Lexus which is relatively cheaper than the neighbor's Ferrari.

One consequence might be that discipleship seeks to harness the internal "impartial spectator." The impartial spectator is a stance that seeks to be apart from one's subjective position. It may be an attempt to take a view that is apart from one's own, or seek to understand a view as if one is from a distance, or is not involved. As Adam Smith said, "Susceptible to misuse as it may be, the presence of this impartial spectator, alongside the natural human desire for moral approval, is the loving design of the ultimate impartial spectator: God." This technique, developed through discipleship and prayer, can be how one can manage rivalry, so that the psyche can be so constituted to be aware of social norms that make both markets and society possible.[10]

Options for Christians

One way Jesus saves through changing how individuals relate to each other. Salvation alters the reasons individuals compare themselves with family, friends, neighbors, and strangers. Faith in Christ begins a liberation from what accompanies a status anxiety that justifies acquisitiveness. It loosens the bondage from the compulsion to compare to idols.

Examples of this liberation include an eagerness to provide for those who are less fortunate (Prov 14:31, Prov 19:17, 28:8). The sense of obligation does not arise from compulsion or guilt from having more, but from an acknowledgement of the other person's humanity. Instead of the physical abstraction of money, Jesus means individuals become the new "coin." Generosity begins by trusting in one's own salvation. But generosity also creates a practice that brings redemption.

The atonement reminds believers they are dependent upon others and God's grace. The faithful cannot deny being instinctively, subconsciously materially, cosmically interdependent with the world and others. Individuality is therefore a pleasant illusion that masks how lives are shaped by other people. As such, no person's individual wealth arises solely from their own hard work. And what makes such work worthy is not what it accumulates, but its creative activity, its pleasure, and its meaning to others.

Modeling Jesus redirects envy and resentment, not by diminishing fairness and mercy, but through affirming being satisfied with what God has given. The acquisitive, the ones who seek wealth for its own sake, risk their own lives because they are easily, blindingly, caught up in an intensified, dynamic of comparison with what is ultimately meaningless. The wealth is their reward, but that's all they have, when there is much more worth seeking.

The apostles demonstrated that an emotional consequence of salvation facilitates the capacity to share our common work and value our life together. This does not require abandoning a market economy, but acknowledging that wisely sharing resources to build together rather than only accumulate individually is a part of the Christian charism. A non-violent atonement can be congruent with a commercial economy that minimizes violence through rewarding voluntary exchange, but a salvific economy puts markets in context, aligning work with other networks that provide meaning and joy, and not only the pleasure of accumulation. The market is to serve leisure and joy—the Sabbath.

The atonement does not require completely abdicating a neoclassical model that counts costs and benefits. Instead, counting can be expanded to acknowledge the value of what cannot be counted easily, such as the time and relationships. The Sabbath, having time for rest, worship, and leisure, counts more than all our toil. By diminishing the value of accumulation, the atonement leads to allocating resources differently. It will encourage the building of non-financial networks of relationships. Discipleship will mean building the capacity for deeper relationships and stronger networks. This cannot be calculated financially, but only by each person, one by one. On people, the church should spend abundantly and promiscuously.

The Atonement and Prosperity

> [24] "But woe to you who are rich,
> for you have received your consolation.
> [25] "Woe to you who are full now,
> for you will be hungry.
> "Woe to you who are laughing now,
> for you will mourn and weep." *Luke 6:24–25*

> "It is almost as if, seen from the perspective of the kingdom, all property is theft. Fair nor not, the text does not distinguish good wealth from bad." David Bentley Hart, Introduction, *The New Testament*, XXX

Accumulating wealth is appealing. It is a convenient way to demonstrate power, success, and glory. It calls the attention of others. Wealth creates opportunities and choices. It allows people to be generous and giving without the chafing of direct personal sacrifice. The church, however, implies only that while working and striving has its place, seeking wealth for its own sake is a mistake, a sin. It suggests the possibility of a shared life as blessed by God, and even that the blessings of the market itself depends on other values worth having in themselves, such as benevolence and trust.

It is possible that the blessings of accumulated wealth may be precipitated upon practices and virtues of frugality, planning, and conscientiousness. The industrialist who has arisen from the dark pools of poverty in the slums who has, through sheer force of will, recognized opportunities and carefully measured what is required to acquire money and power may have some admirable qualities. But there is no justification to assume such a person is the only sort who requires emulating. There are other kinds of lives worth living.

Scripture warns against owning wealth. After all, greed, envy, and hoarding corrode a relationship with God and each other. Acquisitive desire is a universal drive of both the poor and the rich, each the have-nots, the have-somes, the have-mores, and the have-it-alls, but it has disastrous consequences. Individuals are inclined to compare with their peers and those who have more, but as wealth accumulates at the top, the classes self-segregate, which means security guards and private entrances reduce the discomfort of engaging those who have less. The wealthy begin to pay attention to people around them less[11] and risk having less empathy[12] with the poor. This has broader social consequences as segregation occurs.

When there are few counterbalances and less social integration, wealthy individuals may risk being overconfident and overestimate their own ability to understand complex systems. Wealth can shield one from inconvenience, discomfort, and cognitive dissonance. Those who depend on the wealthy for compensation may be limited in their ability to offer feedback that others may take for granted. Being successful, furthermore, becomes a signpost for success, and reinforces itself, but it can also diminish the capacity to handle frustrations, disappointments, and failure.

Another trap for the prosperous is the propensity to understand themselves as fundamentally distinct and independent from the systems they inhabit. They may be unable to distinguish between work and chance, or want and need. Their time and their relationships can more easily be quantified. Furthermore, the desire to consolidate and acquire more wealth crowds out other virtues worth having. The pursuit of having more money takes time and effort which crowds out time used for other purposes that have value, such as building friendships.

Because of the limits of the prosperous, outside institutions besides the market need to inform, create, and enforce rules of restraint. Political institutions in a republic should limit the totalizing power of the few, so that the values of accumulating do not replace values such as creativity and service. Market discipline does not create the only virtues worth having, and wealth should not have power over the life and death of others. For this reason, other institutions are morally justified to check and restrain that power.

The church has a role in shaping individual responses in markets. It can be an example of what a sharing economy looks like. This need not require a flattening out of incomes, but a recognition that a careful understanding of incentives and planning can harness our resources for the common good. The church forms people in ways that help reward curiosity and discernment. It can provide spaces for empathy and honesty, developing leaders who are prosperous, generous, and thankful. The church reminds and invites those who have wealth that they remain dependent upon the labor of others, our natural resources, and upon God herself. Their perception of individual freedom is solely dependent upon the vast interdependence upon a very complex interrelated network of exchanges that provide their wealth.

The emotional challenges are difficult. Luxuries, which are by their nature scarce, have been shown to precipitate selfishness and entitlement. They reinforce a sense of uniqueness, and thus the wealthy become a focus for envy, a model for others to emulate, which includes the path of the miser, who fetishizes cheapness but only uses money to attract more money. But neither the way of luxury or miserliness quite get at what is to be done. It may be that the first, and primary step, is that the church fosters reflection and personal discernment regarding wealth, because different contexts will require different choices. The parable of the rich man and Lazarus, for example, exemplifies how the rich man who didn't know how well he lived, a risk for anyone who accumulates wealth. Even in heaven it is possible for the rich man to be disappointed when one compares oneself with God.

Mimetic theory explains the compulsion to compare. The wealthy compare themselves to other rich people, cloistering themselves among individuals who think and act the same. The wealthy imitate each other and their tastes, seeking unique experiences, specifically unique experiences are only possible by having money. They set themselves aside, concealing their dependence upon the state and their interdependence within the market for their wealth. The concentration of wealth facilitates the ability for the rich to reduce strangers to numbers, as replaceable rather than also as individuals with independent lives and thoughts.

The church does not shame individuals solely for their prosperity or ambition. The disciple need not envy nor become a rival with persons who are prosperous. It may, instead, engage and challenge them to consider ways their wealth can move, circulate, and leave a legacy, reminding them that prosperity is not only because of hard work, but through fortune, inheritance, and interdependence. Fostering a reflective life creates a healthy emotional distance from the pretty baubles that are captivating, reminding that prosperity remains ephemeral.

If the church cannot mandate or *demand* the rich give their wealth away, it may be enough to affirm that money should be made into something concrete—that it should be used to make or buy things—and move among people. Both the rich and the poor are invited to use their resources more deeply to develop the spiritual riches of the church—to engage the sacred scripture and participate in common prayer. And the church may enter places of the wealthy, into its country clubs and its palaces, with confidence and without contempt or envy. The prosperous are sinners like others, who merely have the opportunity to find redemption through a generosity that few others are able to match. Redemption is found in giving.

By being saved in Jesus Christ, the wealthy learn the capacity to be radically generous because they are given a model of how to lose. Through modeling Jesus, they may learn to be open to how their endowments and inheritances are relatively enchanting, but absolutely unnecessary to a life worth living. Through

Jesus, they would unlearn the urge to compare themselves to only the prosperous, but be connected to the less fortunate, and make our common condition as the people of God. Instead of being rivals with others, they can be collaborators. This is the needle. It may be unlikely, but with God all things are possible.

The atonement saves us from the vagaries of the market. Individuals and churches are free from needing to compare themselves to others. Perhaps the disciple learns how to be downwardly mobile, can discern between what one wants and what one needs, to learn to know when one has enough, and renounce the fear of losing. Being saved means knowing what types of desire are worth having, and learning that with God's grace one knows when one has enough.

Notes

1. S. Mark Heim, *Saved from Sacrifice* (Grand Rapids: Eerdmans, 2006), 245.
2. Heim, 246–7.
3. James Gustafson, *Can Ethics Be Christian* (Chicago: University of Chicago, 1973), 55.
4. Kathryn Tanner, *Economy of Grace* (Minneapolis: Augsburg, 2005), 65.
5. Luke Timothy Johnson, *Sharing Possessions: What Faith Demands*. (Grand Rapids: Eerdsmans, 1981), 86.
6. Robert E. Lane, *The Loss of Happiness in Market Democracies* (New Haven: Yale, 2000), 158.
7. Robert Frank and Philip Cook, *The Winner-Take-All Society* (New York: Free Press, 1995), 201–203.
8. Heim, 322.
9. James Alison, *Undergoing God* (New York: Continuum, 2006), 62.
10. Adam Smith, *The Theory of Moral Sentiments*, ed. Knud Haakonssen (New York: Cambridge, 2002), 65 III.v., 5–6, 191–2.
11. Pia Dietze and Eric D. Knowles, *Social Class and the Motivational Relevance of Other Human Beings: Evidence From Visual Attention*, http://journals.sagepub.com/doi/full/10.1177/0956797616667721.
12. Michael E. W. Varnum, Chris Blais, Ryan S. Hampton, Gene A. Brewer, *Social Class Affects Neural Empathic Responses* (Springer-Verlag: Berlin Heidelberg, 2015), https://asumaclab.files.wordpress.com/2014/08/social-class-affects-neural-empathic-responses.pdf.

6 The Church and Salvation in a Commercial World

Jesus saves. The church teaches that this matters, and it changes how individuals relate to others and the world. Through Jesus, individuals can discern how to reject the rivalry that invites anxiety and tension. They can identify the roots of dissatisfaction that cause rivalry to become a spiritual and social problem within a commercial economy.

The church has a response to rivalry. It has sought to manage rivalry through various practices, such as having a regular rule of life. It has cultivated various habits to manage and diminish rivalry between institutions. It has sought to reorient individuals away from the dominance of the market by not only counting its finances, but counting the number of persons it impacts.

I am rector of a pastoral sized parish in White Plains, New York. The institution purchases paper and hire plumbers. It leases a copier and it rents properties. The church hires contractors to repair the gutters and fix the leaks, and sometimes the church has its volunteers. The church buys energy and pays taxes on non-religious income properties. Before 2008, the church had investments.

In the congregation, work is done by people who are paid and unpaid. Compensation may include cash, flexible working hours, and good feelings. We pay to enhance our worship and to outsource our accounting. A thrift shop, rental units, and outside organizations contribute to our bottom line. The diocese takes care of payroll. This shows that a church is a small corporation, but a distinct one. It is private, but also public and not-for-profit. But most descriptively, we are in relationship with both the market and our community.

The Anglican Ascetic Theologian Martin Thornton, in *The Function of Theology*, writes, "Applied theology, sometimes called ascetic theology… is used to guide individual Christians in their uniquely personal interpretation of discipleship, according to temperament and circumstances."[1] In this tradition, this book has sought to apply some theological insights to the mechanics of a shared life, and seek a better understanding of the market and of human desire in order to enhance and direct the work of the church.

In the first chapter, I showed that God seeks to reduce the tension that arises out of an economic system based on acquisitive desire. He does this by restraining envy and by liberating societies from a market system based on debt. In the second chapter, I showed how economists break down human behavior in markets, showing that while money provides many things, it does not provide happiness or meaning. In the third chapter, I showed how theologians critiqued the value neutral claims of economics while inviting a deeper understanding of desire. In the fourth chapter I explained the mechanics of desire and compared societies based on obligation with those based on the market, showing how mimetic theory could explain behavior in both. And last, I explained how Jesus as a model of mimetic behavior might direct disciples and the church.

In this chapter, I suggest what following Jesus might look like in the current context. Following Jesus invites one to distinguish between wants and needs, to practice restraint for the sake of peace, to learn to have enough, and to harness money for higher priorities such as time, friendship, and family. The church already has the foundations for being effective in a way that is consistent and sustainable, especially if it can find ways to apply, for example, Benedictine practices into parish life.

The condition that *Jesus saves* implies making different choices as participants, makers, and consumers in a market economy. If Jesus saves, one has recognized that individuals also have models in other individuals, communities, and firms. Individuals are governed and shaped by these models. Therefore, individuals may discern, through the help of such models, how to decide between using a bicycle, a used car, or a Lexus for their primary mode of travel. Understanding models may help one distinguish why one chooses a camping vacation and spending every winter in Aspen. It may help distinguish between when to assert or submit, or when to be a follower or a leader. It may help show when the market or charity are better distributors of wealth. Models are a sort of map, and following Mark Taylor, when in uncharted territory, maps matter[2].

I have shown how soteriology has economic consequences, and illustrated how it impacts governance. While I do not think there is a single way as each congregation and diocese is called to act, rivalry everywhere is an expense because it requires management. Management costs. Following Jesus is how the church diminishes that transaction cost by making him a model that facilitates management. Therefore, the church is called to build disciples who understand and can manage their rivalry for their mutual flourishing. This is a real world impact of Jesus saving grace.

Following Jesus in the economy is about proper governance as the management of rivalry, not solely about deciding how to spend money. Governance focuses on ways to design appropriate solutions to the tensions that arise when desires conflict. For example, the Sabbath and a Jubilee year exemplify governance designed to manage a complex social system that liberates individuals from sin or debt. An emphasis on governance maintains a moral stance that arises out of faith, even if it may refrain from making grander claims about economic systems.

Governing is not a series of checklists, but about a range of practices. This includes how churches administer. After all, churches have much to say about consumerism, governance, and policy, because the church exists to build networks and connect people. By modeling Jesus, churches teach people to redirect the spirit of rivalry, not merely as unreflective obedience, but identifying what wants are worth having. The church redirects the disciple not from only wanting more cash to live, but teaches the mechanics of building a community: pot-luck suppers, fasting and feasting, a shared meal instead of the choice between luxury and starvation. These everyday events are ways one builds relationships, and from there institutions. Following Jesus can help us both reorganize corporations and administer government bureaucracies.

Without presuming to be the final word, I suggest that understanding and directing desire identifies several ways for individuals to model Jesus. This is to steer people away from the need or feeling to become God, have God's knowledge, or being called to be crucified. Instead, following Jesus includes several compatible ways which are non-rivalrous with each other. There is no single way to follow Jesus, nor should one make a rival out of the ways not chosen. But there are a few signposts worth noting.

One skill is to learn how to manage loss, to make peace with absence, and to become indifferent to what the world, in particular the world of commerce, values. Through prayer one can learn the habit of renunciation. Discipleship, therefore, is *in part* an everyday sense of freedom from the seeking of more material goods. While it does not require a renunciation of all things, a spiritual life that is dedicated to modeling Jesus develops the ability to halt the immediacy of wanting.

Another skill fostered by discipleship is a sensitivity to how the market increases dissatisfaction, as it segments classes of persons and invites comparison between them. Branding, quality, utility, and beauty, as markers of comparison, are distinct, but learned. Individuals may discern whether they are considering questions that make them rivals with others, or if they are making decisions based on other reasons. Rivalry and modeling, however, go deep. One may not choose a Mercedes because they think it makes them look rich, but because it goes fast. But rivalry is still implicit, for valuing speed has itself been modeled. It's possible to remain unaware of how one has developed the values one has. It may be impossible to go all the way down to address every level of rivalry, but it can be a fruitful practice that can provide other benefits. One Christian organization, for example, takes this direction by directing its members to only buy used cars, eschewing new ones. They redirect away from the need for the newest thing.

The practice of reframing desire *does not* require frugality. Elevating "self-sacrifice" also camouflages the forms of slavery brought into being by mimetic desire: "Wanting to be God-like through wealth only mirrors wanting to be God-like through renunciation."[3] Christian discipline does not require grand acts of supererogation because the disciple should not seek to be a rival to Jesus, but needs first to seek to restrain rivalry from its violent ends. In other words, reframing desire allows us to avoid sanctifying suffering, and allows us to acknowledge that restraining desire is not suffering. A market economy neither requires precarity and suffering, nor should its discipline be elevated as moral and just. In any case Jesus has saved us from the need to accumulate and have more than all others, to be like God.

Some constraint among disciples is clear. The authority in scripture constrains acquisitive desire because the power of the market, of money and debt, creates conflict in communities in how it extracts labor and holds individuals in bondage through compulsion. Therefore, it seeks to regulate and restrain our desire and place market networks under the control of other sorts of arrangements, such as the law, the Torah, Christ, the church, or the government. Scripture liberates individuals especially through exhorting the practice of the Sabbath.

A few counterarguments can be made: Christians should not be concerned about the market but solely prioritize personal relationships and pastoral concerns, and let the market do what it does. They should abstain from making any sort of political judgment on the contours of the economy. In this sense, religious obligation can offer no clear guidance to market choices, but presents one vision of the good life among many, incidental to a prior truth and secondary to the commitment to the "freedom" in economism. A responsibility to others or a sense of regulating personal activity, therefore, is not a proper object of economic study, but themselves commodities, a matter of personal choice and freedom, in the marketplace of values.

Furthermore, the counterargument goes that religious concern for the needs of others interferes with economic efficiency, an intrinsic good in itself. The virtues of work arise when people work at a subsistence level, making enough to survive, where industry and discipline are guaranteed by necessity and precarity. Therefore, if government unconditionally supports poor people, or charities support the *wrong* people, they diminish the incentive to work and the virtues that arise thereof. Supporting charities, or a social net, incentivizes sloth rather than encourages self-reliance. The desire of the wealthy for luxury helps create industry among the poor; therefore, only in the most desperate of situations, such as natural disasters (and even then, this may not be an obligation), can mutual aid be morally justifiable.

In addition, it is impossible to identify what actions are distinctively *Christian*. However, Christians do build institutions and make choices. They buy and sell, coordinate activities, assess costs and benefits. They forgive sins and make gifts. They may forgo credit cards, buy only used cars, or only use cash. But we may justify our decisions because we recognize ourselves through the eyes of Jesus, who undermines the mimetic rivalry that creates idols and diminishes our capacity to love one another and recognize our interdependence.

These arguments are found wanting. Christians make moral claims and resist the financializaton of our everyday experience. Scripture describes the human condition as idolatrous, acquisitive, and prone to envy, while generosity and charity are invitations toward an encounter with God and evidences of redemption. By following Jesus, one is saved from the mimetic activity that makes us prone toward idolatry and is now invited into a new mimesis liberated from the world's focus on the ephemeral. Instead an individual follows into relationships that are not driven by envy, but by magnanimity—love freely given.

The church already seeks to form disciples that truncate this desire. Its practices offer a solid foundation for forming persons who have a different model of being. The sacraments, the triune rule of prayer, and the Benedictine rule, for example, offer stable and practical habits that offer a realistic foundation for organizing a life. The church does not need to revamp our institutions, but examine them realistically, and focus on its strengths. The church can align its practices and its power to build leaders and reorganize the economy.

Anglicanism as part of the broader part of both reformed and catholic Christianity develops mimetic activity through a shared prayer life fostered by our institutions. The Trinitarian (and Benedictine) nature of personal prayer, the Daily Office, and the Eucharist can be understood as a rule to help us diminish and regulate our feelings of rivalry. It offers expansive emotional references that deepen self-awareness. It helps eschew idealism or utopianism while also giving every person a time for reflection and common prayer. It helps individuals by teaching a disciple to recognize comparison, and thereby direct our choices in such a way that we can flourish.

Managing Rivalry

A central role for churches, their leaders, and their constituents is managing rivalry. This will include addressing issues in managing information, identifying roles, and aligning an organization's task. Running organizations requires emotional competence. Effective governance must include both the relevant knowledge of the specific enterprise and the spiritual and emotional ability to manage the personal desires of those with an interest in the organization or firm.

Rivalry is easily concealed. It may not always appear as a conflict, but arise as sentiment, such as, "we've always done it this way," or "we're not like that other church," or as nostalgia and attachment. It can also ground a desire to be unattached as well. One can be a rival with rivalry and idealize having no rivals at all. Becoming a hedge-fund manager rivals working altruistically, while working to pay bills is contrasted with enthusiasm. Instead, a disciple treats each choice with a clearer sense of value. A follower of Jesus understands relative worth in the world to absolute worth in Jesus, and accepts reasonable personal constraints as a cost for a meaningful and holy life.

I will outline a few ways our practices seek to diminish rivalry. These are not comprehensive or final, but express inclinations in the church that can orient its work.

Creating Disciples: Prayer, Eucharist, and the Apostolate

Church practices already reflect and shape how we engage the market. Anglicanism, as a branch of Christianity, inclines toward the practical and public, rather than to the perfectionist and doctrinal. Consequently, until the return of the Savior, we can both affirm personal transformation and public policy as individuals who are part of a congregation while also raising our collective voices in public, or seek power over the mechanisms of the state. Our DNA affirms that the state, economy, and church are each distinct and intertwined. The church participates in the public square, commerce and statecraft, with scripture, tradition, and reason. We may be not be experts in all things, but we affirm attempts to govern wealth responsibly. With God's grace, we seek to harness wealth on behalf of the Kingdom.

Experiencing rivalry is a common condition; learning how to manage it is a skill essential to being a disciple. We can participate or withdraw when confronted with rivalry and we can participate in rivalrous relationships in a variety of ways. Even Christians participate, when comparing churches, priests, or distinguishing between denominations or traditions. I will outline a few ways the church actively reframes rivalry.

Prayer

One step in redirecting desire and rivalry is through prayer. The mystic Martin Thornton writes, "The essence of prayer must be relationship."[4] Relationships in Christ will need to find a way of managing the way rivalry participates in our common life. By renouncing rivalry, or framing another person as a model that has what one desires, the person who prays begins "with a potentiality for becoming a self." This does not mean an individual becomes a cleaner, more perfect person but instead offers, "construction out of potential, the attaining of unified existence, the creative movement toward authentic selfhood." A person then can make different choices, not merely by resisting temptation but by cultivating the "ability, strength and courage to choose." This is an invitation to draw the self out of rivalry, thereby creating the possibility of an authentic self.[5]

Thornton affirms the interindividual description of the person when he says, "Existence is always personal and yet always "being in the world" and "being with others". A person cannot divide our existence.[6] Prayer shapes the mind to manage the perpetual systems of desire individuals can be seduced by. It helps reorient the habits of comparison that are a part of the market economy, changing the habits of desiring what others have away from the patterns of consumption that do not bring joy.

An ordered prayer life develops practices of recognizing interindividuality. The church pattern does not seek to flatten the self, as our ritual life is not our entire life. Instead, prayer becomes the mechanism to work through rivalrous habits and gain a better understanding of the nature, limits, and direction of our personal desires, helping align the power of our collective life to provoke mutual flourishing. Prayer identifies and manages the way one imitates. Through habits of praising God, and the concomitant distinctions between needs and wants, for example, it is possible to restore a sense of balance and order between what matters and the ephemeral. Silence frees from the rush that disables self-control. Confession inculcates the ability to reset envy. Worship leads into humble service.

As a daily Sabbath, prayer is a time to reflect that can give the capacity to be removed from the hedonic treadmill which confuses wants with needs. The rule of the church, the private devotions, morning and evening prayer, and the Eucharist, establishes these mini-Sabbaths where the constituent elements of desire can be redirected. The ascetic practice allows us to connect with other individuals without comparing ourselves in a commercial way. In community, prayer becomes an alternate mimetic activity that also provides space to examine and redirect mimetic behavior when used to practice being benevolently attuned to other persons.

Prayer has the potential to foster a reimagination of the person. As a part of learning how to engage an economy, it can train a person to manage disappointment, to prepare for risk or loss. Because Jesus is the all-loving arbiter, it's ok to be downwardly mobile, to be second, or third, or last, because prayer is the space where one learns to be liberated from comparison. Prayer can cultivate strength to engage the neighbor, the stranger, and the enemy; it identifies when to commit, and when to walk away. Through Christ, one has what one needs. Prayer is enough because it is our daily Sabbath.

Sacramental Economics: Baptism and Eucharist

Our liturgies reflect how the church allocates what it considers worthy. The liturgy is not identical to how the world works, but it orients us toward the understanding of what is at the core of all human existence. Therefore, in our fundamental sacraments, it's possible to discern what the church thinks about an economy.

Baptism, for example, emphasizes the universal quality of persons, though they may not be productive. Babies do not produce any initial financial value in the short-term. This may show that God's value of a person is beyond the calculation of the actuary or the advertiser. The Eucharist, also, illustrates a distribution of the Body, of a sacrifice. The priest does not administer two hosts to the greater in piety, and withhold it from the indolent and lazy. While there is still administration and a distinction of roles, the gifts are gathered and distributed apart from industry or merit.

Baptism becomes an invitation into a new sort of mimesis that rejects the separation of people into tribes and into a new pattern of life. Baptism is an invitation to see through the eyes of Jesus, through the grace of God. It underscores a fundamental equality before God that does not either mandate conformity, undermine distinctiveness, or even elevate individualism, but affirms that as made in the image of God, individuals are not meant for work, but to be free in Christ.

The rite of baptism describes a renunciation of a rivalry that creates conflict. Rejecting Satan, the evil powers of this world, and sin are each ways of rejecting the origins of dissatisfaction, social tension, and violence. The affirmation of Christ as a model implies a reframing of desire. Furthermore, the five questions that are asked after the public recitation of the creed indicate a specific sort of governance that outlines the mechanics of managing rivalry. Following the apostles' teaching, gathering in fellowship with others, breaking bread together, praying and resisting evil each reflect how rivalry is managed. It acknowledges, also, that this cannot be done completely—as individuals do sin and will require repentance. But by seeking to be an example, or a model, serving Christ in all persons and striving for justice, peace, and dignity, it is possible to illuminate and affirm the direction of Christian practice.

Rituals shape and reflect how individuals are engaged in the world, and in other networks, firms, and institutions. The intention of the church is to form disciples shaped by Christ, and specifically restricting and directing our desires. In economics, this can include a fear of loss, a habit of comparing, opportunism, and limited knowledge, as well as the creative impulse.

The Eucharist suggests an understanding of allocating and distributing resources. The host is not first offered to the most attractive or the one with the largest weapon. It is administered to all who have been baptized. That said, while its egalitarianism is ordered, roles are distinguished. This is to say, *even in the liturgy there is government*. This governance allows disciples freedom to participate in the broader world without worrying about church. The distinction of roles allows for greater efficiency, by reducing its own social transaction costs implicit in rotating leadership.

Communion represents an economy. During the Eucharist, the offering becomes "part of a larger interpretive narrative and social-symbolic practice, at the heart of which are divine grace and call. The grace is the revelation of God's own uncalculating and incalculable self-giving in Christ (italics not added) for the sake of the world."[7] Communicants ingest Christ, which suggests a willingness to be reformed by him. The transaction by which Christ sacrifices is a rehearsal for redirecting desires away from rivalry so that only Christ, the entire body, carries the burden and no more lives need be lost. The bread and wine substitutes are transfigured for the physical body of Christ, allowing those partaking to be liberated from competing with others, or even with Him.

That Jesus says, "do this in remembrance of me" and offers a feast *instead* of putting a real body makes an important distinction. This form of substitution does not deny anyone else a life, but creates a new proportionality. It is possible to make different sorts of calculations letting a shared experience or a shared joy reduce transaction costs implicit in dissatisfaction, disappointment, and anxiety, and establish a non-violent substitution in the name of reconciliation, where there is a newly reformed body in the Church.

The dynamic and habit of praise, silence, reading, moving, ingesting, and blessing in the Eucharistic service constitute a way of governing a life. They shape and reveal what is true. They highlight individual, and cooperative, community, distributing what is most important equally: they affirm the love of thy neighbor and that our lives are interwoven and interdependent.[8] By analogy, an economy will reflect some degree of interdependence. Therefore, the Eucharist affirms interindividuality by distributing and sharing a broken body, reflecting our interdependence and reliance upon other persons while also creating mimetic ritual acts.

A greater breadth of comparison among individuals, expanding the relative comparison, allows for greater amount of freedom: "The various distinctions drawn by pre-modern economic thought—between needs and wants, necessities and luxuries, use and exchange value—all rest on the assumption that some ways of life are intrinsically superior to others."[9] This allows us to better resist sorts of pressures that can cause anxiety, stress, and unhappiness. The church provides a structure that can rearrange the priority of the good life to external rewards and public position. By ingesting Jesus, the model gives individuals the power to reconsider the game, the rat race, the system of materialism that creates a status war with others.

In this way, the church can reduce pressure to consume. While "experience has taught us that material wants know no natural bounds, that they will expand without end unless we consciously restrain them. Capitalism rises precisely on this endless expansion of wants… It has given us wealth beyond measure, but has taken away the chief benefit of wealth: the consciousness of having enough."[10] Baptism and Eucharist remind the disciple that one is rich in following Jesus first.

Within the Eucharist, the practice of confession can also foster a reflection on how rivalry intensifies. Rivalry becomes more difficult to manage when it is concealed. Confession shores up trust through forming a consciousness that can examine desire truthfully. Confession reminds individuals they have disordered desires that do not bring long-term happiness. It admits the feeling of lack and the fear of loss, and through forgiveness orients us to honesty.[11] It gives the strength to eschew rivalry but also engage networks with greater trust and confidence.

Sacraments focus our capacity to identify, diminish, and redirect rivalry, and thereby enhance how Christians participate in outside institutions. Christians develop non-rivalrous networks for their own sake, and help counterbalance institutions that arise solely out of financialization, an addiction to money, and luxury.

Sabbath Economics

The church can respond in at least two distinct ways within an economy. One is as if the immediate return of Jesus is imminent. In such a world, wealth is unnecessary and should be distributed freely. I do not suggest that this is, or is not, our current condition. In another way, the church seeks to direct the economy toward one that has greater meaning, where human beings can better flourish in a world as it waits. It seeks to allow individual growth and creativity, while also teaching people to recognize the difference between absolute and relative wealth. Through distinguishing between wants and needs, for example, it equips the disciple to better understand how to live the good life[12].

I suggest two different ways to understand the good life in Christian terms. The first is reflected in what God demands on the Sabbath, the pinnacle of the week. Individuals work to live, not live to work. The meaning of life is to live in the heart of what God's abundance has already given us. This may have greater social, economic, and ecological consequences.

Sabbath impacts the economy in two ways. The first is that it removes a person outside the realm of commerce. That said, commerce may make some parts of life convenient and can allow time and space to be experienced more capaciously because it can assist in helping individuals allocate time according to what their desires are. But the Sabbath does shape desire in a particular way, one where time seems wasted because it is not *productive*. This space is where individuals need not worry about business, and happiness cannot be reduced to quantities, and a flourishing life need not be linked to the spectacles provided by the market.

Sabbath can be experienced in the various networks that surround or work alongside the market economy. Church communities have networks and skills that already mitigate the market: tag sales and thrift stores alongside charity. They own public housing, run credit unions, and pensions. This book is a celebration of that. These acts are not merely incidental but essential to engaging the world. We do it well. We should do more.

The church affirms the priority of the Sabbath. The Sabbath allows for joy, festivity, rest, and contemplation. None of these is necessarily prior or more important, but they are outside the realm of calculation. They affirm that we are people, firstly, in relationship with other people. A Sabbath economics directs us to value experiences of love, of eating and drinking with those who we care the most for. We work to live, not live to work, and we work efficiently so that we can rest, play, and party.

In an economy where speed intensifies profit, however, this sort of Sabbath-oriented economy would seem strange and self-defeating.[13] The circulation of money is what distributes wealth, and faster circulation allows people to have more of what they want. It could be argued that what we need is not a reduction in speed, but institutional pressure to change the direction of circulation and to redistribute wealth. However, advocating for going slow, for celebrating rest, for affirming leisure, might not conflict with other policies. Most likely, individual behavior could not be expected to redirect the economy on its own. A Sabbath economy could not be a total economy until the end of time. But it might help the church understand how it could redirect its own priorities and wealth.

The church affirms that a Sabbath economy values work, but recognizes that working for a paycheck solely is less desirable to doing work that one loves. However, one may choose a paycheck so that the quality of our leisure time is higher. I do not argue that all work must inherently be fulfilling and enjoyable, but the end of such work is to have time: time with one's family, in one's community, to do politics, to be with God.

There is much at stake. Sabbath time is not identical to having a weekend or a vacation, but includes dedicated time to reflect on what is meaningful or valuable. Thinking, itself, requires time, and a faster economy truncates this skill, allocating it to individuals who can be compensated. Thinking becomes money for the few paid to do so.

Without time, a person's ability to provide emotional and spiritual support to friends, neighbors, and families becomes truncated. They have less time to gather and solve political problems and less time to orient and manage our emotional and spiritual lives. Instead, one then both rewards the reactive part of our brain and then becomes perpetually exhausted. The economist Robert Sidelsky suggests that without time to consider our values, our economic activity is "bound to be simply an envious striving for relative advantage, without any natural terminus."[14] The antidote to striving without purpose is to practice Sabbath time.

Observing the Sabbath diminishes the intensification of mimetic rivalry and also requires the creditor to replace the concern of interest with the concern of people. It releases the debtor from the risk of losing one's freedom. In addition, the time of the Sabbath allows us to discern what truly gives joy. Both economists and psychologists have learned happiness is often fleeting; happiness is generally elusive and ephemeral, but the Sabbath still allows a space in time where individuals can also be curious, be wrong, and change because they are safe to be. It is the space where time and relationships are prioritized over criteria that counts only productivity, or money.

It would be a mistake to reduce the purpose of the economic life, or of Christian life generally, to one of happiness. Although commended in scripture, it would be unrealistic and possibly undesirable in the long run to assume that happiness is the telos of the our spiritual journey. But I suggest that by emphasizing the Sabbath as an orienting goal, and an institutional anchor, the church can emphasize a few habits. If anything, it would be enough to affirm those spaces where purposefulness is considered.

That said, there is a shape to what the Body of Christ considers a higher priority. First of all, scripture is wary of personal debt. Just as our accumulated debt reflects the intensity of our desire, our atonement comes with the forgiveness of debt (Lev 19:30). Debt also has the modern impact of making perpetual work unavoidable, which will contradict the purpose of a human life, of the Sabbath itself.

Restoring practices of slowing down, of the Sabbath, should be a primary consideration of the church. In our highly networked society, it's easy to be consumed by information that affects us little, but consumes most of our attention. To be able to not be rushed, to be unhurried, is one of the primary practices of our spiritual life, to learn to have uninterrupted time, or to interrupt our time with periods of quietness, stillness, and reflection. This includes both habits of reflection, and getting sleep. Our economy should value both of these.

Sabbath economics emphasize the importance of social bonds in organizing our networks. These are not merely our five close friends, but also our neighborhoods, apartment buildings, parties, associations, and other institutions where people engage each other and make decisions. They are the "soft connections", the multiple interactions that enrich our social fabric.

While money disciplines decision-making, applied individually it crowds out calculating benefits for the common good. Prioritizing the Sabbath, however, disciplines a relationship with money. While money also reduces the cost of making transactions and creates substitutions that diminish rivalry, its fundamental purpose is to move, through exchange or charity, for the sake of building human relationships. That is where faith is required and redemption is possible. As Gretchen Rubin, the happiness guru, says about money, "it's a good servant but a bad master."[15]

The Tasks of the Church

The church has a crucial role as a firm and institution in both financial and non-financial networks. Its disciples learn practices that make them better at listening and collaboration with others. The church forms individuals through prayer and the Eucharist. A follower of Christ seeks to rearrange their lives in contrast to the rivalry the world imposes, potentially strengthening communities. At its best, it forms people who seek to build trust, through fostering benevolence, peace, prudence, and temperance. Therefore, it should allocate resources to facilitate this task.

The church also makes financial decisions. It will necessarily seek to ensure that it uses its money well. However, its final goal is not to count the bottom line, but to count the number of persons it has touched, engaged, or transformed. The true coin of the church is the human person. Its currency is the followership of Jesus.

Acknowledge Reality

Clergy and laity have acquisitive desires. Churches have experienced greedy clerics, embezzling treasurers, and invested in poorly thought-out, expensive building projects. This should *not* diminish reasonable ways to allocate wealth responsibly, especially if the church is clear about the purpose of wealth. Until Jesus returns, the church does not need to abandon wealth and abdicate its responsibility for its inheritance. Instead, it can use its resources to serve until the return of Jesus. Money can be steered to build the networks the church is called to build.

Admitting that institutions are complex and imperfect can help with the task to build non-rivalrous networks that are not firstly grounded in accumulating wealth for individuals. Its power builds social connections between various individuals, groups, and institutions. Those networks embody the value of the church.

Wealth Is for Developing Relationships

The skills of reorienting rivalry are firmly present within the Anglican spiritual tradition in a variety of forms. The practices of listening to God through the daily office and sharing the Eucharist redirects us toward non-envious, non-rivalrous relationships with others. Submitting ourselves within the tradition, listening to what has gone before, and engaging it honestly teaches a longer and deeper perspective, away from the enflamed intensity of our environment.

Following Christ allows individuals both to make exchanges in the market and participate in institutions by reorienting our desires. A trust in God permits gratuitous generosity with our wealth, unafraid of losing our status or position. This does not mean that having wealth must always corrode spirituality, but that the direction of church governance is to put a check on envy to reduce the divisions and tensions in the broader culture. As Archbishop William Temple wrote, "If an economic system is abundantly effective in producing and distributing material goods, but creates or intensifies divisions and hostilities between men, that system is condemned because it is a source of wrong personal relationships."[16] The success of the market is "to be judged by its success in facilitating the true ends of human life—religion, art, science and above all, happy human relationships."[17]

As the Anglican Denys Munby clarifies, "We need to be aware of the dangers of our riches; we need also to be ready to enjoy wholeheartedly the good things that God has given us to enjoy and to be thankful for them… We need to be sensitive to the way that material possessions divide man from man and break up human fellowship. We need to be ready to use our abundance in common than for personal and private enjoyment". To paraphrase Munby's quote about a medieval pilgrim's praise for his host: *Frugal at home, liberal in public.*[18]

Anglicans affirm that relationships matters through organizing as churches, dioceses, provinces, or communions. The world's challenges will need to be addressed not only by market networks, but through political and religious ones. While religious leaders should understand counting, the economic way of thinking, followers of Christ will also point to values that resist easy measurement.

Churches mistake the role of communicants when they treat them as consumers of the church. Instead, communicants can be formed like apostles who are equipped to build their broader community through strengthening relationships. They are not only meant to give to the church, but also meant to build stronger institutions by forming and strengthening relationships.

Such a view focuses the task of the church. The church is not solely a welcoming institution, but a sending one. While it has a role to repair the world, and heal the sick, its proclaiming role requires a more precise and sophisticated exploration. It is, in part, to tell the story of Jesus, and be a certain sort of person who recognizes the power of desire and rivalry and its hold on the world. A church should not be afraid, because of previous mismanagement and poor governance, of taking a stand, clarifying roles, or setting rules about how individuals and institutions should govern. It should not be afraid of managing property or buying land because it has not handled them well before. It can invest and spend, knowing it has and will continue to make mistakes.

Church formation, through expressing the salvation of Jesus, restrains, redirects, and rearranges rivalry. Formation implies a willingness to learn self-governance and administer good governance in any firm. Arranging the resources of a discrete network so that abundance flows throughout the greatest number possible requires institutional governance that works through the complicated kinks within human relationships. Corporations can fire free riders and otherwise find ways to reduce their impact in their institutional life through the variety of incentives they have available. Similarly, churches may have useful boundaries that help its members know their limits and train people to know when they have enough. Boundaries are locations where people must stop and consider; they must listen and make a case. They are the spaces where a conversation must be had. The dialogue is itself a way to create commitment, to ensure some kind of bond. These boundaries can help reallocate resources reasonably.

The work of a cleric in particular must be oriented around those willing to be held accountable for the work of being a disciple. *Regular* Christians pattern their lives so that they hold the church together so that it can be a place of health for those who enter. This voluntary role includes the willingness to build commitment mechanisms, relationships where individuals are dedicated a communal life, and cultivate practices that encourage long-term investment. Learning tenacity and endurance help guide people to make choices that can be liberating.

As transaction costs diminish, the market increases the speed of exchange of money for goods and services while also diminishing the importance of the specific human person responsible. The church may commend, however, the particular and specific relationships between people in the creation of a valuable spiritual culture. Furthermore, through coordination, the church can show how calculating the difference between absolute and relative wealth may point to a shared life that can create broader individual flourishing. By harnessing and reorienting the power that relative feeling has over individuals, it becomes possible to strengthen other, non-financial, kinds of networks worth having. The church can then expose how the cultural commitment to economic individualism impoverishes everyone through fostering cultures of collaboration. Churches can show how a *well-managed* shared life offers different sorts of riches.

This is not anything new. It is affirming what churches already do. Churches already demonstrate the value of the shared life. There is joy in the potluck supper, in communal singing, in the mutual aid in times of crises. Congregations inculcate ways to help individuals experience God, and invite them to be transformed by the love of Jesus Christ through his model.

Harness Lay Expertise in Markets

The church has a role to foster better conversations about economics in the public realm. The economist and Anglican Theologian Denys Munby once wrote, "I would be extremely surprised if more than two or three bishops could be found who in the last fifteen years had read two books on economic matters..."[19] What priests, bishops, and conventions can do is exemplified by the Eucharist: gather interested lay people together to address issues of economic concern. Invite union leaders, entrepreneurs, economists, managers, and environmentalists to share their ideas. The role of the church would be to encourage comfort with complex issues.

Munby writes,

> "In all the expert and political controversy, there has been practically no educative endeavor to make clear to the public just where the experts differ because they do not know enough, and where differences arise because different social and political aims and preferences are involved. It is not beyond the wit of man to show some of the complex interrelations between these matters, but it requires an honest confrontation of different points of view, which does not commonly arise in public controversy,"[20]

and continues,

> "What is required is disentangling the complex technical issues from the political, social and moral choices which lie behind them and their midst. What is needed is not a dose of moral authority, but a careful discrimination to discern the real moral issues involved."[21]

Bishops and clergy should avoid making meaningless pronouncements, but instead model building non-financial networks of connected individuals by creating spaces where individuals from different parts of the economy can collaborate. Munby writes, "We could create beautiful, efficient and humane cities in place of megalopolis; we could use and not abuse the opportunities with which the motor-car presents us; we could grapple with the monsters of advertisement, mass-circulation newspapers and vulgarized culture. But it will not be without much hard thinking and much patient work behind the scenes. Neither is much in evidence."[22] The church might not have in its own leadership of bishops and priests the expertise to solve economic problems, but it does have the authority to suggest prayer and reflection about complex issues when bringing its disciples together.

While it might not be possible to identify a specific Christian way to address the ethics of economic behavior, the church has the capacity to gather technically proficient economists who understand how the market shapes our choices. The church, as a non-rivalrous institution, can coordinate thoughtful and experienced people who can disentangle the economic and social issues involved in engaging the market. These groups could address specific challenges and be given authority, when possible, to speak as a common Christian mind. Bishops would be better informed, and the power of the laity, the priesthood of all believers, would be harnessed. Church prelates could bring both liberation theology and the economic way of thinking in conversation. When the church listens to its disciples, who are conscious participants in the market, they identify how they can be more responsive and effective institutions in local economies.

Affirm Good Governance by Incentivizing Emotional Competence

Churches may help congregations learn to manage the sorts of firms where money is more conscientiously reallocated to foster human flourishing. Congregations, because they inculcate some skills through holding meetings, sharing work, and working without financial compensation, can model other institutions such as employee ownership and cooperatives.[23] The effectiveness of such organizations depends on excellent governance and an aligning of incentives that reward commitment.

At its best, the church builds leaders who are emotionally competent ordained and lay persons. In addition, the physical church provides a hub for different sorts of networks to develop and foster various relationships, through recovery programs, schools, or classes. It can build structures that can house networks of friendship of various kinds. Churches gather in non-commercial ways, without market pressures. Individuals are present with one another without worrying about needing money. Twelve-step groups, where individuals manage their addiction, are a notable example of how churches do this. They become physical places where people can gather in ways not mediated by commerce. The church becomes a network, or a network that fosters other networks, through being a non-rivalrous presence that helps people coordinate their version of the good life.

Teaching People When They Have Enough

Churches are laboratories of renunciation. Disciples may renounce revenge, violence, and property. A disciple can renounce a new Ferrari, and instead purchase a new Honda. One can renounce spending money on objects that indicate positional status and choose based on other considerations.

Christian renunciation is not necessarily a competition with those who do not engage in this practice. A monastic can still have a drink at the yacht club. It does not mean becoming rivals with those who do not renounce. Renunciation includes renouncing resentment, that one need be judged for being vulnerable, second rate, for being dependent, or being liberated. Being a hipster or unique or individualistic does not solve the problem of being in relationship with other people. The approval of the cool or the postmodern does not in itself solve the challenges of relating to each another.[24]

Enhancing Local Economies for Service and Mission

Churches should not be afraid of money. At their best, churches can enhance local economies. They run thrift stores that renew the use of clothes and goods. Some fund missions through selling crafts through online stores. Monasteries sell bread, soap, and beer. They work limited hours during the day; they produce limited supplies and are not greedy. They focus on quality and understand work as a spiritual discipline. Their renunciation has the paradoxical effect of increasing wealth because they spend little.

Churches have built not-for-profit hospitals, schools, credit unions and cooperatives. This may include religiously based credit unions like the Episcopal Credit

Union in Los Angeles, or the many smaller ones peppered throughout the country. Harvey Cox suggests that the Vatican bank offer low interest loans to the poor or buy debt and forgive it![25] The church would truly forgive debts—literally. These examples illustrate that the church has the financial ability to liberate.

In other ways, churches can partner with organizations to offer meaningful work, restore human connections, and slow down our lives. In a market economy it transforms money into the material. With good governance, it can develop land trusts and enhance real estate, developing long-term value that impacts communities. As one theologian explains, such institutions are formed by values, including "reciprocity, cooperation/collaboration, interdependence, accountability to the commons, sustainability, and the inclusion of diverse peoples and experiences. Maximizing profits and accumulating material goods and wealth for the sake of luxury are never the ultimate aims of these ventures even though they can be and many are profit-making"[26].

In spite of claims that the church is declining, the church wields enormous economic and social capital. Its endowments, land, and connected members are hubs for the broader networks within our society. If the church were a corporation, it would be one of the largest corporations in the country.

The church is not called to sell its inheritance but to invest and restore it. Instead it should be thinking strategically and practically, calling its stakeholders in specific places together to consider how they can build the wealth in the communities it serves. This is not only charity, but a desire to make long-term relational investments in the places around them.

Churches Building Networks

Prayer forms individuals. But this is only one half of the church's task. The other task is to build and reinforce connections with others. While companionship was not a subject of this book, it frames a responsibility for the church. It is a matter of health and salvation, as the proximity to bodies and the power of synchronicity reduces stress, builds the immune system, and offers a relief from loneliness. There are few places that are fundamentally equipped to build networks of companionship for its own sake.[27] Churches are one of them.

Churches build networks that are less directed by money. They do not first screen persons based on their bank account. Often, evangelism is framed as an invitation to be a friend with God and others. For this reason, the church often thinks of itself as an institution oriented around hospitality, of sharing everyday work of love. This is nothing new.

It bears, however, reinforcing that the church is a place where people learn the skills of cooperation and coordination. The preparation of liturgies, the planning of meetings, potlucks and capital campaigns as well as the identification of causes and problems each requires individuals learn to align actions. The habits of reflection, of taking turns, of being empowered, of listening are each part of what the local church inculcates as part of a Christian rule of life. Churches foster the virtue of commitment and tenacity, crucial aspects of long-term happiness.[28]

Our public life has suffered from a dearth of individuals who are intentional about learning such skills and applying them. Institutions are understood as implicitly oppressive. Being a good follower, someone who participates as a part of a larger project rather than as the center, has become diminished. There are certainly good reasons for this: in a winner takes all society, the stakes are high and joining an institution that doesn't offer financial benefits is a disadvantage.

Churches may seem pre-institutional because they bridge both the private and public person. Individuals do not enter churches formed, competent, or complete, but as sinners. However, the church begins with face to face relationships with individuals, who have contradictory needs and desires, as the building blocks of all institutional and public life. Individuals are made in God's image, and where two or three are gathered, God is present.

Churches bridge financial and non-financial networks. Being aware of the mechanics of counting, the usefulness of money, they foster competence in directing our resources toward the good life. In short, if churches are *to know Christ and to make Christ known*, they will build broad networks of reconciliation. This may illustrate that churches are to allocate resources so that congregations and their leaders build connections—networks of friendships.

Affirming the idea of networks of friendship is one alternative to rivalry. Kathryn Tanner writes, "For all the status warfare, one thing the oppressed are looking for and are attracted to in religion is a way out of the competitive circulation of goods. They hope not for a status to rival the great, but for a circulation of goods without status rivalry"[29]. The mimetic behavior in congregations enhances the creative possibilities that arise when they eschew status and positional goods.

Salvation in Christ affirms the Sabbath, a life of prayer, community, leisure, and feasting, provides the meaning for persons and the reason for living. Markets, by themselves, are not hospitable to this version of the good life[30], finally prioritizing the accumulation of wealth as the indicator of success: "It is not human beings who need adapting to the market; it is the market that needs adapting to human beings."[31]

When churches create an internal culture where individuals do not fear loss, who can become generous, who are not afraid of dependence, they can become more powerful. Disciples can be equipped with these capacities to participate in a multiplicity of networks. Quoting MacIntyre, this may mean a "new monasticism" to reconstruct local community: "we are waiting not for a Godot, but for another—doubtless very different—St. Benedict."[32]

Benedictine Economics

Benedictine spirituality and governance are one model where the life of the church can reorient economic thinking through both prayer and work. I believe that the Benedictine rule provides a realistic way of engaging human frailty and potential, and offers some guidance in managing our institutions, even if monastic practices can not be adapted in their entirety.

A monastic sharing of possessions might not be easily possible in a small church because the amount of social control would be challenging to implement. Furthermore, the interdependence of the market would make it impossible to constrain wealth from leaving communities. However, it does provide some clues to what churches might do.

First, Benedict affirms that formation is important. Institutions model and shape behavior through mentoring, constraining, and leading. This assertion itself runs counter to the idea that individuals can be self-made in important ways. Instead, the first step is to recognize how congregations model sorts of ways to live. Formation can be defined as directed mimetic behavior that trains desire, without necessarily suppressing the perception of individuality. The abbot, or priest, establishes stability through a skill at managing the complexity of human relations, to prevent the snowballing of conflict that may arise in any community, modeling skills of emotional resilience and health. This is how the church builds meaningful connections.

The manager, the abbot, should have the capacity to hold steady, set boundaries, and promote the general welfare in order to accomplish whatever task is at hand. They will have spiritual and emotional resilience. They especially have the role of forming Christians who are able to incorporate new members in the institution. The monastic tradition illustrates how this formation of disciples takes time and effort. Building commitment itself takes resources.

Similarly, the pastor should be able to foster the capacity to manage rivalry, including the skills of disappointment in public and private life, being patient with slow improvement, and an understanding that transformation is rarely immediate. The pastor emphasizes small steps, the good above the perfect, affirming competence and excellence while eschewing a need for perfection.

Congregations can develop neo-monastic patterns of life. For example, rather than affirming superstars, the church affirms that each person in their place has the ability to do decent, meaningful work. Congregations create opportunities for creativity and creating culture. Churches build networks that both give life meaning and reward skill and talent, without succumbing to the external motivations of the market that reward only the singular, the "winners." Everybody has a voice that can sing.

The church also focuses on its role to provide networks of companionship and trust. These skills that require modeling and formation are akin to following a rule of life that affirms visiting, for example, rather than passively watching television. This means clergy will need to harness the financial resources of the church to train people how to connect. Congregations would direct their time and resources to form persons who collaborate. The congregation is a place where the poor and the prosperous can be connected, and the priest need not be a rival with either.

A Benedictine economy emphasizes the work of both reflection and action. While it will also emphasize values important to markets, such as coordination, measurement, planning and incentives, it also understands there are limits. It does not necessarily shy away from capital, but instead of liquidating capital mainly to create money, it directs money to build relationships with others and God.

The Benedictine tradition recognizes that persons are complex, imperfect, and sinful, yet also reflective and industrious. To enhance a good life, the community shares wealth and labor. While in a market individuals are replaceable, replicable, and substitutable, and are needed to buy and sell, a church that embodies monasticism remembers that individuals are specific persons in a time and place. In the market, money is currency. In the monastery or church, people are the coin. They matter first.

By eschewing personal financial acquisitiveness, churches can find ways to embrace simplicity and productivity while participating in the market. It should not be afraid of being a financially strong and powerful institution with substantial resources. The power of money to arrange complex relationships simplifies and lubricates the many activities the Body of Christ does. It helps congregations hire pastors, it creates income for church parishes, and gives parishes options about discerning how they serve.

If used intentionally, however, its purpose is to build people and strong networks. It can provide some cushion to the disruption the financialization of the economy brings. With coordination, it may harness both its non-financial and financial networks to mitigate, challenge, and redirect the egregious abuses in various sectors that do not have a language for the common good. The Body of Christ should not abdicate its authority to the God of the market: it can, and must, demand that its own resources be used for the common good. It can do this through training lay and clergy leaders, providing benefits, supporting building projects, investing wisely, and upholding shareholder accountability.

The Body of Christ is unlikely to become an entirely monastic institution. But the monastic tradition is a sort of economy that helps the church remember its priorities. Churches foster creativity and sociability—a personal connection with God and the capacity to love the neighbor, the stranger, and the enemy. This means a congregation should focus on building lives of reflection and disciples who can learn how to address the tensions in the various networks of social life. Especially in a highly connected economy, where light moves too fast for us to think, one primary role of the church is to hit pause and remember that *there is a body here.*

Similarly, the economist J. M. Keynes believed that the love of money is justified only to the extent it makes us good. The purpose of economic striving should be to make the world better. This accentuates the church's role, that it uses money without fear or adulation, instead harnessing it for the spread of the kingdom.[33]

Episcopacy, Order, and Governance

Our current context is often suspicious of organization, especially religious institutions. In part this is because priests and bishops have often abused or misunderstood their role. However, having a distinct role and responsibility to organize congregations helps align the work effectively. The role of the bishop, in part, is to align local congregations to help one another flourish by diminishing the economic costs that rivalry imposes. This governing skill requires the spiritual and emotional competencies to handle both being a target of rivalry and being a model. Being a target of rivalry means being able to acknowledge the various kinds of reasonable and unreasonable critiques upon leaders that followers have. It acknowledges the role of being seen also means greater scrutiny. The episcopacy provides clarity to leadership because it exposes rather than conceals the natural tendency toward rivalry and comparison. It identifies one person who fills the role of being a rival and a model, liberating the rest of the system from having multiple targets. Therefore, such a person should have the competency to manage rivalry while being emotionally competent enough to align congregations.

Institutional economics illustrates effective management is a skill. Larger organizations will require more emotionally competent individuals. Learning to manage rivalry, and coaching others on how to do the same, is the central task of the ordained priesthood. *Managing rivalry is the primary characteristic of effective governance.*

Anglicanism implicitly affirms that governance is a good. Just as economic, capitalist institutions also require governance that aligns people for the sake of efficiency, religious institutions govern to align people for mission, both within the church and to enhance other institutions. The church calls its members to participate widely, to build multiple, diverse institutions that can create a heterogenous, messy political life.

The church therefore organizes to diminish rivalry in its body. Its primary task is to instill in its leaders and followers the ability to reorient rivalry toward mutual flourishing. To follow Jesus requires praying to be free from from rivalry through the practice of praise to the one in whom there can be no rival; the building of the church creates hearts in whom rivalry is redirected toward a mutual enterprise, the building of the Body.

The episcopacy exposes the natural inclination of large organizations toward centralizing authority. This is understood empirically, not normatively. The benefit of the episcopacy is that it illumines, rather than obscures, this tendency. More centrally, economies of scale will also concentrate symbolic power. There are several reasons this may be so. Not everyone will have time for all the meetings that make up the life of the church. Not everyone is called to everything; governing, as a form of diminishing rivalry, is a skill that takes time and effort to learn, and people may not want to spend their time learning. The rule of the few, in this case, does not *require* that only a few participate more broadly, but highlights that there are distinctions of roles that make institutional sense.

This may allow us to understand one of the primary roles of the episcopacy. Scripture articulates some of its characteristics. One who governs and oversees should be an individual who refrains from engaging in behaviors that inflame or amplify rivalry. This does not require asceticism or poverty, but a sense of satisfaction and gratitude. Scripture does not force poverty upon any person. In a bishop, desire is inoculated, rather than prohibited.

Thus, the bishop's role is to manage rivalry even though s/he is a psychological target for this jockeying for a position of status within the church. Our bishops would thus be individuals who have the best emotional capacity to reduce rivalry or to recognize that their priests will naturally see each other, and their leaders, as rivalrous. What makes the episcopacy useful and powerful is that by making the object of rivalry plain, *it becomes easier to regulate it.*

The bishop is a target, and the miter is the bullseye.

Governance without Perfection: The Mechanics of Grace

The episcopacy is an imperfect system. However, efforts to create perfect systems have been scattered with the blood of innocents and martyrs. Systems that affirm either the rationality of the market, or the consolidation of power in the state, will not contain the complexity of human relationships. People who believe in the free market lobby for government to change the rules in their favor; governments seek to sustain themselves rather than reorganize on behalf of the public good. Bureaucracies defend their interests, while also defending the interests of the most connected. Still, it is not necessary to reject all attempts at efficiency, equality, or humanity. One can hold in tension the frustration that bureaucracies bring, while recognizing that an ordered system often provides a degree of security, freedom, and effectiveness. While organization constrains spontaneity, few great projects have happened without organized people.

The Nobel-prize winning economist and political scientist Elinor Olstrom writes, "policy analysis can never find 'the' answer."[34] No single design can solve all problems. What we can do is remember that we are adaptive. *Organization is how imperfect people get things done.* Imperfect people can be creative, independent, and experimental. They adapt and correct themselves. The institutions persons build, such as the church, do not need to be perfect.

By focusing on forming non-rivalrous leaders, governance can move beyond merely a technical series of checklists. In this way, the Christian participates in economics by fostering stronger emotional lives within our communities, to align individuals to better harness our resources for the common good.

The Virtuous Administration

A competent administration can diminish rivalry and accompanying emotions such as anxiety, fear, and sentimentality. Administration requires virtues, as Adam Smith described in the *Theory of Moral Sentiments*: prudence, benevolence, and self-control (or "command" as he puts it). It means understanding, fundamentally, when one should change one's mind; an ability to distinguish between self-interest and the interest of the institution, and an ability to share the work. Essentially, it is about regulating one's own mimetic urges, and fostering competence in those same feelings within the church. This will entail sharing information, creating patterns of collaboration, and rewarding mutual effort. These require habits of governance.

Therefore, administration does not primarily mean that the work of clergy is relegated to the office, but also the administration of human relations. This skill requires constant development. It means effective negotiation of parties who might not be aware of the power of mimetic behavior in our organizations, and our desire for attention, visibility, and status. This is how the church can reduce the transaction costs of any institution a disciple engages.

There is a tension, however, in the use of time. Developing a bureaucratic checklist may take less time and seem more efficient than cultivating an individual to create a strong institution. However, formation should not merely be understood as a necessary professional skill, but the embodiment of a theological anthropology at the heart of the gospel. A priest should be able to address our propensity toward resentment and rivalry, and create spaces to redirect it through the spiritual practices of the church.

I believe that this invites the question of what looks like an Anglican culture. In addition to the regular habit of prayer and thought in which the clergy are commended, good governors will have habits of reading and writing expansively; have intentional conversations with people both inside and outside of our communities; and identify how parishes create meaningful lives outside of status and positional anxiety.

The Anglican tradition was formed and strengthened by its expanses on reading. Reading cultivates empathy; regular journal keeping provides a reflective space in one's emotional life; visiting congregations are growing congregations; firms that build commitment are more effective in the long run than other sorts of firms; firms that are cooperative, meaning the profits are shared among the workers, can be profitable and competitive in the market. In short, diminishing rivalry requires intentionality, and that these practices are evinced in the church and other institutions.

In an environment where many firms require individuals to work more than fifty to sixty hours a week, the church perhaps develops leaders who can enhance their own networks by being persons who are rivals through Jesus (and thus direct their rivalry for the same of helping others), rather than rivals in the world. They become positive mimetic partners within any institutions where they live. Firms benefit when employees and managers use their spiritual capacities to renounce the mimetic behavior that characterizes our work within institutions, and redirect our public lives toward building firms that, in this way, represent effective ways of building a society that enhances the lives of everyone.

The Church Administers: How to Inculcate Good Governance

The church develops stronger institutions through competent administration. Administration is analogous to ensuring the communion table, daily prayer, and personal devotions orient a life. They organize a personal spirituality and inculcate a practice of reflection upon the breadth of human emotion. The intentional ordering of church life intrinsically creates spaces where there is more time to reflect and have purposeful activity.

Administration impacts effectiveness. Good administration fosters collaboration over time, which requires incentives that require people to control their desires and work. However, these incentives will be different in various firms. Corporations allocate money to incentivize collaboration, churches use persuasion and an internal sense of meaning, and public institutions must represent a broader number of stakeholders.

The importance of emotional, or even spiritual, regulation in management cannot be overstated, even in complex organizations. Organizations require attention to situations where individuals should be equipped to address new challenges, improve checklists, and manage specific rivalries. New challenges will require a willingness to change, risk, and therefore to lose. Emotional regulation will include a capacity to listen and deliver feedback. The church already develops the emotional and spiritual skills as it prepares its business and worship.

Rivalry is not eliminated when redirected. Competition disciplines so that one can move from good to better. However, the roots of a rivalry can be better understood to be redirected so that the individual has the grace to align and reconcile. Sports events are good examples of how rivalry becomes managed. After a sports competition, for example, the teams may engage in a ritual of peace or mutual respect, such as shaking hands, trading jerseys, or even getting together for raucous singing.

Compensation has been one place the church has also sought to manage rivalry. The catholic model of celibacy and communal living among clergy, for example, limited the incentives to gain and inherit property. While it may not be possible to adapt such practices for congregations, it is important to recognize how the relationships of clergy, paid staff, and congregants are also rivalrous systems. Therefore, discerning a compensation strategy that diminishes envy while encouraging competence will be an important challenge for churches.

Funding emotional competence is a cost. Since the fundamental building block of the church is the ability to understand and build relationships, emotional competence should be considered an administrative skill prior to all others. This skill requires, at the very least, a curiosity about other people, and a desire to take the initiative to connect with others. It requires funding, especially if such emotional competence is to be modeled by other people.

This leadership equips people in all kinds of networks. Commercial and planned economies, or capitalism and socialism, each require individuals to participate in institutional life. Institutions such as governments, churches, corporations, and gangs require relational competence that makes administering a task possible. Congregations, by developing discipleship, form people to be the sorts of persons who can administer and build connections in the world.

To inhabit any organization requires an understanding of power, authority, and leadership. It may be that the role of Anglicans and Episcopalians, or any person who considers church important, is to learn the process by which people understand their own rivalries, be aware of their limited knowledge, and learn the relational skills to align together. All firms, whether public or private, require incentives to coordinate and accomplish tasks. The church inculcates these skills widely. Because it understands to live the gospel means recognizing how envy creates idols. The myriad of small acts of working together, even as small as the breath taken in-between the verses of the psalms in the daily office, anticipates the capacity to make the world.

Some Everyday Examples of How the Church Creates Effective Markets Internally

The various institutions of the church already organize effectively. If they did not already have some skills, the church would not have survived. Congregations harness resources together effectively managing rivalry. I will outline a few examples of how this happens. Each one of these examples may experience some degree of conflict, but they reflect how communities are able to gather. In this section I will review some of the ways the church allocates and distributes resources, unpacking some questions worth asking about how they spend, with the intention of guiding people to be more intentional about how they work together.

Shared Meals: Pot Lucks and Soup Kitchens

The shared meal is one of the most central activities in a congregation. They can take a variety of forms—the potluck, the soup kitchen, or the community clambake are several consistent examples. Each one allocates resources differently, and it behooves congregations to be intentional about them.

A church potluck dinner exemplifies how members of a congregation shares resources and food with a minimum amount of governance, spreading out the labor, allowing individuals to decide what they can or should bring. Individuals make cost-benefit assessments. People can bring dishes they've made before; individuals have enough freedom to purchase and make food on their own schedule, and take responsibility themselves for discerning how much they are able to spend, or how much time they have to make for a dinner, or if they want to bring the most interesting dish.

Potlucks raise some economic questions. It may be more efficient for a single person, rather than everyone, to purchase the groceries for an event. A church may provide the standard staples and condiments in their pantry or be responsible for purchasing the meat in quantity. Perhaps it makes more sense to buy meat as a group from a buying club than asking people to buy higher priced smaller packs of hotdogs. There is some trade-off between individual freedom to purchase individually and being governed through delegated roles and using the church credit card.

Individuals in congregations may need to make reasonable economic decisions about when to make food at home versus purchasing pre-made food for an event. Secondly, it may also be justifiable to simply have the food made or delivered by one source or catered. Evangelism might require letting visitors, new members, or the indigent come with nothing. A community can be intentional, but being intentional also costs time. The work of making a food for a community implies a strong commitment. But it is also easier for a wider number of individuals to participate if they know they do not need to. However, allowing people to come without having to pay for a meal can increase a sense of obligation.

Soup kitchens are examples where the congregation contributes to the economy and well-being of a community through service. They spend money on food to nourish others in a space where individuals can also gather and make acquaintances. The resources of the church kitchen, individual labor, and a commitment to charity enhance some sorts of useful connections. A congregation could spend some time analyzing the quality of those relationships and discerning the social costs of charity.

There are also trade-offs between convenience and work. Buying prepared food saves costs, while removing the meditative work of cooking or the shared liveliness of cooking together. Some people do not find cooking soothing, and people might not work together well in the same kitchen. But a reasonable self-assessment can help allocate time and money. More resources allow the church to harness collective buying power to provide more. It could ensure consistency in hospitality more effectively if it were to contract to a firm that provided coffee every Sunday, which would free up time for congregants to focus on other activities. But this also diminishes the role of developing commitment in the community.

Governance matters insofar as it can help a church walk through these choices. It may include the coordinator who ensures that not everyone brings lemon squares to a dinner or ensures that someone purchases utensils. It may include local customs that forbid the buying of sugary drinks or of alcohol. It assigns tasks such as setting up and cleaning. In smaller congregations, this work might be one of habit. The time expended in governing and planning is unnecessary. But as an institution grows, however, anxiety also grows. It behooves an institution to anticipate the challenges of growth by adapting some patterns of organization.

Churches as Businesses

Churches should not be afraid of business practices. After all, churches may operate various sorts of enterprises such as thrift shops or used bookstores or run community development corporations. In these cases, the church provides labor and space so that members of the community can use their resources more effectively. These networks are economic networks that arise out of financial needs for the church, but also allow for members of the community to have property. It is a market network that not only represents a sort of exchange; it also provides a space for fellowship and can broaden a congregation's visibility in a larger community.

Congregations will decide about the management of these institutions, and have clear ideas about where the resources will go. Some will emphasize a mission that is outside the church, and others will want to focus on the deteriorating roof. A thrift shop may want to have separate books from the church. They will need to decide what tasks are done by volunteers, or who is hired, and why. But the central thread remains the same: governance matters, and identifying the trade-offs is crucial to a sustainable enterprise that can build church networks.

On a larger scale, monasteries of various kinds sell hot sauce, lip balm, dog biscuits, fudge, cheese, caskets, and beer. They do not eschew entrepreneurship or work, but do so in proportion to other work that organizes life. Work is not done for its own sake. They do not seek to create supply to meet demand, but depending on their own need. There is some attention and conscientiousness to the work done, and the funds are used to assist the monastic community. The motivation to do the work is not the whip, but the product itself. The motivation provides useful work, worthwhile goods, and a sustainable income. Business is not valued for its own sake, but in proportion to other values worth having.

Churches and Cooperatives

Churches in some ways overlap with cooperative institutions. In cooperatives, participating individuals have a share in the business, where the profits are divided along some equitable amount, usually according to the value of the share. The primary role of the profits is not to encourage speculation but rather to share expenses and burdens at a reasonable rate. They may or may not be for the purpose of profit. Shares are allocated to ensure some degree of democratic participation.

Congregations have some shared habits that already equip them to develop and participate in cooperatives. The physical church, for example, is itself a shared institution held in trust by the congregation. Management is implicitly democratic and decision-making driven by consensus. Consensus is a type of management that also requires relational practice and skill. Most congregations work best with a sort of consultation where members relate to each other to get tasks done.

Cooperatives come in a variety of structures with various tasks. One church in Oregon operates a cooperative tool shed, by which individuals participate in purchasing heavy equipment that no one person will use continuously. Problems of storage, fees, and rules of borrowing privilege are sorts of issues that require non-rivalrous management. It allows individuals to pool resources to purchase goods they may not normally be able to acquire. There are variations upon this theme: it need not be that there is a single shed, but merely an online way to share such tools without difficulty.

Other cooperatives include credit unions and land trusts. Credit unions are federally backed financial institutions by which individuals can leverage their financial resources to save and make loans. Many churches have created their own, and a few larger church bodies operate on behalf of larger communities. While these require substantial resources initially, such institutions can provide a useful counterbalance to predatory financial institutions in poor neighborhoods. The internet is making this kind of collaboration easier, even allowing groups of Episcopalians to potentially help other Episcopalians manage their debt.

Governing People

One consistent area where congregations and churches need to consider the impact of desire, sin, and governance is compensating leadership. Compensation has a role in reducing rivalry. It can include a cash stipend, benefits, and perks such as time flexibility. One of the tensions that arises in churches is the intuition that church staff should not work for money. In such cases, there are psychological trade-offs that are often unspoken. Congregations may be enticed to expect less competence because they pay for enthusiasm. If priests are to be like Jesus, the theory goes, then they should work for close to free, because Jesus himself worked for free.

Such a view reflects some paradoxical thinking about money. It should be clear that money is a simple and efficient way to reduce rivalry. Reasonable compensation can better ensure that staff do not suffer from the anxiety caused by financial precarity. I assume that few people who enter the Episcopal priesthood will be motivated by affluence, but instead are motivated by other kinds of rivalry, such as being visible. Poverty or suffering are not required to serve Jesus.

The tensions are complex. Financial precarity does not attract competent leadership or diminish anxiety. It's possible that a cleric will be devoting more time to raising money than making connections and building disciples. While the two may be synchronous, they are not the same. A reasonable stipend can reduce rivalry to a point where competence and commitment are suitably rewarded, with social recognition substituting for wealth. This means acknowledging honestly to whom clergy compare themselves. The rector of a large cardinal parish with billions of dollars in real estate assets could be compared to a real estate developer, but make less than one third of the salary of a CEO. A bishop may manage a hundred churches, but most are not compensated at the rate of an equivalent businessperson. This illustrates a reasonable balance. Clergy who manage more money and larger firms are paid more than other clergy, but not at a difference that is reflected in the rest of the economy.

The church can develop a realistic, disciplined understanding of what should be expected from clergy and laity. While the hallmark of the spiritually mature is not needing recognition, the truth is that almost everyone likes to be seen, appreciated, and rewarded. Compensation is one location where this matters. Money can help identify where compensation reduces anxiety and rivalry. Comparing clergy to educators, social workers or not-for-profit managers can help guide what a congregation's expectations should be. Furthermore, the church should be honest about envy, and able to create some innovative ways to develop competent pastors in light of the financial challenges priests have.

Because the church does not only inhabit the world of money, it might offer creative ways to organize. A church could reward with compensation that elevates the Sabbath and models a different way of considering work. Offering compensation for thirty-two-hour work weeks with pension, healthcare, and liberal vacations might be inviting for talented individuals who do not want to be guided by the hedonic treadmill. Creative arrangements can support part-time ordained leadership through providing healthcare, a modest housing stipend, and a used car, which allows them some freedom in finding part-time work during the week. Compensating clergy with vacation, healthcare, and freedom can be one way of illustrating how money can be productively exchanged for time.

Property, Endowments, and the Pension Fund

Relatively, the church has the competence to manage wealth for the greater good. If it has good governance it may be able to manage land, endowments and pensions effectively. What should be examined is how churches and congregations already do this well. What is central to this practice is a belief that the church does have the capacity to use wealth responsibly with clear criteria. Land trusts, public housing, or other kinds of property, for example, require some knowledge about how to manage, buy, and allocate property. Endowments also require some degree of intentionality about how they will be managed. The church need not fear wealth, but recognize that it has managed it both triumphantly and disastrously. It should not be afraid of its responsibility, however, to govern for the sake of the larger community and future generations. It must take the initiative and not abdicate its resources by selling its endowment or claiming incompetence.

Without planning, immediate pressing concerns will tempt Churches to sell off their inheritance. However, an organized church could single-handedly address some of the more severe housing shortages that the country is having if it harnessed its resources more effectively. This requires competence, and the church has it. I suggest its fear of rivalry inhibits its confidence in its own capacity. When the church is wary of money because of the tension it creates, it disables its own ability to make sensible choices about how it can invest its own wealth to build stronger non-financial networks, or even better financial ones.

One of the primary examples of Episcopal competence includes the pension fund, a pooled fund that invests in the broader economy. It was the foundation for the social security system in the US. It pays its management well, but its management is dedicated to the purpose and task of the institution. It exemplifies how the church has effectively learned how to govern desire and embody in real time a faith in the salvific work of Jesus.

I began writing this book in part because I believed that the church should engage in markets, because markets matter. I also believed that the church does a *relatively*, rather than absolutely, good job of addressing the economy. Churches exemplify some of the strongest examples of voluntary collaboration in the public sphere and therefore accurately demonstrate the challenges of managing effective firms. Churches have the capacity to corral resources and allocate wealth to create persons who can responsibly manage power in the world.

I refrained from promoting any specific kind of economy. But I attempted to offer a more complex view by affirming rather than eschewing wealth or power, presenting an understanding of reasonable governance as central to what a church offers, and how a church forms its disciples. The church, at its best, forms competent governors.

Modern society creates tensions and rivalries by unleashing desire: "Those arising from power relationships and those arising from the insatiability of human wants. The two work in combination to produce an ethic of acquisitiveness, which dooms society to continuous objectless, wealth-creation—something that did not exist in earlier times, and that remains, in some sense, peculiar to capitalism."[35]

The concentrations of power and people who desire have created a social and spiritual crisis that undermines other values worth having.

It is not my intention to argue for public control over economies, although I believe that our social networks benefit from public institutions that allow for a broader experience of the *good life*—that allow for persons to receive reasonable healthcare, build families, and rest. The church, however, has implicitly created a rule, a habit, or a way, arising from the belief that Jesus saves by protecting us from rivalry with others that can make such a life possible. Within those constraints, the church organizes so that people can seek their own specific meaning.

Governance matters. Although the economist Daniel Finn writes that economics is concerned with four elements, he also alludes to a fifth which has to do with the nature of institutions, of forming or reproducing.[36] This may be one of the primary roles of the church: to help people learn the skills to form institutions that can adapt to the needs of civil society. Without such people, building institutions will be impossible.

By talking about "networks" I've sought to reframe and reaffirm the insight that politics and economics cannot be disentangled. I've described governing structures, the public, and other sorts of relational organizations as networks. The stability of these networks are prior to the market and make the market possible. However, when all networks are financialized and all human relationships transactional, what gives life meaning is crowded out and the social bonds of trust that ground all networks become corroded. Therefore, it is important for the church to engage those networks that also exchange political power, while also shaping broader networks to limit how money destabilizes human relationships based on love and affection.

The prioritization of market forces, not just the market forces in themselves, puts our complex system of interconnecting networks in danger. Furthermore, the market's disposition to free human beings from any difficult face to face interaction, and to unmoor us from our natural environment, primes us for the deception of mass media and propaganda. As one economist wrote, "If it is true that the economy must be deferred to, there is a case not only for constraining the imprudent actions of the prince, but for repressing those of the people, for limiting participation, in short, for crushing anything that could be interpreted by some economist-king as a threat to the proper functioning of the 'delicate watch.'[37] Further, when most citizens are absorbed by making money, fewer people can participate in political power. The time spent making money can kill political life, opening the door for tyranny.[38]

This book affirms that Catholic teaching has been broadly correct in its assessment of the place of market forces. I also more strongly affirm that economics is of central importance to the church. Debt itself reflects the sin in our market networks. The mechanics of desire have to do with money. The wants of individuals are better when shaped by deeper connections that cannot be quantified.

Another crucial insight of mimetic theory is that firms of different kinds imitate each other. Corrupt public institutions will corrupt other networks and vice versa. Institutions, whether governments, the church, or corporations, that expand to help the good of all will be imitated by others. *The zero sum presumption that if the government is big then markets will be small, or if markets are big then government must be small, is wrong*. Instead, because individuals are connected with different sorts of networks, so the health of one will impact the health of the other. Corrupt governing will mean corrupt corporations; self-serving corporations invite self- serving governments. Therefore, any firm that allocates resources for the common good will be a model for other firms. Responsible, non-rivalrous governance can happen where multiple institutions engage each other, not as rivals for the same piece of the pie, but as rivals for the common good.

The church can be pro-commercial or pro-government. Disciples of Jesus can serve in government or be entrepreneurs. They can be cops or they can be CEOs. They can be diligent employees and generous managers. One can both believe that the government has a role in the economy, helping the poor, or be a businessman and do so privately, and still follow the Gospel. But the church cannot assert that the worker and the owner are *always* enemies or that the government is *inherently* incompetent. The church is neither a rival with either government or capitalist firms, but leads *both* of them toward the common good.

It cannot be avoided that politicians will seek to reap personal benefits from their connections; the prosperous will constantly compare themselves to each other in the personal ubiquitous desire for status and honor. These are surely parts of our public life. But a public official, with mixed motivations, can still work for the sake of the public; a person of wealth can give their inheritance to ensure the prosperity of their neighborhood church or a struggling school. Individuals who obey the law even though it chafes or allow for process because it's fair for everyone are closer to this non-rivalrous ideal. In churches, however, are places where one's spirituality matters, a spirituality formed in a community that recognizes that status, honor or even wealth cannot be measured except by first being understood as children of God.

The church has data about how financial networks work in communities. It runs soup kitchens and thrift shops, day care centers and not-for-profit schools. It has investments and properties. At the very least, the church can report what it sees to the public, as a public institution, as part of other economic and political networks. By offering its experience, it contributes to the public conversation about orienting economic life. This does not mean it has the final word or the power to compel. However, it may form those who have proclaimed Jesus as Savior, and invites those committed to see their own lives through the lens of Jesus to understand their own lives as worthy, apart from our status or position. A Christian need not be seen because she knows that her Father sees. Each can be seated last at the table, because every person will have enough.

The church itself is a form of governing that contains its own economy. It administers wealth, shares resources, and addresses costs and benefits. As the humanist political scientist Arthur F. Bentley notes, "The church and organized religion are phenomena of government in the widest sense from start to finish, and sometimes of government in a differentiated form akin to the state." He then says, "a corporation is a government through and through. It has been forced into corporate form by the struggling of the interests upon one another, by the struggling of wider groups with the intra-corporation groups."[39]

This is because, like in government, churches are groups of people. Bentley writes, "All phenomena of government are phenomena of groups pressing one another, forming one another, and pushing out new groups and group representatives to mediate the adjustments."[40] This insight emphasizes the relationality inherent in the work of any institution. The clergy, as governors of the church, as managers, are engaging in some sort of group activity. The church, within its body, is already a government, and we have interests. These "interests" are defined by our actions.[41]

The primary activity of the church is to build disciples by forming relationships that overcome rivalry in Christ's name. This work includes both those who are called by the church to live in such relationships as the ordained, but also businesspeople, journalists, elected officials, teachers, and truckers. The work of the managers of our institutions, its priests, is to encourage and model such relationships. The church also reminds us that in the process of governing our economy, values matter. It affirms interdependence and a shared public life. The church's currency, its coin, is the human person. That's what the church counts. By taking this view, the church can slow the corrosion of all institutional life. The purpose of coin, of money, is always in the service of the real coin, the human person.

Without a deeper understanding of the institutions within those markets, financializing diminishes how societies work. The speed of capital puts enormous pressures on all social institutions, including capitalist ones. It forces all firms to react without long-term intentions; with less accountability, it corrodes the trust that is also the foundation of market society. This is detrimental for the relationships that make our networks thrive.

The Republic requires a wide variety of groups and networks that offer differing types of mimetic behavior. The church is one network that encourages individuals to be persuaded by Christ, and this is learned when there is a diversity of groups in which individuals engage a wide variety of behaviors, agendas, and desires. At its best, the main role of the church is to train people to be trustworthy in any institution.

The church provides an alternative voice. It holds corporations and governments responsible. It builds networks of outside organizations. It may not avoid the messiness of public life but can still shape it with intentionality. By building leadership with emotional skills, in individuals who have the desire to connect and share, the church can reconcile, rebuild, and reconnect the many different networks that make a human life meaningful. In short, by being saved by desire through Jesus, the church can seek to know Christ, and to make Christ known.

Future Possibilities

I have first suggested the threefold rule of the church, the Daily Office, the Eucharist, and Personal Prayer, remains an essential grounding for organizing a community away from rivalry so that it can better engage economic networks. I wish to restore the idea that the church as a community of prayer has economic and redemptive value, because the skill of reflection builds stronger networks by diminishing rivalry and creating emotional stability. The church has a deep capacity to build stronger institutions of all kinds because it illustrates how governance can redirect desire away from personal accumulation toward shared mutual flourishing. When churches send reflective individuals to become a part of multiple networks, individuals bring multiple models into conversation with each other, diminishing rivalry by inoculating against the Balkanization of our public institutions.

I have not in detail discussed issues that arise out of communities of color, feminism, or the environment. I think there are several suggestive paths that can arise out of further dialogue with these ecosystems of thought. Certainly rivalry is a part of the tension and violence that has arisen in our broader economy, and the reality is that the financialization of the market was a part of the history of slavery.

While I have alluded to slavery as a part of debt, I have not discussed it as a part of race. Furthermore, there are also ways that women have been considered the objects of exchange in markets, and the atonement suggests directions of understanding a redemption away from patriarchy that I did not examine. Lastly, the economics of the environment deserves further discussion, because every person is indebted to the network of the natural world, and not learning to live cooperatively within it remains a stumbling block that may threaten our entire planet.

Institutions matter. The hostility toward institutions reveals only that the church has lacked clarity about its role, illustrating that organization is how a broken, sinful, and imperfect people can get things done. At its best, the church participates in an economy by creating disciples. The church creates individuals who have the skill of listening and the tenacity to work together. This is what prayer does, and what the Eucharist represents.

Churches thus become networks, hubs, of relationships that are not finally moderated by commerce. They count individuals with bodies, minds, and faces. Therefore, the work of a priest is to learn how to listen to people, to work with them, and to train others to do the same. The role of clergy is to be communicators, connectors, and collaborators in their community, thereby making other institutions also more effective.

I believe that the church can hope communities re-center their networks if they are intentional about raising the following questions in practice. For example:

1) Expand what is considered a resource. Money, time, labor, and networks are distinct but interrelated. For some people, time is easily quantified into financial value, but the Sabbath encourages us to think of time as prior to money. While money can help us discipline the use of time, it is often in wasted time where we may experience God. Identifying and analyzing local resources should be a regular habit in congregations, and not an incidental practice.

   While I have not discussed the need for meaningful work, congregations also harness the opportunity for offering shared projects that can make individuals and communities feel proud. Congregations routinely may gather people to paint, build, and garden together. They may also use this economy to teach technical skills to one another and do so for less expense.

   Congregations can also be networks that direct people to smaller, competent businesses. Individuals who work in the market by having shops and offering products may share with each other special deals or at least an assurance of honesty and trust. Congregations become stronger when they build their networks, their relationships with other institutions.

2) Churches operate in a variety of scales. They may purchase from Amazon, the local used bookstore, or even operate a Sunday Morning bookstore itself. For large events, a church may use a caterer, and for smaller events be a potluck. It may take the choir out on the church credit card to create a stronger commitment. But churches could benefit by being intentional about understanding what scale they are operating in and what it will take to strengthen bonds between them and the community. Sometimes saving money is more important; sometimes time is money. But administrative intentionality can help harness resources and direct them to be more effective. What makes a church more powerful is when it can connect its local network to other local networks, and become a hub of relationships in a community.
3) The church has the role of forming persons to deepen their emotional capacities through prayer and action. By developing these skills, individuals become better at collaborating and committing, managing loss, fostering stability, and having the confidence to initiate projects. A good formation program will ground people who can discern between wants and needs, and reorient the tendency to compare so that they can be more immediately generous.
4) Develop personal practices that can help reorient a relationship with money and deepen connections with other networks. This can include, but is not limited to:
    1. A regular habit of prayer, (e.g. the Daily Office or a gratitude journal)
    2. Creating a personal rule about TV and Social Media
    3. Eschewing convenience for collaboration
    4. Having at least one creative outlet that requires regular practice
    5. Examining one's own personal debt
    6. Creating a personal rule about reflection and participation in the market
5) Remember these principles:
    1. The purpose of money is to move. Exchanging and giving is redemptive.
    2. It is possible to have enough. Satisfaction in having things is a blessing.
    3. Everyone is formed by someone else and their environment.

4. Jesus forms us, and this takes attention and practice.
5. Competent governance is a gift and skill that is worth recognizing.
6. Wants and needs remain distinct. (see #2)

Rivalry is an expense in all sorts of institutions. It creates dissatisfaction in the economy. It is why institutions of various kinds are built. Because individuals compare, seek the attention of others, and want to be connected with friends and neighbors, tensions rise and fall depending on the habits, rituals, and practices that direct them. These are costs, and therefore they are economic.

Economics is a serious spiritual matter of ultimate concern, not a secondary one. Markets matter, as they have arisen out of the ways communities have sought to manage sorts of tension and dissatisfaction in the world. Jesus arose as a response to reveal that the roots of dissatisfaction arise from a misplaced understanding of how God moves. Instead, followers of Christ have a new model in Christ, who makes it possible to live in the world without being seduced by the dissatisfaction of others.

This is not a plea toward a utopian vision of the future, or a necessarily belief that this will hasten the coming of the kingdom. But in a world where institutions matter, where sin remains a daily reality of our very human condition, the capacity to live in the world well as a response to Jesus remains possible. I believe that the church can recognize its strengths and live into them. Our inheritance is real. It has already changed the world. It can continue to hold in tension between the needs of the world as it is and the possibility of what it can be by equipping its disciples to build concrete relationships, using its immense resources to strengthen networks of friendships across all different sectors of the deeply interconnected world it inhabits.

By affirming that the risen Lord has saved us, as the Body of Christ, can we show the world what it means to be alive.

Notes

1. Martin Thornton, *The Function of Theology* (New York: Seabury, 1968), 26.
2. Mark Taylor, *Confidence Games: Money and Markets in a World without Redemption* (Chicago: University of Chicago, 2008), 329.
3. René Girard, *Things Hidden Since the Foundation of the World* (London: Continuum, 2003), 236.
4. Martin Thornton, *Prayer* (Cowley: Cambridge, 1988), 50.
5. Thornton, 60–61.

6. Thorton, 62.
7. Stephen Barton, "Money Matters," in *Engaging Economics*, Bruce Longenecker and K. D. Liebengood (Grand Rapids: Eerdmans, 2009), 59.
8. Episcopal Church, *The Book of Common Prayer and Administration of the Sacraments and Other Rites and Ceremonies of the Church; Together with the Psalter or Psalms of David According to the Use of the Episcopal Church* (New York: Seabury Press, 1979), 351.
9. Robert and Edward Skidelsky, *How Much Is Enough: Money and the Good Life* (New York: Other Press, 2012), 93.
10. Skidelsky, *How Much is Enough? Money and the Good Life*, 69.
11. Dan Ariely, *The Honest Truth About Dishonesty* (New York: Harper Collins, 2013), 249–50. He shows in *The Hidden Truth about Dishonesty* the temptations of dishonesty. Individuals justify cheating, especially when there are no consequences. He suggests, however, that reminders and rituals like confession can help counteract dishonesty by helping recollect our duties to one another. The habits of confession replace and disrupt our inclination to fudge. Confession resets inclinations.
12. Skidelsky, *How Much is Enough? Money and the Good Life.*
13. David Harvey, *The Enigma of Capital and the Crises of Capitalism* (New York: Oxford, 2010), 41.
14. Skidelsky, 150.
15. Gretchen Rubin, *The Happiness Project* (New York: Harper Collins USA, 2016), 190.
16. William Temple, *Christianity and Social Order* (Reading: Shepheard-Walwyn, 1987), 82.
17. Temple, 83.
18. DL Munby, *God and the Rich Society* (London: Oxford, 1961), 56.
19. Munby, 161.
20. Munby, 167.
21. Munby, 168.
22. Munby, 174.
23. Kate Pickett and Richard Wilkinson, *The Spirit Level: Why Greater Equality Makes Societies Stronger* (New York: Bloomsbury, 2011), 255–263.
24. Girard, *Things Hidden*, 286–7.
25. Harvey Cox, *The Market as God* (Cambridge: Harvard, 2016), 98.
26. Elizabeth L Hinson-Hasty, *The Problem of Wealth: A Christian Response to a Culture of Affluence* (Markyknoll, New York: Orbis, 2017), 160.
27. Robert Lane, *The Loss of Happiness in Market Democracies* (New Haven: Yale, 2000), 82–87.
28. Richard Layard, *Happiness: Lessons from a New Science* (London: Penguin, 2011), 103–4.
29. Kathryn Tanner, *Economy of Grace* (Minneapolis: Augsburg, 2005), 24.
30. Skidelsky, HME, 93.
31. Skidelsky, HME, 138.

32. Skidelsky, HME, 185.
33. Robert Skidelsky, *Keynes: The Return of the Master* (New York: Public Affairs, 2009), 133.
34. Elinor Olstrom, *Understanding Institutional Diversity* (Princeton: Princeton, 2005), 254.
35. Skidelsky, HME, 180.
36. Finn, MEM, 138–139.
37. Albert O. Hirschmann, *The Passions and the Interests, Political Arguments for Capitalism Before its Triumph* (Princeton: Princeton, 1977), 124.
38. Hirschmann, 125.
39. Arthur F. Bentley, *The Process of Government* (Cambridge: Belknap, 1967), 267–8.
40. Bentley, 269.
41. Bentley, 271.

Bibliography

Alison, James. *Broken Hearts and New Creations: Intimations of a Great Reversal.* New York: Continuum, 2010.

Alison, James. *The Joy of Being Wrong: Original Sin Through Easter Eyes.* New York: Crossroad, 1998.

Alison, James. *Undergoing God: Dispatches From the Scene of a Break-in.* New York: Continuum, 2006.

Agamben, Giorgio. *The Kingdom and the Glory: For a Theological Genealogy of Economy and Government.* Trans. by Lorenzo Chiesa. Stanford: Stanford, 2011.

Anderson, Gary. *Charity: The Place of the Poor in the Biblical Tradition.* New Haven: Yale, 2013.

———. *Sin: A History.* New Haven: Yale, 2009.

Ariely, Daniel. *The Honest Truth About Dishonesty.* New York: Harper Collins, 2013.

Atwood, Margaret. *Payback: Debt and the Shadow Side of Wealth.* Toronto: Anansi, 2008.

Avila, Charles. *Ownership: Early Christian Teaching.* Eugene Or: Wipf and Stock, 1983.

Baker, David. *Tight Fists or Open Hands? Wealth and Poverty in Old Testament Law.* Grand Rapids: Eerdmans, 2009.

Baptist, Edward E. *The Half Has Never Been Told: Slavery and the Making of American Capitalism.* New York: Basic, 2016.

Bell, Daniel M. *The Economy of Desire: Christianity and Capitalism in a Postmodern World.* Grand Rapids: Baker, 2012.

Bentley, Arthur F. *The Process of Government.* Cambridge: Belknap, 1967.

Berry, Wendell. *What Matters? Economics for a Renewed Commonwealth.* Berkeley: Counterpoint, 2010.

Bauman, Yoram and Grady Klein. *The Cartoon Introduction to Economics, Vol 1*. New York: Hill & Wang, 2010.

———. *The Cartoon Introduction to Economics, Vol 2*. New York: Hill & Wang, 2012.

Benedict XVI. *Caritatis in Veritate*. Vatican City: Vatican Website, 2009.

Betz, Hans Dieter. *2 Corinthians 8 and 9: A Commentary on Two Administrative Letters of the Apostle Paul.* Philadelphia: Fortress, 1985.

Blank, Rebecca. *Do Justice: Linking Faith and Economic Life.* Cleveland: United Church Press, 1992.

Boer, Roland. *The Sacred Economy of Ancient Israel.* Louisville: John Knox, 2015.

Brown, Peter. *Through the Eye of a Needle: Wealth, the fall of Rome, and the Making of Christianity in the West, 350–550 AD*. Princeton: Princeton, 2012.

Carter, John and Michael Irons. "Are Economists Different, and If So, Why?" *Journal of Economic Perspectives*, 5 (Spring, 1991) 171–177.

Cavanaugh, William T. *Being Consumed: Economics and Christian Desire*. Grand Rapids: Eerdmans, 2008.

Chang, Ha-Joon. *Bad Samaritans: The Myth of Free Trade and The Secret History of Capitalism*. New York: Bloomsbury, 2008.

Cialdini, Robert. *Influence: The Psychology of Persuasion*. New York: Harper Collins, 2007.

Claassens, L. Juliana M. *The God Who Provides: Biblical Images of the God Who Feeds*. Nashville: Abingdon, 2004.

Coase, R. H. *The Firm, the Market, and the Law*. Chicago: University of Chicago, 1988.

Cobb, John. *Sustaining the Common Good.* Cleveland: Pilgrim, 1994.

Cox, Harvey. *The Market as God.* Cambridge: Harvard, 2016.

Crosby, Michael. *House of Disciples: Church, Economics and Justice in Matthew*. Maryknoll: Orbis, 1988.

Dietze, Pia and Eric. D. Knowles. "Social Class and the Motivational Relevance of Other Human Beings." *Psychological Science* 27, no. 11 (Oct, 2016): 1517–1527. https://doi.org/10.1177/0956797616667721

Dominguez, Joe and Vicki Robin. *Your Money or Your Life*. New York: Penguin, 2008.

Dumouchel, Paul. *The Ambivalence of Scarcity and Other Essays*. East Lansing: MSU, 2014.

Dupuy, Jean-Pierre. *Economy and the Future: A Crisis of Faith*. Trans. by M. B Debevoise. East Lansing: MSU, 2014.

Dupuy, Jean-Pierre. *The Mark of the Sacred.* Trans. by M. B Debevoise. Stanford: Stanford, 2013.

Durham, John, *Word Biblical Commentary, Vol 3: Exodus*. Waco: Word Books, 1987.

Episcopal Church. *The Book of Common Prayer and Administration of the Sacraments and Other Rites and Ceremonies of the Church; Together with the Psalter or Psalms of David According to the Use of the Episcopal Church*. New York: Seabury Press, 1979.

Finn, Daniel K. *Christian Economic Ethics: History and Implications.* Minneapolis: Fortress, 2013.

———. *Distant Markets, Distant Harms: Economic Complicity and Christian Ethics*. New York: Oxford, 2014.

———. *The Moral Ecology of Markets: Assessing Claims about Markets and Justice.* New York: Cambridge, 2006.

Fischer, John Martin. *The Metaphysics of Free Will.* Cambridge, MA: Blackwell, 1997.

Francis. *Encyclical letter Laudato si' of the Holy Father Francis.* 1st ed. Vatican City: Vatican Web Site, 2015.

Frank, Robert H. *The Darwin Economy: Liberty, Competition, and the Common Good.* Princeton: Princeton, 2012.

Frank, Robert. *The Economic Naturalist's Field Guide: Common Sense Principles for Troubled Times.* New York: Basic Books, 2009.

———. *Luxury Fever: Weighting the Cost of Excess.* Princeton: Princeton, 2010.

Frank, Robert and Philip Cook. *The Winner-Take-All Society.* New York: Free Press, 1995.

Friedman, Benjamin. *The Moral Consequences of Economic Growth.* New York: Vintage, 2005.

Girard, René. *I See Satan Fall Like Lightning.* Maryknoll: Orbis, 2004.

Girard, René. *The One by Whom Scandal Comes.* East Lansing: MSU, 2014.

Girard, René, J-M. Oughourlian, G. Lefort, S. Bann, and M. L Metteer. *Things Hidden Since the Foundation of the World.* London: Continuum, 2003.

Glass, Z. "Land, Slave Labor and Law: Engaging Ancient Israel's Economy," *Journal for the Study of the Old Testament* 91 (2000):27–39.

Gnus, Rober Karl. *You Shall Not Steal: Community and Property in the Biblical Tradition.* Maryknoll: Orbis, 1982.

Gorringe, Timothy. *Capital and the Kingdom: Theological Ethics and Economic Order.* Maryknoll: Orbis, 1994.

Graeber, David. *Debt.* New York: Melville, 2011.

Greenspan, Alan. "Never Saw it Coming," *Foreign Affairs* (Nov/Dec 2013).

Gustafson, James. *Can Ethics Be Christian.* Chicago: University of Chicago, 1973.

Haan, Roelf. *The Economics of Honor: Biblica Reflections on Money and Property.* Grand Rapids: Eerdmans, 2009.

Hart, David Bentley. *The New Testament: A Translation.* New Haven: Yale, 2017.

Harvey, David. *The Condition of Postmodernity.* Malden: Blackwell, 1990.

———. *The Enigma of Capital and the Crises of Capitalism.* New York: Oxford, 2010.

Heim, S. Mark. *Saved from Sacrifice: A Theology of the Cross.* Grand Rapids: Eerdmans, 2006.

Hengel, Martin. *Property and Riches in the Early Church.* Philadelphia: Fortress, 1974.

Heyne, Paul. *The Economic Way of Thinking, Eighth Edition.* Upper Saddle River: Prentice Hall, 1997.

Heyne, Paul T. *Are Economists Basically Immoral?: And Other Essays on Economics, Ethics, and Religion*, ed Geoffrey Brennan and A.M.C. Waterman. Carmel, In: Liberty Fund, 2008.

Hinson-Hasty, Elizabeth. *The Problem of Wealth. A Christian Response to a Culture of Affluence.* Maryknoll: Orbis, 2017.

Hirschmann, Albert O. *Shifting Involvements: Private Interest and Public Action.* Princeton: Princeton, 1982.

Hirschmann, Albert O. *The Essential Hirschman*, ed. Jeremy Adelman. Princeton: Princeton, 2015.

Hirschmann, Albert O. *The Passions and the Interests: Political Arguments for Capitalism Before Its Triumph.* Princeton: Princeton, 1977.

Holmes, Stephen and Cass R. Sunstein. *The Cost of Rights: Why Liberty Depends on Taxes.* New York: W.W. Norton, 2000.

Horsley, Richard A. *Covenant Economics: A Biblical Vision of Justice for All.* Louisville: Westminister John Knox, 2009.

Johnson, Luke Timothy. *Sharing Possessions: What Faith Demands*. Grand Rapids: Eerdsmans, 1981.

Kahneman, Daniel, Jack Knetsch, and Richard Thaler. "Fairness and the Assumptions of Economics," *Journal of Business* 59 (1986): S286–S300.

Kanter, Rosabeth Moss. *Commitment and Community.* Cambridge: Harvard, 1972.

Kasser, Tim. *The High Price of Materialism*. Cambridge: MIT, 2002.

Kirwan, Michael. *Girard and Theology*. London: T&T Clarke, 2009.

Lane, Robert E. *The Loss of Happiness in Market Democracies*. New Haven: Yale, 2000.

Layard, Richard. *Happiness: Lessons from a New Science*. London: Penguin, 2011.

Leo XIII. *Rerum Novarum. (May 15, 1891)*. Vatican City: Vatican Website, 2018.

Leshem, Dotan. *The Origins of Neoliberalism: Modeling the Economy From Jesus to Foucault*. New York: Columbia, 2016.

Levine, Amy-Jill. *Short Stories by Jesus*. New York: HarperOne, 2014.

Lindblom, Charles. *Politics and Markets: The World's Political-Economic System*. New York: Basic, 1977.

Long, D. Stephen. *Divine Economy: Theology and the Market.* New York: Routledge, 2003.

Longenecker, Bruce and Kelly D. Liebengood, eds. *Engaging Economics*. Grand Rapids: Eerdmans, 2009.

Longenecker, Bruce. *Remember the Poor: Paul, Poverty and the Greco-Roman World.* Grand Rapids: Eerdmans, 2010.

Mansbridge, Jane J. *Beyond Self-Interest*. Chicago: University of Chicago Press, 1990.

Marwell, Gerald and Ruth Ames. "Economists Free Ride, Does Anyone Else?" *Journal of Public Economics* 15 (1981): 295–310.

McKibben, Bill. *Deep Economy: The Wealth of Communities and the Durable Future*. New York: Henry Holt, 2007.

McRorie, Christina. "The Emptiness of Modern Economics: Why the Dismal Science Needs a Richer Moral Anthropology." *Hedgehog Review* 16, no. 3 (Fall 2014) 121–129.

Meeks, M. Douglas. *God the Economist: The Doctrine of God and Political Economy*. Minneapolis: Fortress Pr., 1991.

Morris, Ian, and Joseph Gilbert Manning. *The Ancient Economy: Evidence and Models*. Stanford: Stanford University Press, 2007.

Moxnes, Halvor. *The Economy of the Kingdom: Social Conflict and Economic Relations in Luke's Gospel.* Philadelphia: Fortress, 1988.

Munby, D. L. *God and the Rich Society.* London: Oxford, 1961.

Novak, Michael. *The Catholic Ethic and the Spirit of Capitalism.* New York: Free Press, 1993.

———. *The Spirit of Democratic Capitalism*. New York: Simon and Schuster, 1982.

———. *Toward a Theology of the Corporation*. Washington, DC: American Enterprise Institute, 1983.

Ostrom, Elinor. *Governing the Commons: The Evolution of Institutions for Collective Action*. New York: Cambridge, 2011.

Ostrom, Elinor. *Understanding Institutional Diversity.* Princeton: Princeton, 2005.

Oughourlian, Jean-Michel. *The Genesis of Desire.* Trans. by Eugene Webb. East Lansing: MSU, 2010.

The Oxford Handbook of Christianity and Economics, ed. Paul Oslington. New York: Oxford, 2014.

Palaver, Wolfgang. *René Girard's Mimetic Theory.* Translated by Gabriel Borrud. East Lansing: MSU, 2015.

Pickett, Kate and Richard Wilkinson. *The Spirit Level: Why Greater Equality Makes Societies Stronger.* New York: Bloomsbury, 2011.

Piketty, Thomas. *Capital in the Twenty-First Century.* Cambridge: Belknap, 2014.

Polanyi, Karl, Conrad M. Arensberg, and Harry W. Pearson. *Trade and Market in the Early Empires: Economies in History and Theory.* Glencoe, IL: Free Press, 1957.

Preston, Ronald. *Religion and the Ambiguities of Capitalism.* Cleveland: Pilgrim, 1993.

———. *Religion and the Persistence of Capitalism.* London: SCM, 1979.

Rubin, Gretchen. *The Happiness Project.* New York: Harper Collins USA, 2016.

Sandel, Michael. *What Money Can't Buy: The Moral Limits of Markets.* New York: Farrar, Strauss and Giroux, 2012.

Schor, Juliet B. *The Overworked American: The Unexpected Decline of Leisure.* New York: Basic Books, 1992.

Schweiker, William and Charles Mathewes. *Having: Property and Possession in Religious and Social Life.* Grand Rapids: Eerdmans, 2004.

Seaborn, Richard. *Money and the Early Greek Mind: Homer, Philosophy, Tragedy.* New York: Cambridge, 2004.

Skidelsky, Robert. *Keynes: The Return of the Master.* New York: Public Affairs, 2009.

Skidelsky, Robert and Edward Skidelsky. *How Much Is Enough: Money and the Good Life.* New York: Other Press, 2012.

Singh, Devin. *Divine Currency: The Theological Power of Money in the West.* Stanford: Stanford, 2018.

Smith, Adam. *The Theory of Moral Sentiments*, ed. Knud Haakonssen. New York: Cambridge University Press, 2002.

———. *The Wealth of Nations*, ed. Edwin Cannan. New York: Modern Library, 2000.

Stackhouse, Max. *Public Theology and Political Economy.* Grand Rapids: Eerdmans, 1987.

Stiglitz, Joseph E. *The Great Divide: Unequal Societies and What We Can Do About Them.* New York: Norton, 2015.

———. *The Price of Inequality: How Today's Divided Society Endangers Our Future.* New York: Norton, 2015.

Tanner, Kathryn. *Economy of Grace.* Minneapolis: Augsburg, 2005.

Temple, William. *Christianity and Social Order.* Reading: Shepheard-Walwyn, 1987.

———. *Prayer.* Cowley: Cambridge, 1988.

Thornton, Martin. *The Function of Theology.* New York: Seabury, 1968.

Taylor, Mark C. *After God.* Chicago: University of Chicago, 2007.

———. *Confidence Games: Money and Markets in a World without Redemption.* Chicago: University of Chicago, 2008.

———. *The Moment of Complexity: Emerging Network Culture.* Chicago: University of Chicago, 2001.

———. *Speed Limits: Where Time Went and Why We Have So Little Left.* New Haven: Yale, 2014.

Tawney, R. H. *Religion and the Rise of Capitalism*. Brooklyn: Verso, 2015.
Thaler, Richard. *Misbehaving: The Making of Behavioral Economics*. New York: Norton, 2015.
Thaler, Richard. H. and Cass R. Sunstein. *Nudge: Improving Decisions About Health, Wealth, And Happiness*. New Haven: Yale, 2008.
Turak, August. *Business Secrets of the Trappist Monks*. New York: Columbia Business, 2013.
Varnum, M. E. W., C. Blais, R. S. Hampton, Gene A. Brewer, "Social Class Affects Neural Empathic Responses," *Cult. Brain* 3, no. 122 (2015), https://doi.org/10.1007/s40167-015-0031-2.
Veblen, Thorstein. *The Theory of the Leisure Class*. New York: Oxford, 2009.
Wheeler, Sondra Ely. *Wealth as Peril and Obligation: The New Testament on Possessions*. Grand Rapids: Eerdmans, 1995.
Williamson, Oliver E. *The Economic Institutions of Capitalism*. New York: Free Press, 1985.
———. *The Mechanism of Governance*. New York: Oxford, 1996.
Yuran, Noam. *What Money Wants*. Stanford: Stanford, 2014.
Wright, Christopher J. H. *God's People in God's Land: Family Land and Property in the Old Testament*. Grand Rapids: Eerdmans, 1990.

Index

A

administration, virtuous
mimetic behavior reduced and, 180
reading cultivates empathy, 179–180
rivalry diminished by, 179
After God (Taylor), 111
almsgiving
capitalism and, 51
generosity and, 43–45, 50
Amos, wealth creation struggle and, 23
ancient economy vs. modern markets, 51
Anderson, Gary
on giving money to the poor (Daniel), 43
on mechanics of debt and sin, 34
Sin: A History, 12–13
Anglicanism, 158–159, 177
Animal Spirits (Keynes), 86
apostles, modeling Jesus and, 147
Arrow, Kenneth, on trustworthiness, 69
ascetic theology, 154
atonement, impact of
consequences of, 146
impartial spectator and, 146
non-violent, 147
shifting desires and, 146
atonement, prosperity and
being saved means knowing types of desire worth having, 151
church does not shame for prosperity or ambition, 150
church's role and, 149
emotional challenges and, 149–150
limits of prosperous, 149
Mimetic Theory and, 150
parable of rich man and Lazarus, 150
scripture warns against wealth, 148–149
wealthy who are saved become generous, 150–151

B

baptism, new pattern of life and, 160–163
Being Consumed: Economics and Christian Desire (Cavanaugh), Cavanaugh, William, 113
Bell, Daniel
  critique of desire by, 108–109
  theologian reflecting on economics, 100
Benedictine economics
  creativity in congregations, 175
  eschewing personal financial acquisitiveness, 175–176
  managing rivalry, 175
  modeling skills and, 174
  monastic tradition and, 176
  work of reflection and action, 175
Bentley, Arthur F., on economy of church, 190
Betz, Hans Deiter, on language of debt, 33–34
bishop, role of, 178
Body of Christ, The, defined, 3
Boer, Roland
  on coinage, 18–19
  Sacred Economy of Ancient Israel, The, 9–11
bounded rationality (insufficient knowledge), 79–80
  TCE and, 66
Brown, Peter
  on Christian giving, 41–42, 46
  on generosity, 43
Buchanan, James, value-free economics and, 84

C

Capital (Piketty), 88
Capital and the Kingdom (Gorringe), 102
capitalism. *See also* Tanner, Kathryn
  Christianity directs desire differently, 108–109
  Gorringe on, 103–104
  never having enough and, 163
Catholic social teaching, 111–113
  building non-financial networks of relationships, 148
  common good and the Sabbath, 112–113
  market as subordinate to other values, 111–112
  mechanics of desire and, 113
  prior ethic required, 112
Cavanaugh, William, *Being Consumed: Economics and Christian Desire*, 113
Chardin, Teilhard de, Catholic theologian, 110
Christian options
  discipleship and stronger networks, 147–148
  modeling Jesus and, 147
  salvation alters relationships, 146–147
Christianity, market distinct from, 109
Christianity and economics, Jesus and, 3–4
Christ's resurrection, significance of, 139–140
church, tasks of, 166
  commitment to economic individualism, 169
  roles of the church, 168
  value of shared life and, 169
  work of a cleric and, 168
church and salvation in a commercial world, 153–194
  overview, 4–5, 153–158
  Benedictine economics, 174–176
  building networks, 172–174
  church tasks, 166
  churches as businesses, 184–85
  creating disciples: prayer, Eucharist, and Apostolate, 159
  creating effective markets, 182

emotional competence incentivized, 170–171
enhancing local economies, 171–172
enough is enough, 171
episcopacy, order, and governance, 176–178
future possibilities, 191–194
good governance and, 180–181
governance without perfection, 178
governing people, 185–186
lay expertise in markets, 169–170
managing rivalry, 158
prayer, 159–160
property, endowments, and pension fund, 186–191
reality acknowledged, 166–167
Sabbath economics, 163–166
sacramental economics: baptism and Eucharist, 160–163
shared meals and, 182–183
virtuous administration, 179–180
wealth and relationships, 167–169

churches
collaboration over time, 180
counting, 180
discipleship and, 181
emotional regulation and, 180
funding emotional competence and, 181
good governance and, 180
governing skills required, 177
leadership and, 181
local economies for service and mission, 171–174
managing rivalry and, 177
motivations of disciples for satisfaction, 93–94
as networks, 171
relationship building and, 92
religious institutions suspect, 176
rivalry redirected, not eliminated, 180–181
sports events and, 181
teaching people when they have had enough, 171–172
twelve-step groups and, 171

churches, acquisitive desires and, 166–167

churches as firms, 69–71
non-monetary exchanges and, 71
rivalry and, 71
TCE and, 70–71
transaction costs and, 70

churches: creating effective markets internally
alternative vice and, 191
building disciples as main activity, 190
as businesses, 183–184
containing its own economy, 190
cooperatives and, 184–185
corruption and, 189
experience of church contributes, 190
forming competent governors, 187–188
governing people, 185–186
managing wealth and, 186–191
as phenomena of government, 190
prioritization of market forces, 188–189
property management and, 186–187
shared meals, 182–183
training people to be trustworthy as role, 191
worker and owner not always enemies, 190

Coase, R.H., on firms, 64–65

Communion, social-symbolic practice, 162

Confidence Games (Taylor), 110–111

counting, 57–58
problems with, 81
why individuals count, 84

covetousness, 26–27

Cox, Harvey, 109–110
on acquisitiveness, 110
on market as religious faith, 109
market distinct from Christianity, 109
on market's impact, 109–110

D

debt, 33–34, 165
  See also Jesus: envy, debt, and empire
Decalogue, 26
decision-making
  costs of, 67
  Keynes and, 86–87
  overconfidence and, 79–80
  unpredictability and, 77–78
Dempsey, Bernard
  conflict rejected by, 102
  Functional Economy and, 101
desire
  to accumulate and, 27
  for approval, 86
  created by advertising, 113
  at heart of problem, 51
  incentives and, 78
  Long on crucial problem of, 102
  mechanics of, 85
  problem of, 108–109
  as root of envy, 26
  self-interest and, 78
  See also Bell, Daniel
desire, learning to, 119–137
  overview, 4, 119–120
  economics and Mimetic Theory, 130
  imitation and, 122–123
  individual freedom and Mimetic Theory and, 127–130
  individualism and mimetic theory, 126–127
  market's impact on social solidarity, 131–137
  Mimetic Theory and, 120–121
  models and, 121
  rivalry and, 123–125
desires
  acquisition of more and conflicting, 115
  church and the good life, 115
  Girard, on, 122
  imitation and, 122
  origins of, 123
  scarcity and, 124
  spiritual impact revealed by Jesus responding to, 115
disappointment, causes of, 80–81
discipleship, as economic discipline, 5
Dumochel, Paul, 134
Dupuy, Jean-Pierre
  on indifference toward human life, 83
  on perpetual growth of markets, 83
  on religion-economy link, 99
  on selfishness, 135

E

economic consequences of being saved, 140–144
  atonement and, 144
  Christian approach to economics and, 140
  Christ's death and resurrection are decisive, 141
  church must redirect rivalry, 142
  cross as end to suffering, 143
  desire to be seen and, 144
  eschewing rivalry as a model and, 144
  Jesus as model, 143–144
  Jesus does not guarantee salvation, 143
  markets presumed to be mutually beneficial, 140
  markets redirect energy of desire away from sacrifice, 143
  reorienting rivalry and, 141–142
  salvation includes modeling, 144
  sin rooted in mimetic rivalry and, 141
  techniques offered by Jesus for cultivating nonrivalous self, 142
  Trinity and, 140–141
  understanding rivalry, 141
economic thinking critiqued
  conflicts of interest, 73
  coordination of strangers and, 74
  economics as value-neutral, 71–72

human interaction removed and, 73
invisible hand metaphor and, 72–73
market as "serviceable mechanism," 74
money and power, 72
political roots of allocating sources, 73–74
scarcity and desire, 73
TCE and, 71
Economic Way of Thinking, The (Heyne), 2
economics, engaging, 55–94
overview, 4, 55–57
calculator, or *homo economicus*, 76
comparing ourselves to others, 78–79
critiques of economic thinking, 71–74
disappointment and, 80–81
envy and, 84–85, 87–88
governance and, 68–69
incompleteness of humanity model and, 81–82
market and firms, 64–65
market critiques and, 82–84
market problems and, 88–91
markets as a transaction cost, 65–68
networks and governance, 92–94
risk, loss aversion, and bounded rationality, 79–80
self-interest defined, 74–75
Smith, Adam, 85–86
true needs addressed, 91–92
understanding economics and morality, 57–59, 94n2
See also churches as firms; Heyne, Paul; markets defined
economics and Mimetic Theory, desire, learning to, 130
economists
assumptions used by, 57–58
counting matters, 57–58
economy, agricultural, 12
Economy of Grace (Tanner), 106
emotional challenges, difficulty of, 148
endowment
defined, 79, 88
element of envy, 87–88
envy
corruption and, 27
economics and, 84
elements of, 26–27, 87–88
intensified by wealth, 28
media and, 88
mitigating through cultural conditioning, 93
episcopacy
benefit of, 177
as imperfect system, 179
equality in relationships, Wilkinson, Richard on, 90
Eucharist
confession and, 163
distributed apart from merit, 161–162
expression of God's economy, 112–113
frees from our debts, 42
symbol of revolutionary corporation of church, 103

F

Fable of the Bees (Mandeville), 58
financial crash of 2008, 1, 77
Finn, Daniel
on contemporary economists, 82
on four elements of economics, 188
on harms caused to others require redress, 113–114
on limits on "free" markets, 64
on markets, 59
Moral Ecology of Markets, The, 84
on relationship of wealth to the community, 22
on self-interest as a type of egoism, 75
on trust and social systems, 90
Fischer, John Martin, *Metaphysics of Free Will, The*, 127
Frank, Robert
on imbalance in consumption patterns, 89
Luxury Fever, 89

on mitigating envy through cultural conditioning, 93
on wealth as "good thing," 92
Friedman, Ben, on results of improvement in growth, 91
Friedman, Milton, value-free economics and, 84
Function of Theology, The (Thornton), 154
Functional Economy, Dempsey and, 101
future possibilities
affirmation of Body of Christ demonstrates being alive, 194
church operates in a variety of scales, 193
communities of feminism and color not addressed, 191–192
creating disciples and, 192
deepening emotional capacities of disciples, 193
not a plea toward utopian vision, 194
principles to remember, 193–194
re-centering networks and, 192–193
reorienting relationship with money, 193
rivalry as expense in every institution, 194
threefold rule of the church, 191

G

generosity, economy of, 42–47
almsgiving and, 43–45, 50
Eucharist and, 42
giving as duty of all Christians, 45, 46–47
"individualism" and, 47
property ownership and, 45–46, 50
redemption and, 43, 49
sharing of wealth and, 49
See also Anderson, Gary; Brown, Peter; Hengel, Martin; Johnson, Luke T.
Girard, René
on desire, 122
on the intensity of mimetic behavior, 129
Mimetic Theory and, 120
on rivalry and prestige, 135
Things Hidden Since the Foundation of the World., 120–122
golden calf image, 22
Gorringe, Timothy
Capital and the Kingdom, 102
critique of views by author, 104
proposals of, 103–104
rejection of market economics in church teachings, 102–103
theologian reflecting on economics, 100
governance
and behavior, 66
as cost of working together, 68
quality of, 68–69
Governing the Commons (Ostrom), 92–93
grace, mechanics of, 179
grace and God's generosity, 106–108
Graeber, David
on debt, 13
on money as symbol of life-debt, 19
Greenspan, Alan, on financial crash of 2008, 77

H

haggling, 61, 73
happiness, 90
Hart, David Bentley, on condemnation of wealth, 41
Harvey, David
on expansion of market network through capital, 62
on markets, 59
on money and power, 72
Hayek, Friedrich, value-free economics and, 84
Heim, S. Mark
on cross seeking end to suffering, 143
on impact of resurrection, 142
Hengel, Martin
on generosity, 45
harsh critique by Gorringe, 103

Heyne, Paul
Economic Way of Thinking, The (Heyne), 2
on markets, 59, 60
on money as common denominator in market, 63
on purposive action in economics, 57
on scarcity as sacrifice, 63
on storytelling, 1
Hirschman, A.O.
on disappointment, 80
on economics and self-interest, 78
on money as threat to social order, 72
Hirschmann, Albert O., on self-interest as virtue, 75
homo economicus, 57, 76, 79
Hosea, wealth creation struggle and, 22–23
how Jesus saves, 139–151
overview, 4, 139–140
atonement and prosperity, 148–151
atonement impact and, 146
economic consequences of being saved, 140–144
how sin gets in the way, 145
options for Christians, 146–148

I

idolatry
community and, 20–22
golden calf image and, 22
prohibitions against, 20–21
tension with true worship, 21–22
imitation
desire formed by, 122–123
models and, 122–123
impartial spectator, 146
incarnation, doctrine of the, 30
invisible hand metaphor, 72–73, 85–86, 88, 110
Isaiah, 23–24
Israel, ancient, networks in, 9

J

Jeremiah, temple sermon and, 23
Jesus, money and, 24–26
Jesus and abundance, 35–37
Jesus counts, 34–35
Jesus critiques the master to the household, 34
Jesus: envy, debt, and empire, 32–37
abundance and market economy, 35–36
on abundance parable ("lilies of the field), 34–35
abundance shown by anointing, 36–37
competition between the disciples (Mk 10:35–44), 32
counting what cannot be measured by money, 35, 50–51
economy of abundance and, 36
envy and, 50–51
forgiveness of debts, 33–34, 49
Lazarus's story, 32
master-to-household relationship and, 34
parable of guests, 32
parables highlight impact of monetary market-based networks, 37
parables on loss and gain, 34–35
power of envy diminished, 32
See also Anderson, Gary; Betz, Hans Deiter; Levine, Amy Jill
Jesus exhorts the forgiveness of deb*ts* (Matthew 6:12), 33–34
Jesus saves, 148–151
Anglicanism and, 158–159, 177
author's congregation and, 153–154
being saved from mimetic activity toward idolatry, 157–158
counterarguments and, 157
governing and, 155
Jesus as model, 155–156, 162
making choices and, 154–155
power of desire exposed, 140
rearranging economic choices and, 139
reframing desire and, 156

rejection of rivalry and, 153
sin rooted in mimetic rivalry and, 141–142
as source of liberation, 139
transformation of life, 141
Jezebel, 27–28
Johnson, Luke T.
on generosity, 45
ill-gotten wealth and, 27
on possessions, 30
Johnson, Luke Timothy
harsh critique by Gorringe, 103
on the idolatrous impulse, 144
Jubilee years
canceling of economic debts and, 13, 14
redemption and, 43
the Sabbath and, 47–48

K

Keynes, John Maynard
Animal Spirits, 86
decision-making and, 77, 86
on love of money, 176
King Ahab and Naboth (1 Kings 21), 27–28
kinship, umbrella of, 10–11

L

Lane, Richard, on church as shield from social threats of market, 92
Laudato Si, 112
Layard, Richard
on benefits of cooperation, 93
on happiness, 90
Lazarus's story, 150
learning to desire. *See* desire, learning to
Levine, Amy Jill
on abundance parable ("lilies of the field), 36
on experiencing loss, 34–35
on mustard seed parable, 36
Long, David
on restoring meaning to market, 100–102
theologian reflecting on economics, 100
theology of radical orthodoxy and, 102
Longenecker, Bruce
on Paul's notion of "love," 39
Remembering the Poor, 39
loss aversion principle
defined, 79
power of, 92
Thaler on, 88
luxuries, scarcity generates desire, 150
Luxury Fever (Frank), 89

M

Malthus, Thomas, 58
Mandeville, Bernard, 58
market, impact on social solidarity, 131–137
indifference and, 132, 133, 136
intensity of social bonds and, 131
Jesus exposes the costs of rivalry and, 137
Jesus offers idea of being nobody and still be loved, 135
market hides mimetic roots, 132
market liberate desires, 133
market weakens social solidarity, 133
resentment and envy arise from mimetic behavior, 134
sacrifice as original exchange between community, victim, and God, 136–137
scarcity generates desire, 134
market and other networks, 16–17
Nehemiah 5:3–7, 16
1 Samuel 8:1–22, 16, 17
market critiques
counting and, 84
liberty as primary value, 84

limitations of economics, 82–83
moral critiques of growth and, 82–83
time as ultimate scarce resource, 83
markets, networks, and institutions, 113–115
markets defined, 59–64
capital flows and, 62–63
coercive nature of, 113–114
cooperation and, 61–62
coordination and trustworthiness, 60–66
dynamic motion of capital and, 62
extra-market institutions and, 60–61
faith in economics and, 63, 69
governance and behavior, 66
haggling and, 61, 73
laws limiting freedom and, 64
market as a firm, 64–65
as networks, 59
pricing and, 62–63
scarcity as sacrifice, 63
as systems of relating, 59–60
Transaction Cost Economics (TCE) and, 66
See also Finn, Daniel; Harvey, David; Heyne, Paul; Ostrom, Elinor; Taylor, Mark
markets: lay expertise and, 169–170
materialism, 145
Meeks, W. Douglas, 99
Metaphysics of Free Will, The (Fischer), 127
Milbank, John, radical Orthodoxy of, 102
Mill, J.S., 76
mimesis, defined, 120
mimetic behavior reduced and. *See* imitation
Mimetic Theory (MT)
to boast in Christ, 129
compulsion to compare and, 150
described, 4, 120–121
economics and, 130–131
Girard, René and, 120–121
God as the model, 127
increasing freedom, 128
individual freedom and, 127–131
individualism and, 126–127
original sin and, 129–130
rituals and, 128–129
rivalry and, 123–124
modeling Jesus
apostles and, 147
Christian options and, 147
salvation and, 144
modeling skills, Benedictine economics and, 174
money
choices offered increase freedom, 114
envy, status, and, 11, 27–28
interest and, 14–15
Jesus and, 24–26
perils of, 40–42
power of, 49
in scripture, 19, 20, 28
sin and, 13, 50
understanding, 1–4, 18–19
See also Seaborn, Richard
money, perils of, 40–43
giving as duty of all Christians, 42
money not corrupting in itself, 40–41
1 Timothy 6 (text), 40
See also Brown, Peter; Hart, David Bentley
Moral Ecology of Markets, The (Finn), 84
motivations of individuals
forms of comparison and, 78
"keeping up with the Joneses" and, 78
relationship to other people and, 78–79
Munby, Denys Lawrence
on dangers of riches, 167
on an expanding economy, 89–90
on lack of educative efforts of economic concert, 169–170
on market as "serviceable mechanism," 74
on need for property rights, 29, 30

N

Naboth and King Ahab, 27–28
needs, addressing
  church networks and, 92
  economic growth and, 91
Nehemiah 5:3–7, 16
networks
  defined, 9
  economics and, 58
  governance and, 92–94
  impact of, 58
  oikonomia, 58
  religion as a, 110–111
  voluntary, 92, 93
Novak, Michael
  free-market view of, 100
  on market and power of creativity, 104–105
  views on governing and restraining desire, 105

O

Oberlin Student Cooperative Association (O.S.C.A), cooperative living and, 1–2
oikonomia, economic network, 58
on abundance and having things, 28–32
  scriptural narrative on, 28–29
  tension and, 29
1 Samuel 8:1–22, 16
opportunism, 67
O.S.C.A (Oberlin Student Cooperative Association), cooperative living and, 1–2
Ostrom, Elinor
  on creativity of imperfect people, 179
  on firms, 64
  Governing the Commons, 92–93
  on voluntary communities and shared resources, 93
  on "working rules" of institutions, 60–61
ownership, honoring
  common courtesies and, 31
  Deuteronomy on, 31–32
  private property eschewed, 50
  scripture and, 30–31

P

parables, 32, 34–35, 36, 37, 150
Paul's letter (2 Corinthians 8:7–15; 9:1–12), 39
  early Christian communities and the poor, 39
  explanation of, 38–39
  relationship between wealthy and poor, 50
  text of, 37–38
  See also Longenecker, Bruce
Pickett, Kate, on equality in relationships, 90
Piketty, Thomas
  Capital, 88
  on centralization of wealth, 88
possessions, 30
prayer
  as mini-Sabbaths, 160
  redirecting desire and rivalry, 159
property rights, 29
prophets and idols, condemnation of ill-gotten wealth by, 27

R

reading scripture, 7–53
  overview, 4, 7–9
  on abundance and having things, 28–32
  approach to economics and, 9–12
  covetousness, property, and god's law, 26–27

economy of generosity, 42–47
envy, status, and money, 27–28
idolatry and community, 20–22
interdependence and redemption, 37–39, 50
money and Jesus, 24–26
networks in ancient Israel, 9
peace and a spiritual economy, 49–51
perils of money, 40–42
prophets and idols, 22–24
Sabbath, the, 47–48
sacrifice, 20
sin and debt, 12—13
understanding money, 18–19
usury and interest, 14–15
See also Jesus and abundance; Jesus counts; Jesus critiques the master to the household; Jesus: envy, debt, and empire; Jesus exhorts the forgiveness of deb*ts* (Matthew 6:12); market and other networks
redemption, defined, 43
Regulation Theory, 9–12
money and Jesus, 10–11
See also Boer, Roland
religion and economics link
long provenance of, 99–100
theologians reflecting on economics, 100
trust and, 100
Remembering the Poor (Longenecker), 39
risk-taking, 79
rivalry
biblical relationships and, 26
defined, 123
managing, 125, 158
ubiquity of, 124
Rubin, Gretchen, on money, 166

S

Sabbath, the
the market and, 147
markets and, 12
purpose of, 47–48
Sabbath economics, 163–166
good life and, 163
happiness and, 165
how Sabbath impacts economy, 163–164
Sabbath time and, 164–165
social bonds and, 166
Sacred Economy of Ancient Israel, The (Boer), 9–10
sacrifice
changing nature of, 20
money as substitute for, 111
Sandel, Michael
on things money cannot buy, 114
the value of acting without compensation, 115
scripture, 27–28
Seaborn, Richard, 17
on money characteristics, 18
self-interest
comparison to others, 78–79
decision making and, 77
desire and, 78
economics and, 75
making rational choices and, 77–78, 79
market network and, 74–75
measuring economic, 76
moral worth and, 76
opportunism and, 67
Sermon on the Mount, 24, 33
sin
debt and, 12–13, 25, 119
economics and, 119
See also Anderson, Gary; Graeber, David
Sin: A History (Anderson), 12–13
sin gets in the way
broken relationship with God, 145
concealing the source of the desire, 145
materialism and, 145
Smith, Adam
on effects of being wealthy and poor, 133
on individual self-concept, 82

on presence of impartial spectator, 146
Theory of Moral Sentiments, 82, 85–86
social solidarity, market and, 131
storytelling, churches and, 1

T

Tanner, Kathryn
on capitalism, 107
critique of views by author, 108
on dimensions of desire, 108
Economy of Grace, 106
on ownership, 107
theologian reflecting on economics, 100
Taylor, Mark
After God, 111
Confidence Games, 110–111
on "faith in economics," 63
invisible hand metaphor and, 110
on mechanics of market religion, 111
playing in markets equated to poker game, 110
on religion as a network, 110–111
on religion-economy link, 99
TCE (Transaction Cost Economics), 66, 67–68, 70–71
Temple, William (archbishop), on market success, 167
Ten Commandments, 123
Tenth Commandment, The, 26
Thaler, Richard, 86
loss aversion, and, 88
theologians reflecting on economics, 100. *See also* Bell, Daniel; Gorringe, Timothy; Long, David; Taylor, Mark; Tanner, Kathryn
theological responses, 99–117
overview, 4, 99–100, 120
Bell: the problem of desire, 108–109
Catholic social teaching, 111–113
Cox: how the market is like a God, 109–110
desire, 115
Gorringe chooses life, 102–104
Long: restoring meaning to the market, 100–102
market and power of creativity, 104–105
markets, networks, and institutions, 113–115
Tanner: grace and God's generosity, 106–108
Taylor: religion as a network, 110–111
See also Bell, Daniel; Gorringe, Timothy; Long, David; Novak, Michael; Tanner, Kathryn; Taylor, Mark
Theory of Moral Sentiments (Smith), 82, 85, 179
Things Hidden Since the Foundation of the World (Girard), 120–122
Thornton, Martin, 154
on existence, 159–160
Transaction Cost Economics (TCE), 66, 67–68, 70–71
Trinity, doctrine of, 140–141
atonement and, 140–141
trust
building, 60–65, 90, 93
in social systems, 90

U

usury and interest, 14
See also Graeber, David

V

Veblen, Thorstein, 85

W

wealth
  Anglican tradition and, 167
  creation struggle and, 50, 92
  developing relationships and, 166–167, 168
  scripture warns against, 148–149
wealthy
  by being saved by Jesus, 150–151
  knowing types of desire worth having, 151
whoring, as sin, 23
Wilkinson, Richard, on equality in relationships, 90
Williamson, Oliver
  on economizing as means, not end, 69
  on organization is not oligarchy, 69
  on transaction costs and governance structures, 66, 68

Studies in Episcopal and Anglican Theology

C. K. Robertson
General Editor

"The links which bind us to that historic past are not fetters upon the free and enterprising spirit which is essential to progress." (Encyclical Letter of the Fifth Lambeth Conference of Bishops, 1908)

In these early years of the twenty-first century, we who claim an Anglican identity are reminded again of the importance of both our historic past and an enterprising spirit as we engage numerous theological issues and controversies which occupy our time, energy, and imagination. Through the work of both established and emerging scholars within the Episcopal Church and the worldwide Anglican Communion, this series explores a broad range of topics, including ecumenical and interfaith relations, human sexuality and gender equality, biblical authority and ecclesial structures, ministry theory and praxis, sacramental theology, and religious foundations for advocacy. Volumes in the series are in the form of monographs, revised dissertations, and compilations of essays.

For further information about the series, as well as the submission of proposals or manuscripts, please contact:

The Rev. Canon C. K. Robertson, Ph.D.
Canon to the Presiding Bishop, The Episcopal Church
Distinguished Visiting Professor, General Theological Seminary
815 2nd Ave., New York, NY 10017
e-mail:crobertson@episcopalchurch.org

To order other books in this series, please contact our Customer Service Department:

Or browse online by series:

www.ingramcontent.com/pod-product-compliance
Ingram Content Group UK Ltd.
Pitfield, Milton Keynes, MK11 3LW, UK
UKHW021008120926
8556IPUK00028B/205